WESTERN CIVILIZATION BITES BACK

by

JONATHAN BOWDEN

EDITED BY GREG JOHNSON

Counter-Currents Publishing Ltd.
San Francisco
2014

Cover design by
Kevin I. Slaughter

Cover image:
Peter Paul Rubens, "The Tiger Hunt," 1615–1616

Published in the United States by
COUNTER-CURRENTS PUBLISHING LTD.
P.O. Box 22638
San Francisco, CA 94122
USA
http://www.counter-currents.com/

Hardcover ISBN: 978-1-935965-76-3
Paperback ISBN: 978-1-935965-77-0
E-book ISBN: 978-1-935965-78-7

Library of Congress Cataloging-in-Publication Data

Bowden, Jonathan, 1962-2012, author.
Western civilization bites back / by Jonathan Bowden ; edited by Greg Johnson.
pages cm
Includes bibliographical references and index.
ISBN 978-1-935965-76-3 (hardcover : alk. paper) -- ISBN 978-1-935965-77-0 (pbk. : alk. paper) -- ISBN 978-1-935965-78-7 (electronic book : alk. paper)
1. Civilization, Western--Philosophy. 2. Paganism. 3. Religion and culture. 4. Hopkins, Bill, 1928-2011--Criticism and interpretation. I. Johnson, Greg, 1971- editor. II. Title.

CB19.B599 2013
909'.09821--dc23

2013037545

CONTENTS

EDITOR'S FOREWORD

Western Civilization Bites Back collects transcripts of seven lectures by Jonathan Bowden, supplemented by three shorter published pieces and the transcript of Jonathan's last interview. As with all of Jonathan's works, these pieces range as far and wide as his vast learning, powerful imagination, and genius for seeing connections could take him. But I have strung them together on a common thread: Bowden's conviction that the crisis of the white race is ultimately moral, both in cause and in cure.

The moral cause is the dominant Christian and liberal values system which elevates weakness over strength, equality over excellence, humility over pride, the guilty conscience over the innocence of becoming. This moral programming has been used to demoralize and dispossess whites not just for our many collective crimes and mistakes but also for our greatness: for the beauty of our people and their magnificent achievements in philosophy and letters, art and architecture, science and technology, exploration and statesmanship—excellences which other races seldom equal and scarcely ever surpass.

Christian and liberal values have never been consistent with biological flourishing and cultural greatness, and their dominance has led, inexorably, to whites being essentially "talked out" of planetary dominance and onto the path of extinction within the span of less than a century—an astonishing reversal of fortunes in a historical blink of the eye.

Talk of equality and pity led, first, to a pervasive lowering of standards and the raising—even privileging—of the marginalized *within* white communities. Then the same moral pleading was used to bring about the inclusion, equality, and eventual hegemony of Jews and other non-whites within our societies. Once Jews gained sufficient control over education, culture, and the mass media, the path from white guilt to white dispossession has been immensely accelerated.

Even the massive use of coercion to advance white dispossession—for example, the American Civil War, the Bolshevik

Revolution, the Second World War, and the pervasive drive to criminalize ethnocentric speech and thought throughout white societies—could not have happened before whites—specifically elite whites in positions of power and influence—had been essentially *talked into* them on moral grounds.

The moral cure for our decline is what Nietzsche called a transvaluation of values: the creation of a new moral hierarchy—or the return of a very old one—that is consistent with the biological and cultural flourishing of our race. We need a value system that is both pre-Christian and biological, a value system that prizes the striving of life for differentiation, struggle, and excellence.

Effecting this transvaluation is an inescapably intellectual and thus elitist project involving the deconstruction of the hegemonic value system and the formulation and propagation of a healthy alternative.

But there is a sense in which transvaluation is deeply populist and subintellectual, for the root of it is our people's recovery of spontaneous animal vitality—our *will* to persist as individuals and to live on through our race—and a simple *refusal* to be robbed of our heritage and destiny by egalitarian sob stories. It is the *refusal* to be bogged down in morbid conscientiousness, self-examination, and guilt in the name of naïve, spontaneous, vital self-assertion.

This is the sense of Bowden's recommendation that we just "step over" the guilt trips and tales of woe. Vital beings with a sense of destiny and a drive for glory cannot be bothered with spurious historical crimes and mistakes *or even real ones.*

Answering the arguments of those who wish to swindle us out of our future is all well and good. But a healthy organism cannot be talked out of its existence, period. Thus the deeper victory is to arrive at the conviction that all such arguments simply do not matter. Winning an argument is nothing compared to this triumph of the will.

In editing these transcriptions, I punctuated for maximum intelligibility, added the first names of many historical figures, supplied a few missing words, deleted a few false starts, and added the minimum necessary sprinkling of explanatory and corrective notes. The passages that appear in quotation marks in Jonathan's speeches are, of course, usually his paraphrases, not exact quotes. Those who wish to consult the original recordings at www.counter-currents.com will see that nothing extraneous has been added and nothing essential removed.

I wish to thank Michael Woodbridge, Jonathan's literary executor, for his blessing on this project; Michael Polignano, for recording "Western Civilization Bites Back" and Jonathan's last interview and then recovering the latter recording from a broken flash drive; and all the individuals who recorded and made available Jonathan's lectures.

I wish to thank Michael Polignano for transcribing "Western Civilization Bites Back," "Credo: A Nietzschean Testment," and "Western Civilization: A Bullet Through Steel"; Davied E. Clarke for transcribing "Marxism and the Frankfurt School" and "Revisionism: Hard and Soft, Left and Right"; V. S. for transcribing "Hans-Jürgen Syberberg: Leni Riefenstahl's Heir?" and "Bill Hopkins: An Anti-Humanist Life"; V. S. and S. F. for transcribing Jonathan's last interview; and the many loyal readers of Counter-Currents/*North American New Right* who helped us complete and correct these transcripts after they were placed online.

I also wish to thank Matthew Peters and Tim Reus for their careful proofreading; Kevin Slaughter for his always excellent design work; and all the friends and supporters of Counter-Currents without whom this book, and all of the others, would be impossible.

Finally, I wish to thank Kevin MacDonald, Adrian Davies, and Tom Sunić for their promotional quotes.

Once again, this book is for Jonathan.

Greg Johnson
San Francisco
September 15, 2013

WESTERN CIVILIZATION BITES BACK*

Well, I don't really speak to a topic, but you need something to fasten your mind on when you're engaged in a speech. Speeches are about energy, and are about power, and about how you utilize power and how you channel it. I'm what's called a mediumistic speaker, so I hear the voice instant by instant before I speak, and when you stand up you hear what you're going to say a fraction of a second before it comes out of your mouth. What I'd like to talk about is Western civilization and how we can save it.

Now the crisis of the West is ongoing, and everybody knows what it is. In the circumstances of the United States—I've only ever been here twice—the prognosis for decay is well-advanced. The people who created the United States are on the defensive: they're on the defensive psychologically, and emotionally, and linguistically, and culturally. People are comfortable, at least those that are, and a lot hit by recession, but everyone is worried about what the future will hold. Demographically, the people in this room could well be a minority in 40 years, maybe less than 40 years, maybe more than 40 years; maybe it doesn't matter if it's 40 years or 44 or 64 or 35.

What matters is that you've become a minority now. You've become a minority mentally, because these things happen to people mentally and psycho-spiritually before they have a physical impact. I think people are preparing to be a minority now, long before it happens. I was well aware that President Bill Clinton was once asked about his commitment to political correctness, and he said whites *need* political correctness. He said white Europeans, white Americans need it because they're going to be a minority relatively soon, and you need to play all of those

---

* A transcript by Michael Polignano of the keynote speech given at a Counter-Currents gathering in California on February 25, 2012.

vanguard games whereby you play off each group against every other group, you make sure that your protest is in early whenever you're insulted, or you feel there's the prospect that you might be insulted

And an insult in this trajectory, in this terrain can mean anything. It can mean the denial of future prospect that you might have expected to own and honor. It can be the denial of something which is your right as you perceive it. Your right to dominate the cultural space here in the United States. That the United States is a post-European society. That all of its architecture—Judeo-Christian and otherwise—seems to have the impress of old Europe upon it. I speak as a European obviously, who doesn't know the United States that well. But everything that's glorious about the United States is largely created by the people in this room, and those to whom they relate.

Now, the problem that we're finding is that people are giving away the inheritance that they brought up. It's as if you have a family business, and you've inherited it from a grandfather, and you inherit it from a father, and you have this patriarchal chain of hard work and understanding and excellence and fulfillment, and it comes down to you through the generational sort of structures of the past—and you decided to give it away. You decided to squander it.

It's very reminiscent of the aristocratic families in Europe: in the era before the Great War, there were big blowouts in aristocracy where people would gamble away their entire fortune, *because they were bored.* Because they were bored with the Third Republic's lifestyle, in French terms, in Francophone terms, of endless summers in the sun where people were pining for the destruction which Europeans would wreak on themselves in the Great War, the war that was to end all wars: a war of such manifold destructiveness that people didn't think there would be another one, and yet within a generation there was another one that was even more destructive.

And that war is the crucial event of the last century, because everything that exists now is a rebounded correction, as it's perceived, of that struggle and what occurred in it. Even in the United States, it's almost as if we as a group won that war and lost that war simultaneously, irrespective of what side our forebears fought on. In the United States you fought against Nazi Germany, you fought against Fascist Italy, you fought against Imperial Japan in the Pacific theater, and yet in a strange way you're the losers of that war. You've turned into the apostates of that war, retrospectively, and you've partly done it to yourselves, as all continental European people and post-European people have all over the world. That war has been wrenched out of history, and is used as an ideological totem in relation to everything that occurs.

Whether or not the next 18 months or the next six months we're going to see an attack on Iran, and the Islamic Republic of Iran, is in its own way an extension of post-1945 events. In all sorts of ways, the attack in Iraq which occurred a couple of years ago had as much to do in many people's minds with the symmetries and the re-symmetries, of the 1939 through '45 conflicts and everything that resulted from it, than it had anything to do with the dictator in the Iraqi desert. He was a Sunni nationalist, and he held the Kurds down in the North and the Shia down in the South, and America invaded—you remember all this?—America invaded in order to remake the world safe for democracy!

There's no democracy in Iraq now. All that's happened is the Sunnis have lost power, and the Shias have come up, and the great new hatred, which is Iran, dominates post-war Iraq. America launched a war that cost $2 trillion in order to bring to power Iranian sponsorship and Iranian surrogates inside Iraq. So you have the odd situation now that Iran manifests power through conquered Iraq, conquered under American guns and aegis, with a bit of support from Britain in the South, where the Shia and oil are, and that power that Shia arc of power runs through Iraq to Lebanon and the Israeli border.

And you'll find that all of these disputes are intimately connected with the society that was created in 1948 in Israel, and which didn't exist before. And the need to keep that society safe, the need to watch out for it, the need to prize open this prospect of villainy against it, the need to go to war—conceptually and actually—anyone against anyone who might threaten it in the future, never mind in the present.

This war, if it ever were to occur with Iran, has been looming for many years. Many years. Ahmadinejad's speech has almost nothing to do with the Iranian desire to destroy Israel *per se*, although you could argue that an extraordinarily foolish speech in many respects. But all he said in Farsi was that the society that was created falsely, and to the detriment of the Palestinians, should cease to exist within world history. Which is a pretty nebulous and "student-fist-in-the-air" sort of speech, but it's been seized upon to deny the Iranians the prospect of nuclear weapons and to enable the West, through the United States, in yet more warfare: *more warfare for peace*.

I remember Harry Elmer Barnes once edited a compilation in book form, called *Perpetual War for Perpetual Peace*. And since 1945, we've had war after war: confined to the zero-sum game of the Cold War and now extending beyond it—whereby all of these wars were are fought *allegedly* for us, *allegedly* for our betterment, *allegedly* for our safety, *allegedly* for our security, and always on the basis of our patriotism.

The bulk of patriotic people from the Right would regard what I'm saying as unpatriotic, because in a Sarah Palin sort of a way, they believe that one should stick up for the West—and our allies—against perceived enemies. Many of these enemies may not be friends of ours, but they are not enemies in the real sense. The enemies that we face here in the West, here in California, are internal. They're internal to our own societies. They're even internal to our own minds.

The greatest enemy that we have—to slightly adapt Roosevelt's slogan about fear, that there's nothing to be afraid of except fear itself—the greatest enemy we have is raised in our own mind. The grammar of self-intolerance is what we have imposed and allowed others to impose upon us. Political correctness is a white European grammar, which we've been taught, and we've stumbled through the early phases of, and yet we've learned this grammar and the methodology that lies behind it very well.

And we've learned it to such a degree that we can't have an incorrect thought now, without a spasm of guilt that associates with it and goes along with it. Every time we think of a self-affirmative statement, it's undercut immediately by the idea that there's something wrong, or something queasy, or something quasi-genocidal, or something not quite right, or something morally ill about us if we have that thought. And this extends out beyond racial and ethnic questions to all other questions. To questions of gender, to questions of group identity and belonging, to questions of cultural affirmation, to questions of history.

Think about what it will be like when white Americans are 10% of the population of the United States—or 12%—15%—or even 25%. Political correctness will not save you from the marginalization of your history and traditions, which will occur because it's not much fun being a minority. Which is why all minorities seek through their vanguards to take majorities down. And they seem to take them down physically, conceptually, actually, legally, philosophically, and in other ways. And they form alliances with like-minded groups that wish to do to majorities what minorities feel that they ought to, because it's a question of survival. Everyone's interested in surviving, and even getting along with each other in a relatively quiescent and "PC" way is just another way of surviving. Maybe in the current circumstances it's the *only* way in which multiple group-based societies *can* survive.

The Bill Clinton metaphysic is that everyone should mind their own business, and everyone should get along with each other. But it denies the crucial harbinger of identity, which is the heart of all existence and *becoming*—in Nietzschean terms, or in neo-pagan terms. All real identity is underpinned by what existed before you. The societies that are being created are *tabula rasa* societies, where you've got essentially a blank piece of paper, and what an American is, is written upon this piece of paper, the way you ask a child to do a diagram or an image and they do a face with a smile. And that's your new American: your new American is straight off the boat, he's a face with a smile and two dots for the eyes.

Where is the history of what it means to be an American? Where is the historical trajectory which relates to what you are now and to what you have achieved? And if that *tabula rasa* is such that everything that you have ever achieved in the past is smoothed-down and removed, what will it mean to be an American? What will it mean to be an American—a de-hyphenated American, deconstructed to the degree that doesn't even occur—because that is all that will exist in the future. "Americans" will be those that wish to be American.

Osama bin Laden and the al-Qaeda network once did a poll in accordance with their own resources, and a third of the people who live in the Third World would like to come and live in the United States. That's a third of the global population outside Europe, outside Japan, outside developed East Asia, outside the new bourgeois India—200 million out of the billion on the subcontinent who have raised themselves up to a middle-class standard of life and wish to stay on the subcontinent—but a third of those that are outside of those bourgeois remits want to come here. And when they say "the United States," they mean "the West." They mean "Western Europe," "Northern Europe," "Southern Europe," and the new Eastern Europe.

The new Eastern Europe is rather really interesting and will have a lot to say about the future of European man in the next century or so. Eastern Europe was preserved by communism from the decadence of the liberalism which has semi-destroyed Western Europe (and points to the west of that). Communism was a strange non-exultation. Communism was a strange doctrine, because it preserved under permafrost many of the characteristic social chapters of what it means to be a European. Communism was pretty hellish to live under, particularly materially, and it was almost always the most deformed, the most warped, and the most degraded parts of the society that had been put in charge of you.

I remember someone I know was imprisoned in East Germany in a Stasi prison for putting a slogan on Lenin's finger. Do you remember those statues with Lenin's finger, where Lenin addresses the masses, like this? There were hundreds of them in all of the Eastern European societies. And they used to appear in mass posters in East Germany. And one of his friends—very stupidly given the society that East Germany was—put a bubble, a sort of Marvel Comics bubble, on the end of the finger. And the bubble said "Hitler was right!" And he stepped back to observe—this was this chap and his cousin, and they were on a holiday in East Germany—which is an unusual type of a holiday even then—and he stepped back to examine his handiwork, and said to his relative, "What do you think about that, Bob?" And Bob turned around and there were eight Stasi, *eight Stasi*—one, two, three, four, five, six, seven, eight—in their requisite leather jackets and trench coats, because they all had the same uniform. And he got 18 months in a Stasi prison breaking rocks and living on black bread and onions. And that Stasi prison was notorious in East Germany, in East Berlin. And that Stasi condemned him for "acts contrary to proletarian justice and the will of the Socialist Republic." He was condemned for being out of kilter with the masses in history.

East Germany is now a state that no longer exists. It's been agglomerated into Western and greater Germany. The Wall has come down, the Stasi have demobilized and are no longer evident, yet in a strange way a spirit of Marxism is abroad in the West. A spirit of Marxism is abroad in the United States, unbelievably so! The number of American Marxist-Leninists you could have gotten in a few taxis to a certain extent, and yet this element of cultural Marxism is abroad in the United States, as it is in Western Europe, as it is in Northern and to a certain extent Southern Europe, as it is much less evidently so in post-communist Eastern Europe, where there's been an enormous reaction against it.

It's taken a little bit of time to examine why Marxism, of all things, has ended up culturally influential in the United States. It's got little to do with economic theory; it's got much more to do with self-hatred and negation. Guilt. The extending of your own mental remit into groups that don't care for you, or that purposefully wish you ill. And it's got a lot more to do with the architectonics of the Frankfurt School, and its ability to morph and to merge into the general liberal currency of the last 50 years.

Since the Second World War, white Europeans have felt guilty about being themselves and have been made to feel guilty and are being encouraged to feel more guilty than they have at any other time in their history. There is no period in our history where we have faced such evident self-hatred and such evident insults upon ourselves which are harmful to the prospects of our children's lives, and their children, and generations as yet unborn. Is this a phase that we've gone through, or is it something slightly more sinister and ulterior than that? These are questions which we need to analyze.

Why, here in the United States, is there such guilt about the majority identity when the United States could point to, in its own cognizance, an exemplary war record against Germany and Japan, being on the victor's side, being on the victor's table? And yet the guilt for alleged and prior atrocity is such that all white Americans feel ashamed about any push forward in relation to the prospect of their own identity. It's quite shocking how, since 1960—I was born in 1962—the West has lost its fiber and has collapsed internally and morally in terms of its spirituality and in terms of its sense of itself.

Fifty years is a blip historically; it's a click of the fingers. And yet for 50 years we've see nothing but funk, nothing but a failure of nerve, nothing but a self-expiration, nothing but the degree to which the historical destiny of the European peoples has been traduced—and has been traduced by elements of themselves and their own leadership, who have accepted at face value the fact that much of what was wrong with the modern world is morally our responsibility and not that of any other group. And that if we ever dare to assert ourselves again in any meaningful way, that we are in turn co-responsible with some of the worst events of human history.

Now, let's unpackage this a bit. Communism in the 20th century killed tens of millions. *Tens of millions.* When Mao met Edward Heath, who was the British prime minister, in 1972 in the Forbidden City, he said "I'm regarded as the worst mass murderer in human history." Of course he said this in Mandarin and this sort of thing, he had to be exhaustively translated by Foreign Office Sinologists and so on, and Edward Heath was rather shocked by this, and said "And what's your view of this, Chairman?"—a politician's answer, he just reflected it back upon Mao—and Mao said, after the laborious translation had intervened, "I'm rather proud of it, actually"—being the worst mass murderer in human history.

Don't forget the Great Leap Forward, the enormous famine that devastated much of rural China and which was in fact a great leap backwards; claimed by mainstream historians to have claimed 46 million lives—*46 million lives*—it's so large that the human mind balks at it basically. Once you get beyond the body count of a couple thousand, the brain falls silent and listens to these numbers and internal calculus almost in a fantastical way. But even if a scintilla of that is true, and the truth is most of the communist atrocities and most of the worst sort of data that can be leveled against those regimes turns out to be quite true.

When the Soviet Union collapsed, the KGB figures for those that suffered under Stalin were halfway in the range between what the apologetic individuals in the West said about the regime—the sort of revisionists, if you like, of the Soviet sort—and the exterminationists in Western countries, who tended to be conservative and who tended to be religious. The actual body count was halfway in between. Whether communism killed 100 million in the 20th century is up for grabs. Whether it killed 20 million or between 20 and 100 million is up for grabs.

And yet everywhere one looks the soft Left, the Left untainted by communist atrocity, is everywhere apparent and appears to be everywhere triumphant.

The trick that the soft Left has learned is that if you disavow the hard edge of Leftist slaughter and Siberian camps and Stasi prison cells and you instead excel in the polymorphous rebellions of Herbert Marcuse and the student Left of the 1960s, you can actually influence the whole soft spectrum from the moderate Right, through the Center, through the Center-Left, through the general-Left/generic-Left, through the soft Left, up to the softest accretions of the hard Left and to the moderate-hard Left. An enormous spectrum—two-thirds of the political spectrum—can be influenced by Marxist ideas shorn of their hard-edge Stalinist and Maoist filters.

No one wants to know about Jean-Paul Sartre now, even in France. Partly because he embraced Maoism at the end of his career. He embraced Maoism, with Simone de Beauvoir, and André Gorz, and these other people right at the end of his career. He edited a Maoist paper. This was at a time when Pol Pot was wreaking extraordinary havoc in Indochina.

And yet the ideas that these people stood for—the idea that the family is a gun in the hands of the bourgeois class, the idea that humor itself is a gun in the hands of the bourgeois class, the idea that there's something uniquely oppressive about being male, that there's something uniquely oppressive about being a Caucasian, that there's something uniquely oppressive about the Western historical destiny—all these ideas have been shorn of their human rights abuses in Eastern Europe and Central Asia and far Eastern Asia, and have been reflected back into the West and onto the West. To the degree that you can't set up a student group in an American university now—unless you're under relatively deep cover—to oppose this sort of thing because the ideas themselves are so hegemonic.

Why has this occurred? Why can't Counter-Currents exist on American campuses? Why isn't there a Counter-Currents group or something of a similar order at Berkeley, for example? Why is the idea that there could be such a group at Berkeley absurd, and almost risible, and produces a mild smile? Why isn't there? Because the physical danger that such a group would be in is largely exaggerated. It's the moral, mental, and spiritual danger that afflicts our people and that afflicts the young and would-be radical amongst our people, that is the thing to look to.

Why has this occurred? It's occurred because the radical Left with a culturally Marxian agenda, scorned by the Stalinist hard line that they were quick to repudiate, marched through the institutions in the United States and elsewhere from the cultural and social revolution of the 1960s and has marched through those institutions for 50-odd years to such a degree that the whole of the media—mainstream—the whole of mainstream politicking outside of the Rightist and libertarian allowed areas of dissent in the Republican Party and their European equivalents are controlled by nexus of ideas and interconnected thought processes which determine moral valency and morality.

Everyone in this room is regarded as immoral by the ruling dispensation in the United States, and that's very important, because it prevents people from identifying with ideas which are, quite transparently, in their own interest. If people think an idea is immoral they will shun you, particularly in an era of media exposure. The idea that identifying with yourself and with your own past is somehow immoral is one of the chief factors whereby the identity of post-European people in the United States has been turned: turned back upon themselves, turned back in a vice-like constriction where it can be used to destroy people and disarm them. Because if you've disarmed yourself before the struggle begins, you're easy meat and easy prey for what's coming. And the future in America is darker than the past. Unless there is a desire amongst people of European ancestry to step outside of the vortex, the zone of chaos which they have allowed to be created for themselves over the last 50 years.

If people think that the circumstances of American life are ill-disposed to your future identity now, what's it going to be like in 50 years? What's it going to be like in 150 years? In 150 years white Americans could be maybe 20% of the population. This is the future that faces you. And your culture will be disprivileged. Forget political correctness. Political correctness works when minorities aggregate together in a vanguard way. It doesn't work when majorities fall and stagger into minority status and then look around for allies now that they are themselves a minority in the hope that somehow they will achieve fairness and equity. Because these things are not about fairness and equity. They are about who can set the standard and the tone for the cultural domination of a civic space. And if it's not the white identity in the United States—if it's not post-Europeanism in the USA—it will be other forms of identity. Some of them fractured, broken-down, mixed, and otherwise marginal.

To European eyes the Obama presidency is the signification of America's decline. You have a situation where it used to be only B-listed Hollywood films that would show a powerful black executive President ruling in the Oval Office. Almost a psychic preparation for the real thing. And now the real thing has occurred. With the Obama presidency, you see the future the United States writ large. And from an external point of view, it will be difficult to unseat Obama, because the Republicans are doing all his work for him, it seems at the present time, and I speak as someone who obviously isn't an American.

The Obama presidency epitomizes the willed decline of majority instinct in the society, because if you don't feel it's at all offensive that somebody that does not relate to the majority—axioms, forms of entitlement, forms of belief, and historical precedent here in the United States—is actually President of your Union, is President of your society, is your Commander-in-Chief; if the Israeli planes need to be refueled over the Persian Gulf when they attack Iran at some time in the next year to two years to six months, Obama will give the order for that to occur. And he will do so in the name of everyone in this room; everyone beyond this room. And he will do so because he still speaks as the most powerful man in the world.

So the most powerful Western country is now led by a non-Westerner. Something which would've been unthinkable in the 1960s, I would imagine; unthinkable in the 1970s, but is now evidently thinkable and thinkable to such a degree that I think a lot of the anger about it which is manifested in libertarian currents like the Tea Party movement, seems to have evaporated. I speak as an outsider obviously, but it seemed to me that halfway through the Obama presidency there was a mild cultural insurgency against his regime which found a way to channel itself so that it didn't mention racial questions. And that's what the Tea Party movement and libertarianism was about.

And that's what libertarianism is. Libertarianism is the allowed Right wing for people who wish to make Ron Paulesque points but can't go the whole distance, and in many ways can't go the whole distance under the present dispensation, because many people feel constrained about who they know, and who they're married to, and who did what their job is, in relation to how explicit they can be in terms of how they reject the current American and European power structures.

Our people are used to being in charge. That's why they find it so psychologically and emotionally forbidding when they're no longer in charge. That's why they feel so bereft in contemporary Western societies, because to fall from a majority and a purpose and position of power, to a more desiccated and a more jaundiced view of oneself and one's own capabilities, is quite a wrench.

Everything that I've said about the United States could've been said about my own country if one goes back 50 or 60 years. There was a time early in the 20th century when you could argue Britain was most powerful society in the world. Britain is now a shadow of a shadow of its former state. It is in a precarious and culturally quite a terrible situation. It has decided in its near-death throes to yoke its star to the contemporary United States. Everything about modern Britain is Americana taken to a different level and repositioned in Western Europe. Almost all of our models, speaking as a Briton, are American now. Almost all of our wars are American-led. We always tag along as a sort of surrogate or executive vessel.

All of our politically-correct trajectory has in some ways come retrospectively from the radical Left fringes of the 1960s, and has been filtered by both an indigenous and a transatlantic Left. And we've allowed all this to occur to ourselves, because we have been inured to the prospect of suffering.

And we've been inured to it through plenty. There are many who believe that while Western people suffer no economic distress and while the fridge is full, and while there are several sort of four-wheel drive vehicles in the yard outside, people will never resort to an anti-regime attitude, and their default position will always be one of resignation in relation to what is coming. Particularly when they consider that they can negotiate their way out of what is occurring. The problem is that what may well occur in the future will be nonnegotiable, particularly when it hits.

There are those who believe that the white South African Boers or Afrikaners reposition themselves within their own society so as to have a sort of whites-only republic or an area of the country which is theirs. I think that's an important yardstick that you put out there as a metaphorization. But my private view is more pessimistic than that. I feel that unless you can actually so soak a proportion or a quadrant of the union with yourself that to split away from it at some unforeseeable time means that you've got a totally post-European enclave. I feel such things, such games are not really worth the candle, because when you give up the control of a state for duration—particularly the control of the most powerful republic the world has ever seen—you're partly doomed when you've done that. My view is you never restyle from the desire to be the governing echelon of one of the world's most powerful societies.

It is true that the United States is in a radical—and from a European perspective, terminal—decline. Partly because the European empires of the past—British, French, German, Dutch, Spanish, German and elsewhere—can see the writing on the wall. All of the precedents—of indebtedness, of being beholden to China in relation to the manipulation of the debt and its economic management, by having an ally such as Israel that wags the tail of the dog to such a degree that it's almost in charge of the Middle Eastern policy of the United States of America—you could say Cuban-Americans are in charge of America's Cuban policy, yet the policy towards that tiny and redundant Stalinist island is not as important, by any stretch of the imagination, as the policy towards Israel in the Middle East is in relation to the crucible of world expectation.

The CIA don't get many things right, but they predict a war in the Middle East involving nuclear weapons in the next 25 years, because the depth of the hatred on both sides is so great. No one can stop other countries getting nuclear weapons; this is the irony of the present Iranian situation. Thirty-four other countries are developing, 34 other countries are developing nuclear weapons as we speak, including Brazil, and South Africa, and Argentina, and Saudi Arabia, and so on. And there's many societies, such as South Korea and Japan and modern Germany, that could develop these weapons overnight if they chose to do so.

The *point* of an increasingly destructive and an increasingly bifurcated and divided world is to reconstitute yourself in such a way as you are least threatened by its exigencies. If you are least threatened by them you have the biggest possibility of reviving your own culture. I regard the cultural health of the civilization to be the elixir of its development and its authorization, its preferment in its sense of itself. Without that cultural overhang and extension, you cannot be worthy of the inheritance of European identity. If you allow your culture to be transparently disfigured by forces which are external and internal to it, and which you could have controlled in previous incarnations, you will witness your own death knell. And you will witness it in your own lifetime.

But this is not necessarily to harp totally upon the negative, this speech of mine. Because I regard initiatives like Counter-Currents as very important. Counter-Currents is, to my estimation, a sort of Right-wing university. A sort of free access Right-wing university on the internet, a radical Right-wing university. The whole point now is that higher education has locked off the Right end of the spectrum. You can learn about conservative ideas, you can learn about liberal ideas, you can learn about socialist ideas, you can learn about Marxist ideas in the university context; you can learn about all forms of pan-religiosity and so forth.

But you can't learn about radical Right-wing ideas in the university context unless it's adversarial, unless you're deconstructive, unless you're against these ideas in a prior way. "I'm writing a thesis at the moment," somebody would say, "about the far Right in the United States." But the premise for such a remark if they were talking to a fellow university lecturer, would be "I'm writing it from an adversarial point of view." Because nobody can ever say that they were writing it from a friendly, or an effective, or non-adversarial point of view; because it's a viewpoint to which you must be opposed, because all right-minded people are allegedly opposed to it.

The truth is most right-minded people are only opposed to it because they believe that they *ought* to be. They believe that their own niceness and their sense of themselves and their sense of what their neighbors think of them is tied up with the reflexivity of reverse negation, as I call it. "We will not align ourselves with these haters." "We will not align ourselves with these people who are depicted by the media in such a bad way." "We will not align ourselves with people who could be held to be in some ways morally responsible for events in the past that we wish to have nothing to do with." This is the majority sentiment.

Only when you can break through that permafrost—only when you can get into the majority sentiment and begin to turn it around—will there be a change here in the United States or elsewhere. One of the things that can force a change is the impact of more and more transmigration and migrations of peoples. All peoples indeed, which the future holds open for us. The degree to which the world is now shrinking, and although there are now more Caucasians than ever before, our proportion of overall mankind is going progressively downwards as we have one to two children per family and we do not replicate ourselves to the degree that other peoples are doing elsewhere around the world.

But it's not necessarily something about which we should be completely negative. The prospect of negativity is so great with our people and with our predilections to look upon the worst side of things particularly when our back is against the wall, that we forget the advantages that we have at the present time. Technology, and the creation by our group of many of the instruments of this technology, are so fulsome and so extensive that we can communicate with almost everyone on Earth—and we can communicate amongst ourselves—instantaneously at the flick of a button or a switch.

Nobody who wishes to learn about Western civilization and is volitionally moving towards learning about it, cannot do so at the present time. It used to be that only a fraction of our societies could ever hold in their minds anything about our past, certainly in an academic or vocational way. Now we have the prospect that vast millions of our people can access the Western tradition of the flick of a switch, and this is all to the good.

The problem is that they retain in their minds a mindset which filters out much of the excellence of the Western tradition. Because only when you realize that what we painted, what we built, and what we wrote, and what we self-dramatized, and what we composed musically, had to do with concepts of our own *strength,* of our own *becoming,* of our own purpose of glory—only when you realize that that was the underpinning for much of what was valued, only then will you really accord value and respect to the precedence of the past. If you rip out—for the fear of being hostile to anyone else—all prospect of group identity that is based upon strength, you will end up with a very weak and very effeminate and a very fey doctrine of your own culture, and that is what is occurring at the present time.

Alex Kurtagić is a friend of mine who's known to certain people in this room, and he wrote a very interesting article a couple of years ago about the decline of the modern face. The decline of the modern face. It was an article in physiognomy, which is quite a technique of analysis in the 19th century. Have you noticed that most people when they're photographed today wish to look as nice as possible, as reflexive as possible, as open-hearted as possible? They're pleading to be liked. Whereas he dug up all of these photographs of missionaries from the late 19th century and Shakers from New England—remember that cult called the Shakers?—they used to have these ecstatic dances, they all died out because they were frightened of sexual intercourse—which of course will occur, because if you're frightened of the one you will certainly meet the other. But the face of these Shakers was furious. Even just to pose nicely for the camera they would look like this. They would look with a demonic intensity and ferocity and sense of themselves and sense of courageous purpose and that sort of thing.

Today you're regarded as mentally ill if you look like that for your own portrait, aren't you? And yet what they were doing is they were putting on a face. They were putting on the way in which they wish to be perceived by the world. It was like sitting for portrait, sitting for an oil portrait. You didn't show your weakest or your most reflexive or your most kind-hearted side; that, if it existed, was for private use. This was a public face. And in the decline of the West's public face you can see writ large the decline in the spirit of ourselves which has occurred over the past last century, and which has accelerated over the last century.

People say today that men are less masculine than they used to be. That men have been emasculated by feminism. That maleness itself is so under threat that most men don't even wish to mention the concept, certainly not in polite society. There's nothing more fascistic than a recrudescent male, is the general idea. If you cannot even—and these are ideas that are outside of the racial box, outside of the culturally-specific area, still important ideas in relation to political correctness—but they are a softer area in which it's possible to be more radical one would have imagined; and yet even here one sees funk, and one sees decline, and one sees an acceptance of that which will lead to the destruction of forms of identity which existed in the past and that need to exist in the present and the future, if there is to be a future.

To have a future, people need to be aware of their past, and they need to be aware of the glory of that past. I believe there are celebrations at the present time in the United States—if celebrations is the word—about the Civil War. The Civil War is American experience of extraordinary intensity and drama, whereby the most elitist experiment ever decided upon on the North American continent was extirpated and destroyed by armed force.

Henry Miller is an unusual character in all sorts of ways, and ended up in Big Sur. Henry Miller wrote a book quite against type and against what you'd imagine his own predilections to be, called *The Air-Conditioned Nightmare*. He wrote it in 1942 after he had a car journey all around United States of America. In this book he makes several dissentient remarks, one of which he says the South—the old South—is to him the most beautiful part of the United States. People here around the Californian coast might not wish to hear that, but he reckoned that the old South was the only aristocratic society—based as it was upon slavery, of course—that was created here in the North Americas. And that it was an elitist society of an old European sort, the nature of which had to be extirpated if you were to have modern America.

What do you do about the Confederacy, and what do you do about the Civil War? You basically probably prefigure the black and the female experience, you marginalize the white South, and you marginalize those who fought on behalf of racial consciousness at that time. You marginalize all those people in the North—weren't they called "copperheads"—the people in the North who sympathized with the South—a venomous snake, you see. Why is that when radical forms of white identity are dealt with in the historical tradition, they are always dealt with from a perspective of demonization?

When Haitian militants massacred the white population of

Haiti, they would be considered by contemporary historiography to be more radical variations of blackness, more radical variations of militaristic Republicanism in Haiti at that time. But they would not necessarily be condemned for what they did. There would be an attempt to evaluate and to explain and to provide extenuating circumstances within the discourse.

Why isn't that done for the white South? Why isn't there an attempted social experiment on the American soil perceived as one of the trajectories in white politics at that particular time? Why is the double standard of double moral jeopardy applied by the historians of our own group to more radical formulations of Caucasian identity here in the United States, or as then it was the dis-United United States? Why have people allowed a situation to emerge whereby our own historical reckoning and our own traditions of self are turned against us in such a radical way that it's almost impossible—except by the recession to the absolute right—to defend oneself?

Let's face it, many people do not want to come on to the Right end of the spectrum, and right at the end of that spectrum as well, in order to defend themselves. They would like to be in the middle. Most people are comfortable in the middle. They're comfortable when they're with their fellows, when they're part of a crowd and feel that they're mainstream. This is an extraordinary problem that we face: the degree to which people do not wish to stand alone. And it's understandable that they don't wish to stand alone, particularly at this time. We must provide them with the courage to do this, and Counter-Currents is one of the means by which people can educate themselves to defend themselves and their own honor and future prospects.

Counter-Currents is what I personally believe the best, most educative Right-wing site that I've come across, and it's used by an enormous plethora of people who want information about their own past and their own future. There's a great wealth of material on it, and it provides this tertiary education of the mind in a radical Right sensibility. I believe that this is crucial if we're to have a future.

There are various other websites like Alternative Right and others, the Voice of Reason network, exist to furnish, in my opinion, in a more direct and concrete—and everyday and populist sense—the work that Counter-Currents does. Obviously one wants to see much more of this, and there's no doubt that the Right has gravitated to the internet in order to get around the censorship that exists almost everywhere else. Because these views are censored almost everywhere else.

Political correctness is a methodology and a grammar. It is designed to restrict the prospect of a thought before the thought is even enunciated. Chairman Mao had the idea of "magic words." Magic words. "Racism" is a magic word. Use it, and people fall apart. People begin to disengage even from their own desire to defend themselves. All of the other "-isms": sexism, disableism, classism, ageism, homophobia, Islamaphobia, all the others are pale reflections, in other and slightly less crucial areas, of the original one: "racism."

"Racism" is a term developed by Leon Trotsky in an article in the Left oppositionist journal in the Soviet Union in 1926 or 1927. It is now universalized from its dissentient communist origins—don't forget Trotsky was on the way out of the Communist Party of the Soviet Union as Stalin engineered his disposal and the disposal the Left opposition that he led—and that word has been extracted now to such a degree that it is a universal. It's universal, it's become a moral lexicon of engagement and disengagement. If you wish to condemn somebody in contemporary discourse, you say that they are a racist. And there's a degree to which nobody can refute what you're saying in the present dispensation.

Only when people gain the courage and the conviction to read what is on Counter-Currents, to internalize it, and to defend their own possibilities—of development, biologically and culturally—will we see a change here in America and elsewhere. Only when people are prepared not to fall down and beg for mercy in relation to the past—or the *Shoah*, which is a sort of a Moloch, sort of a ceremonial device which is used in order to shame nearly all Caucasian, Aryan, and Indo-European people; it's become a religious totem, a pseudo-religious totem, which is wheeled out and shunted around and made use of so that people fall down and beg for mercy even before they've opened their own mouths. They're begging for mercy even for the prospect of opening their own mouths.

And although I'm saying nothing the people in this room don't already know, it's important to realize that these psychological constructs for the majority of our people are deeply crippling and deeply negative in their effects. You have a situation now where people have so loaded upon themselves the untrammeled forces of guilt and the absence of self-preservation that almost any healthy instinctual or virile capacity is beyond them, except as a reaction to a prior threat.

Only when we recover the sense of dynamism that we seem to have partly lost will we have a future: here in the United States, here in California, or in the Western world as a whole. Many other groups in this world wonder about what is happened to us, wonder what has happened to our energy. Don't be surprised if you learn that many of the elites in foreign countries, in India and China and so on, view with bemused amazement the trajectory of the present West, the degree to which the West is so self-hating: about its own music, about its own art, about its own architecture, about its own military history—other groups in the world are amazed at this, but will seek to take advantage of it, because why wouldn't they? In the circumstances of group competition which this globe entertains, all groups are partly in competition for scarce resources against all other groups. It doesn't have to be as merciless as all that.

But it *is* real, and it is extant, and it is ongoing.

Mass immigration into Britain began with the Nationality Act in 1948, which was passed by the Clement Attlee government. And Attlee, who was the then Labor Prime Minister, in a landslide victory that Labor won immediately after the Second World War, said that, "If the races of the world are mixed together there will be no more war." "If the races of the world are mixed together there will be no more war." And he took that idea from the anti-colonial movement of the 1920s and the 1930s.

What you get instead is the internalization of divisions and a bellyaching of a globalist sort *inside* societies instead of between them. So all that happens is the group dynamics which were nation-state oriented and national in the past three to five centuries become *internal,* because human competition and the dynamics of group difference are such that they will *always exist,* no matter what you do. They will exist inside multiracial marriages. They will exist inside multiracial schools. They will exist inside multiracial cities. They will exist within multiethnic housing developments. And they will certainly exist within multiracial societies.

What then happens, is that each group creates a vanguard that negotiates with the other groups about how big a slice of the pie that they get. And the future politics of societies like United States is the negotiation that occurs electorally—and between elections—between the groups. Obama's elections are a snapshot. The ball goes on, there's a flash, and he's there for an instant, because for that moment the trajectory of forces between working-class whites who vote Center-Left, between women who are more inclined to vote Center-Left than Center-Right, between black Americans who will vote overwhelmingly for Obama—even though he is of mixed race—because they consider him to be one of themselves; towards Latinos, who will vote for an alternative candidate from the Democratic Center-Left because they feel that they will get more of a space under the sun under such a dispensation than they would from a white Republican; together with the apathy of those who don't vote or those who vote for other candidates; together with the trajectory at that moment of that particular electoral cycle where the Republicans were deeply depressed, where there was a deep alienation from the Jr. Bush second presidency, where there was deep malaise in the society because of the forced nature of the Iraq war, which had created convulsion and dissent within the society; and where you had an enormous economic depression which led to an economic vote for Obama, which may be partially repeated next time but was certainly evident then. That's a snapshot. All elections are, are snapshots out of the forces that are in coalition at a particular time. And yet notice how broken-down and how ethnically fractious that coalition is to be.

The prospect of white Republicans being elected—except to lower levels—probably decreases with each year of demographic change in the United States. Even the number of years Obama has been in probably changes the thing in a game-changing way to his advantage. For each year that goes on—my understanding is that America is now a third non-white?—essentially it's a two-thirds/one-third society—but many Western Europeans still conceive of the United States as a white European society. There was even bemused surprise in parts of Western Europe that a non-white president had been elected. But anyone who knows the United States relatively knowledgeably, and who knows of the Kennedys' desire to extend immigration out to the whole world, and to end the previous Europeans-only, whites-only immigration policy which had subsisted from the 1920s, I believe. Everyone knows that realizes that the new political dispensation in the United States is contrary to—and hostile to—the indigenous majority that lives here.

Why won't Caucasian and European people wake up to Eurocentric verities? The truth is they feel there's always an excuse to put off the prospect of that waking up, and they are always moments—particularly of media intrusiveness—that people fear in their own lives. One of the major halting elements in the re-energization of our own people is the mass media. And it's the control of the mass media by forces which are uniquely inimical to our future development. The mass media plays upon every segment of the masses that exist in contemporary Western society—churns them up, holds them against each other, reroutes them, messes up the agenda of everyone that has his own subtext to begin with, which it is forcing and corralling the points of energy in this society towards. Everyone can see this who watches the mass media with half a mind. Then there's just the effect of "prolefeed" as George Orwell called it in *Nineteen Eighty-Four*, whereby the masses are just fed a cultural industry of excess and exploitative infotainment and entertainment for their own edification, and which is an important part of the overall project.

Only when you can break through the carapace of the mass media, with all its multiple gorgon-like heads and its hydra-like amphitheater—only when you can break through that, using the internet, have you a chance to embolden the necessary vanguard of our own population. All change and all radical and all revolutionary change is led by minorities. And it always occurs top-down, even though the minority may be the throwing-forwards of a focus or a group tendency that is more generic and more general.

What the Right has to do here in the United States is to build vanguards. Build as many and as purposeful ones as possible. Build them in such a way as they can't be broken down externally and defeated internally. One of the uses of the internet is it gets around the extraordinary backbiting and rivalry, even as it expresses it, that exists between different Right-wing individuals and groups. Because people who have a naturally decisive and quasi-authoritarian mindset always believe that they are right. This is why the Right is extraordinarily difficult to arrange and manage and bring forward. Everyone who's ever been prominent in a Right-wing group knows it involves herding cats. And the reason for that is because of the bloody-mindedness of the maverick people who are part of these tendencies of opinion. Because you have to be bloody-minded in order to attack against that which is comfortable, and that which is "in the zone," and that which is the managed expectation of mediocrity in decline that is going on at the present time.

The first speaker this morning, Greg Johnson, talked about decadence. And the debate as to whether it's just a decline—whereas just as I drop this pad it falls to the floor—is it just a decline, or is it a *willed* decline? Is there a force which is moving this pad down to the floor, metaphorically, and keeping it there, and putting a boot on it once it's there so that's it's got no prospect of rising up again, or a hand would creep forward and wrench it up from under the boot and raise it back up to the table? That's a debate that one can have, but one of the things that is most important to realize is that we have our own destiny before us.

There are more of us than ever before, we are better educated in the mass than ever before, unbelievable though that may sound. When the Boer War happened in 1899, the British did an audit of the slums in Britain, and found that a quarter of the working-class men who came forward to fight in that war were so riddled with disease, and had been so badly educated, that they were militarily of no use. And Winston Churchill said at the time that "an empire that can't flush its own toilet isn't much use." One of very few radical social statements of any sort, glosses or otherwise, that Churchill ever made.

So we have enormous advantages that exist now. But we must not allow comfort and ease to sleepwalk us towards oblivion. Comfort and ease are the enemy of a decisive cultural breakthrough and a decisive implementation of the politics of the future. We have to forget the last 50 to 60 years, but remember the lessons that we should draw from it. And the lessons that we should draw from it is to believe totally in ourselves.

There's an organization in Ireland called Sinn Féin, which in Gaelic means "ourselves alone." And ourselves, we are the locomotive of our own destiny. We ourselves will determine what the role that European people have in the United States will be well into the next century. We must not allow other groups to determine it for us. Only when we are fit for power will we find the means to re-exercise it in our own societies. What is happening here and elsewhere in the West is the biggest test that Western people have faced for a very long period. In the past threats are always perceived as external. Another nation, another dictator, another aggressor, another imperial rivalry. In this filament of Empire, in the scramble for Africa at the end of the 19th century, and so on.

All the enemies that we now face are internal. And the biggest enemies that we face are in our own minds. The feeling that we shouldn't say this, shouldn't write this, shouldn't speak this, shouldn't think this. These are the biggest enemies that we have. We're too riddled with post-Christian guilt. We're too riddled with philo-Semitism. We're too riddled with a sense of failure, funk, and futility in relation to the European, the Classical, and the High Middle Ages past. We're too defensive. We're not aggressive and assertive enough as a group.

Many white people feel bereft because the leadership that we look to, the upper bourgeois tier—the most educated part of our own society—seem to have left the majority. The elite has gone global and sees itself as part of a global elite, and the traditional brokers of power from the university lecturer to your senior businessman, to your senior lawyer and so on, always seem to be on the side of giving the line away. And that's because in the present day it suffices and works for you to be on the side that gives away what the past has bequeathed to you.

What will it take for the bulk of people who leave Western universities to have the middle or common denominator view of the people in this room? It will take an earthquake. But it's not that difficult to achieve, once you get people thinking in a dissentient way. This involves very much raising the game.

In some ways we have no freedom of speech in Europe. There's no First Amendment "right" in Europe. Everyone who speaks in Europe and wishes to avoid a prison cell has to adopt in some ways a stylized and rather abstract form of language. Anti-revisionist laws exist in most of the Western European societies. Britain is slightly unusual in not having them. But that is also rather like the old Hollywood censorship which improved a lot of filmmaking because people had become more indirect and more artistic in the way in which they treated things. It can cause people to raise their game. And I'm very much in favor of Right-wing views being put in the highest rather than the lowest or the median way. I'm very much in favor of appealing to new elites, and getting them to come forward rather than making populist appeals when we're not in the right electoral cycle for that.

I was involved with a nationalist party in Britain for quite a long time. With a project that seemed to have failed and come to nothing, even though people were elected to the European Parliament. But at the end of the day people are only changed when their cultural sensibilities shifts. And when there is a release of *energy*, and a release of *power*, and a release of *self-assertion*. That is the change that you seek. Electoral change and advantage results from that, rather than the other way around. Getting a few people elected will not suffice, in my view, at the present time. What will suffice is a counter-current, and a counter-cultural revolution, which reverses the processes of the 1960s.

The Marxians have marched through the institutions of the last 50 years because the doors were swinging open for them.

They hardly had to kick them down because they were swinging open for them.

All the doors are shut to us. We must find ways to work our way around these doors and reconnect with the new minds of our upcoming generations.

One of the reasons that this will happen is that people in the Western world at the moment are chronically bored. There's a boredom that has settled upon our people. You can sense it. There's a spiritual torpor out there. And the most exciting ideas, the most threatening ideas, the most psychopathological ideas, the ideas which are beyond all other ideas, are the ideas which are in this room. They are the most dangerous ideas, and therefore they have a subtle attraction to radical and dissident minds.

Don't forget that everything which has occurred in the last 50 years was once so dissident that the people in the 1920s—those who advocate the ultra-liberalism of today—had to meet in secret, because they were frightened of revealing what their views were to the generality, and to their own families, and to work colleagues. See how the entire notion of what it was to be "progressive" or "reactionary" or "unprogressive" or "traditionalist" or otherwise has changed around in a hundred years.

We are now the people stalking. We are now the people who are afraid of media revelation. We are the people who are taught to be frightened and ashamed of our own views. The whole thing has been reversed in a hundred years.

But there is a natural tendency to kick; there is a natural tendency to kick against the system which is in place. And politically-correct liberalism is an enormous target to be attacked. And it is fun to attack it. And it is life-affirming to attack it. And to traduce it and to kick its bottom and to run 'round and to be chased by it and to be opposed by all these po-faced zealots and that sort of thing.

It's entertaining, and that's one of the things that people have to realize that will attract many people to our side. The bloody-mindedness of it, the useful cantankerousness of it. Everyone likes a rebel up to a point, as long as they're not personally and they're not adversely affected by the consequences of such radicalism. And what we need to do is position ourselves in the way that the *International Times* and '60s radicals did the other way around.

If we become the lightning rod for cultural revolution in the West, you will see, in the future, student movements that are loyal to the Right rather than Left, even if these terms break down and in increasingly group-based societies no longer have any meaning, as is occurring. But we still use them because it's an affordable shorthand.

But never forget the thrill of transgression. Right-wing ideas are *transgressive*. And are therefore interesting, and sexy. Herbert Marcuse once wrote about the eroticism of the Right. Susan Sontag did as well. And the Right is more erotic than the Left, is more exciting than the Left. The Left is boring, the Left is extraordinarily grungy and erotically unexciting, you know, despite its prevalence and its penchant for decadence. There's a degree to which it is not as radically outside the box.

And my view is that people will be attracted in the future not by reason. They will read up with their reason once they have decided to emotionally commit. The important thing is to get people emotionally. And it's to appeal to the forces and wellsprings in their mind which are eternal, and which underpin rationality. The power of irrational belief as spiritual codification, of mystical belief, of belief in identity, of the need for communitarianism, and the need to belong, is immensely powerful. Far more powerful than the anything the Left can offer.

If you can tap these forces of—in some respects—codified irrationalism, if you can bring them to the surface, if you can bottle them, and if you can then add on reason and add in the discourse on Counter-Currents, you will tap the energies of future generations of majority Americans. And you will do so because it appears to be *extraordinarily* interesting. More interesting than anything else. More *threatening* than anything else. More *shocking* than anything else. And that is something that the Right should actually in my view heighten, in a civilized and persuasive way.

One should never lose sight of the reason that people are opposed to our ideas is because they are thrilled to be frightened by them. They are thrilled to be appalled by them. It is the political equivalent of Satanism to many people. I'm saying nothing that is at all original. And in doing so we actually make ourselves *tremendously* attractive at certain levels of consciousness—not to some Southern Baptist chapter, admittedly. But you make yourself tremendously psychologically appealing. You may not have a halo over your head but you are transfigured in a sort of dark and sepulchral light, which makes you deeply spiritually ambivalent to people who exist now. And that contains the prospect of growth and the prospect of renewal.

I personally believe people agree with ideas long before they moved towards them. They have an instinctual saying of "*Yes!*" They say "*Yes!*" to the idea before they completely have worked out all of the formula for themselves. The Counter-Currents of this world exist to provide the formula for people after they've said "*Yes!*" After they've put forward their first step upon the route to identity, and the politics of identity, and the religion of identity.

If I can mention something about that, all the religious divisions that exist amongst people of European ancestry don't really matter. All that you do is you format a doctrine of psychological inequality. If people believe in inequality they can come to it in terms of whatever spiritual system they want. As long as they believe in orders of European inequality, all of the traditions of all of our people can be contained in that.

Thank you very much!

Counter-Currents/*North American New Right*
March 3, 2012

MARXISM & THE FRANKFURT SCHOOL[*]

I'd like to talk in this brief period that I have before me about the Left, and about Marxism in particular, and within that about the Frankfurt School as a particular type of Marxism. We've never had a speech, and we've never had a talk, about the Left before, in these gatherings as the New Right, *per se*.

Now, from one level if you were an extreme Leftist now in the Western world, in Western Europe, maybe parts of Southern Europe (yes and no), and North America, you'd look around, and you'd think there was a cultural desert, that you'd lost completely, that communism had collapsed, that far-Left movements have no votes at all, except residually in Italy, to a much smaller extent in France, and a few places elsewhere. You'd think that the socialist *dream*, that life could be better and more equal and free and so on, had come *crashing down completely*.

And yet, paradoxically, these people have lost a world and yet gained another, because their values, in a subtle way, in a mediated way, in a transliterated way, are the values that exist largely of the society *out there*. And when you go down and remove Sky Sport or put something else on and even there residually, you will find what a Marxist would call "the reification of triumphant values," in other words a soft-Left viewpoint put again and again and again, in *every* media, at *every* level.

Now how has this occurred? That a force that in a *hard* way seems to have lost everywhere: its states have gone down; its military structures have gone down. Its Chinese and Asiatic version is producing a mass, super-capitalist version, with an increasingly "post Left," indeed even racial elite that manage the society technologically and whose ideology is frozen into a type of theology. Many Marxists are in *despair* in this era, and the

---

[*] A transcript by Davied E. Clarke of a speech at the 13th meeting of the New Right in London on January 12, 2008.

Frankfurt School, that we're going to have a bit of a look at in this talk, actually in some ways is a movement of despair both within Marxism and within Western thinking. Yet, this victory in defeat and defeat in victory that we have all around us is something that I want to look at.

In England, in the early part of the 20th century, intellectuals of Left and Right often used to debate with each other. This is really no longer possible now 80, 90 years on. G. K. Chesterton, Hilaire Belloc, George Bernard Shaw, and H. G. Wells knew each other well, often had debates with each other.

The irony is that if you'd turned to them or their audiences, maybe in venues like this, 80-odd years ago and more, that we would have in the early part of the new millennium, a Left-wing, capitalist society, people would have said "You're mad!" The idea that the market can adopt the values of the folded out, libertarian, slightly soft—but not entirely so—Left would have been regarded as perverse by almost *any* social and ideological commentator of that era. But it's what we've got! And it's *all* around us, and it's sort of in the ether; it's all-pervasive. Even to cut against it in a very minor way is to create a shock somewhere. Certainly if you're anyone of any reputation or any foreknowledge in the culture and you make a remark which is "incorrect," and you're known, and you've ventilated it as such, there's a tremor in the web.

Now my interpretation of this is that hard Marxism, strict Marxism-Leninism and various anarchistic and other variants off and to one side of it, have failed, but the trajectory of the ideology itself has succeeded, has morphed, and has transfigured itself in a new way. You have the Left that has come into the Center, taken it, turned it around, and what we'd call liberalism now, either with a small or large "L," is not the liberalism of 50 to 60 years ago. It's not even the liberalism of 150 years ago. The truth is that the people who led Palmerstone's Liberal Party had views which in the middle of the 19th century, could be construed as people who, if not to the Right of this gathering, then wouldn't have been too far away.

The Protestant ideological moralism that underpinned liberal ideas of a traditional sort has been *ripped out*. So it's become a materialist and secularist ideology prone to infiltration and change by forces from its own radical Left.

One of the things that's most germane to the Frankfurt School is the Frankfurt School repudiates those elements of communist practice that liberals don't like: the *harshness*, the *camps*, the belief in struggle, the secret police, the art of the people, and the crushing out of anything that the people don't like. Andrey Vyshinsky *screaming* that ex-comrades should be killed, beheaded, and their families tortured before they die! All in the name of love, and humanity and peace. The French Communist Party organ was *L'Humanité*. Humanity!

Maurice Thorez, who was the leader in the post-war period, was personally trained by Stalin in exile during Vichy to take France, which the Eastern Bloc believed (more so than Italy at that time) was the first Western domino to go within Europe. Get them out of NATO, align them with the Warsaw Pact, create chaos inside the Western Alliance, and so on.

Now, Marxism grows up of course from the 19th century, but before Marx gave state socialism and ideological socialism a pseudo-scientific gloss and formulation, there'd been various other theorists: Saint-Simon, Charles Fourier, Utopian types of socialism, some of them a secularization of Christian, libertarian ideals. Marx was determined to reshape not just the nature of the Left but the nature of philosophy and the Europe of his time and the world for all time!

His type of trajectory relates to a particular view of society that certain intellectuals have—although he never specified it as such, Marx and those of his ilk who came after him, in a wide range of theorists who've almost died out today. There's not *one* major Marxist theoretician, really, who's alive today who's of *any* importance. You get a minor, minor figure like Alex Callinicos, who was associated with the Socialist Workers Party at one time, who occasionally bobs up. But these are people of almost no importance whatsoever.

Jean Baudrillard and major theorists like this are cynical, materialistic liberals and libertarians who laugh and sneer at everything, and it's all a great game to them, because they're concerned with language, what it means, what it doesn't mean, how it can be repositioned and so on. They're not really Marxists at all. The last really powerful thinker in that trajectory—well there could be two of them, really—are Jean-Paul Sartre in a way and Theodor Adorno, and after them there are just *minor* figures who floated up.

So this entire mass of theory that begins with Marx is part of the idea that intellectuals can totally dominate society. In the Anglophone worldview intellectuals are on the whole praised and privileged to a degree but also accorded a very minor status. In France and in Eastern Europe—which often modeled itself on French patterns of intellectual culture—intellectuals form a class within the society which is very coherent and quite hard-edged.

And it's understood that you do the academic jobs, you do the higher journalistic jobs, you do the par, upper-tier, pre-modern, professional media jobs. You write the books, you run the galleries, and so on. It's not just an inchoate group of individuals; it's a tier with its *own* morals, its *own* way of behaving, its *own* salons which are the parties and groups where this particular subset of intelligent people meet.

I went to an intellectual salon—run by a Continental European, of course—when I was 18, and all the intellectuals were talking about "ordinary people" because *that* is the class division if you're an intellectual. There are those that live for the mind and ordinary people who don't. So they have their own mental class division within that, and Marx in, his own way was a radical twist on some of those ideas. He believed that theory could dominate life and social process to such a degree that it could change the world, and even human nature, forever.

One of the important things about Marxism is its total and utter break with the past, its total and utter break with *all* religious ideas; there is nothing supernatural; they're just human theories and mixed within language. There is *nothing* prior to man; there are *no* eternal values whatsoever; everything is in the now, and everything is based on materialistic precepts which predetermine every aspect of life. This means that in the high regime and ferocity stage, communism represses religion with extreme and often irrational violence.

You always know that a communist movement is falling back

again into social democratic centrism and state socialism when it allows people to adopt a religious preference. After the Soviet collapse when the Communist Party reared up again and in one of Boris Yeltsin's internal elections (one of the ones that his forces won) they had a bit of a chance. They said that Christianity and Orthodox Russian Christianity were now compatible with Marxism-Leninism, which is the key to a weakening of the *resolve for struggle,* because the desire to crush out religious belief, even to the degree of atrocity such as those committed by Pol Pot in Kampuchea for example, where there was an actual attempt to kill *every* self-defining Buddhist in the society, is an attempt to *eradicate* completely that which exists before.

Mao, who was even more psychologically radical than Marx himself, believed—completely contrary to all biological ideas—that *man is a piece of paper.* Man is a white sheet. You can take a man and torture him to a gibbering wreck; you can take a man and say he's a God and then shoot him afterwards. Man is changeable and plastic and can be molded by struggle, or what they called dialectic. Ideology in life and in language and in history. "Give me a man for half an hour, and I'll make him a communist." It's this sort of idea. And occasionally, many of their theories when applied, such as to American prisoners of war in the Korean War for example, had a certain salience.

Maoist behavioral theories worked on these lines. They believed that there is a five percent leadership caucus in all groups, so you take the officers away from the men when you've got them captured. Then you take away the non-commissioned officers. Then you take away the *moral* officers, those amongst the men who the elite amongst the mass of the troops who have personalities that will be known as leadership personalities. In crisis people would look to them. If the officer has fallen, they become the officer. You get rid of them. You remove them. You either shoot them or put them in a separate camp or send them back to the Americans. You want the *mass* that you can mold and destroy and remake.

And they did it with quite a lot of them. Many of them came back to the US three or four years later mouthing sort of Marxist platitudes, you know: "We invaded the Third World, man," you know, "We deserved what we got," and this sort of thing. In the Vietnam War some of these tendencies to deterioration and degeneracy in the American Army became so large that many of them would shoot their own officers rather than go out on patrol, which is one of the many reasons why they ended in a surreal mess prior to surrender. America of course conducted a mass bombing campaign, said they'd won, and then cleared out—a scenario they may repeat in Iraq and Afghanistan in the next couple of years. But to return to our Marxist theory.

Marx emerged really, first in a group of radical German intellectuals called "The Free Ones" ("Die Freien") who used to meet in a beer cellar in the 1840s. In the 1840s, of course, liberalism and nationalism went together as ideologies; now, 150 years on, they're daggers drawn. But in that group in the 1840s there were gathered some of the most radical, "let's change the world" intellectuals in Germany, in central Europe.

Many of them have been forgotten today: Botho Strauss and Otto Strauss have been forgotten; Ludwig Feuerbach is only remembered because Marx wrote an essay about him. Max Stirner is remembered for one book he wrote about extreme individualism. But in the corner of the paintings of The Free Ones as they gathered in this cellar there is a tall gentile Friedrich Engels, the factory owner, the financier of the theorist, and Marx, then with an enormous black beard because he was very young then.

Marx's idea is that you have to *smash* all the theory, particularly all the progressive theory that predated him. That's why he began with *Groundwork* (*Grundrisse*) and *The German Ideology*. And you must clear away all these false and fake "progressive" ideas based on liberal thinking, bourgeois semantics, and utopianism. Everything must be based upon science and upon matter and must be provable and must be empirical. He believed that intellectuals could so interpret the changes in society that they could master the consciousness of a society, change it, and shift it, and force it in directions that even hadn't entirely been predicated on the theory.

The one thing you notice about Marxism is it's a seething vortex of ideas; it's always restless; it's always counter-propositional. Marx will make a statement, then he'll qualify it, then he'll withdraw it, then he'll make another statement which is more radical. And this is part of again what they call "dialectic."

Now the idea of dialectic is based on Hegelian theory, and it's based on an ancient Greek thinker called Heraclitus, who believed that everything is in flux, and everything changes, and everything works on itself. The *fury* with which Marxists fall on each other in intellectual dispute, often about arcane matters which are of no relevance, which in a regime context is a choice between life and death! You advocate the dialecticism of a particular crop cycle, and you get it *wrong*, and the party sides with another, you are shot! And your family's shot! And those that are related to them are shot as well, because ideas are *important*.

The man who thumbs through *The Guardian* on the tube who thinks "Ideas? . . . who cares?" To a Marxist ideas are *life*, and you write them in blood because they're *important*. They suppress artistic forms because they believe they are important enough to merit that. And that's the difference between . . . why they almost conquered a world and did it in various ways.

Now Marxists, on the whole, form two camps in my mind, politically and ideologically. In all Marxist groups you get the rather weak, pacifistic, loving, humanistic people. The vicar's daughter who believes human nature isn't . . . right. If only we could be nicer to each other, if only we could spread more love. You get these people always in ultra-Left and communist groups.

And next to them on the podium, next to them in the auditorium, are your *utterly* nihilistic, ruthless, virtually criminal types who want to use the structure of power when they get it to *crush* those underneath them, don't give a *damn* about ideology, and are actually amongst the most misanthropic people you could ever meet. And you have these *extremes* of the innocent lovey and the sort of sadistic amoralist in the *same group*.

That's why when a Communist regime comes in they have enormous purges, because they have to start by purging their own, to get rid of all the idiots! To get rid of all of those who believed it was "love, love, *love*," and they're led off by the men in leather jackets, because you've got to get rid of those *fools* early!

If a Right-wing regime is formed, and there's a purge, it's because it's people struggling for power. That's what it's about.

Now, Marx, in the British Library, began writing sort of pure theory as a critique. The interesting thing about Marxism is in a strange way its unoriginality. Epistemologically, it's Hegel (and that's the theory about how it thinks about its own theory) and Heraclitus. Politically it's the ultra-Left of its own time fitted in a made to do service.

All of the classical liberal thinkers from Adam Smith onwards who underpinned capitalism as an idea, Marx doesn't think up an original theory in relation to them, he critiques them. All Marxism is a shadow; it's a critique; it's a sort of feeding on the carcass of something which exists before you. You critique it, you turn it around, you re-engineer it, and it comes about on the basis of a negation. So the negation of that which exists before is the key to this type of thinking.

And then you negate the negation, and then you negate the negation of the negation, and you go on and on.

The most radical version of state communism is Trotskyism, the idea that you have a regime that renews itself through *endless* and perpetual struggle. "There is *no* rest!" "There is *no* motion!" Trotsky wrote endless sentences like this "no love, no serenity, no stillness, no motion, *only the struggle*!" And of course Stalin took him at his word, which is why he purged them all from the Party after 1928. But until then, of course, they were giving almost as good as they got, and both sides in that dispute worshiped the parent, Lenin.

Now Lenin was taught his Marxism by Georgi Plekhanov, who was a Menshevik who didn't like the Bolshevik Revolution. Quite a few Marxists who were almost gentle professors of cultural destruction, didn't actually *like* the Bolshevik Revolution, because in actual fact it's contrary to some Marxist theory.

The idea of the Plekhanov school is that if, in a totally undeveloped society, you have a militarist coup by a Left-wing armed group (which is what the Bolshevik Revolution really was) you will end up in an extremely nasty, what we would call today Third World dictatorship.

Which is exactly what happens, because in their theory you

have to allow capitalism and the bourgeois class—which is loathed and yet admired strangely, simultaneously—to reach fruition to create the proletariat industrially, then there must be leaders from the bourgeoisie who split off, form the communist vanguard, link with the proletariat, revolutionize the world, and create *defective* communism, create socialism—the first step. So it's a progressive cycle.

The Leninist way of dealing with dissidents is to just shoot them! That was Lenin at the end. Half his brain was virtually liquid towards the end, massacres on every front, the civil war was going badly. They won that civil war because every man on their own side who retreated more than eight paces, the secret police stood behind them and shot them. And Trotsky introduced that and advocated it in a booklet called "The Necessity of Red Terror." *The Necessity of Red Terror!*

I met Corin Redgrave once who was one of the leaders of the Workers Revolutionary Party, and Redgrave, who's this rather depressive sort of actor, basically, piped up in the middle of this party as he was chain-smoking, and he said, "When we're in power," he said, "we're going to have iron hard, IRON HARD . . . *destruction of the bourgeois class!!*" Like this. And I said, "But Corin, you could be regarded as one of the most bourgeois men in Britain." And he said, "No, *NO!* It's all in the mind."

And of course it *is* all in the mind.

He said something very interesting to me about the extraordinary mental arabesque that this theory can cast. Somebody said, "Well, what about Stalin then, Corin?" And he said "Stalin is the recrudescence of the theory of the class enemy which occurs mentally at the hypostatization within the class that falsifies its ideology and history and is the class enemy at the particular moment of struggle. If you refer to Trotsky's *The History of the Revolution*, chapter 8, paragraph 92, he tells you everything that you need to know about it!"

So it is almost an ersatz religion! Now I've known a few Polish people in my life, and Poles learnt Marxism-Leninism at school after the creation of the Władysław Gomułka's regime after '48. I went to a Catholic school, although I'm not a Catholic (not even a Christian), and you had four periods a week of religious knowledge, and they ripped that out and replaced it with Marxist Leninism, the same four periods!

You learnt the Paris Manuscripts, the early idealistic stuff in 1844, which he then reverses. You then go on to the scientific socialism (so-called) of *The German Ideology* and the *Groundwork* which was only published in East Germany probably under Ulbricht in '67. Then you go on to *Capital* volume one and *Capital* volumes two and three which Engels writes later. Then you go on to Engels' parallel material, which is slightly different to Marx. Then you look at people like Plekhanov.

The irony about this pure theory is that without the mountebanks, without the political criminals, without the guerrilla terrorist figures like Stalin, they would have never got anywhere, because they married this theory to sectarian propaganda and conspiratorialism by small, violent, and often criminal groups.

And this is a rival tradition that goes back to the French Revolution. If you look at people like François-Noël Babeuf in the 1790s, but in particular it's Louis Auguste Blanqui's tradition in the 19th century. Small, close-knit, revolutionary bands that almost no-one's heard of, swim around these theoretical groups, wait for a crisis in society to use armed force at a crucial and strategic moment, and then build a structure on the basis of the theory, which often hardens just into a secular theology whilst they're really concerned with the exercising of pure power.

I saw a thing which interested me recently in *Forbes* magazine in the United States which has a rich list, and it said that Fidel Castro's personal fortune was 70 million US dollars. *Seventy million US dollars!* And they described him as a "communist prince."

And there is an interesting side to these types, because often they take illicit and semi-secret shares in state owned industries. The families that owned the original sugar and tobacco industries in old Cuba would be shot or heaved out of the state. They would *re-appropriate in the name of the masses.* Which means? A slice for the Castro family! And of course it might be quite small in terms of equity when it's taken, but over 50-odd years it builds up to an enormous fund.

And yet many communists or Marxists that I've known are in some ways not particularly materialistic people. The whole point in the communist movement is that you often owned nothing. Often you left very little, except for these monarch types that I've just mentioned, because *they lived* for the re-creation of man! They believed in a total change in almost all areas of society. Probably the most extreme communist experiment of all was Pol Pot's in Kampuchea.

Now Pol Pot of course wasn't his real name, it in some ways means "political potential," which is what Maoist instructors in China called him: "Political Potential," Pol Pot. He had political potential.

Pot himself was a nerdy little man with a lopsided smile and a sadistic desire to impose a type of peasant-based, anarchistic Marxist theory.

One of the interesting things is when he was a student—and Indochina is strongly influenced by French imperialism of course—when he was a student in Paris he sat in on lectures by Sartre, by de Beauvoir, by a feminist theorist called Julia Kristeva, who was also a Maoist at the time, and he sort of wrote down things that they said, but in a sort of cretinous, future sadistic way like: "The family is a gun in the hands of the bourgeois class. Destroy the family! Yes! *Destroy the family!* Make everyone live in communes, destroy the bond between mother and child, and husband and wife, everyone is therefore part of the masses, and then it's *wonderful!!*"

When he got the chance to do it in a society with gangs of terroristic teenagers, many of them out of their minds on drugs and so on, he did it!

He put people in large barns, and if you said you wanted to see your uncle he said: "I'm your uncle." And the person was dragged out, and their head beaten in with the butt of a machine gun, because you weren't worthy of a bullet.

So that is the sort of sort of high theory that these French Parisian literati types—that have hardly ever had a problem in their lives at all, who're rebelling against the norms of their own culture, almost as play—give the language and the sort of action theater to these types who internalize it all. And although most of them just remain Gerard Healy-like idle dreamers on the margins of Western society, if they ever really got the chance to do it, *they would impose it,* because they believe that it's morally right to make that imposition.

And the idea that these theories are "morally right" is important in relation to their reception at a later time, because I believe that contemporary liberalism has recycled a large number of these theories and treated them, purged of nasty Soviet and Maoist and other accretions, as something normative, as something given.

Seventy years ago, many of the values that face you in the media and elsewhere would, amongst normal and apolitical people, have Fbeen regarded as abhorrent. Now they are normative and even to speak out against them is to essentially embrace thought criminality.

But there's a degree to which the reason this has occurred is because a *hybrid* has developed between post-war secular liberalism and the Marxism of the past, and this is what I'd like to discuss.

The Frankfurt School grew up in Germany as a particular response to modern life. Marxism believes in crisis; everything is in crisis. The family's in crisis; class relations are in crisis; race—which they don't accept as a social concept because it's an anthropological concept and isn't reducible to economic materialism, but does exist because it exists in the mind of reactionaries and so on.

They think that the endless critique of what has gone before prepares new grounds and vistas of struggle, so the purpose of the Frankfurt School was to critique all Marxism, to bring back a more purified and critically intelligent form of the dialectic, which could be used in modernity.

The Frankfurt School is quite complicated because there's a strong streak of pessimism and despair in it which is very unusual in Marxism. Another very unusual thing is that very Germanic forms of Marxism such as those proffered by Leo Löwenthal, by Max Horkheimer, by Theodor Adorno, by Franz Neumann, and others who were prominent in the school, linked to forms of Anglo-Saxon, American, and imperialist thought. Why is this? Because of the existence of fascist governments in central Europe in a certain time, all of these types sought refuge in the United States.

When Adorno was at the University of California and the Frankfurt School had been closed down by a certain notorious government in Germany at that time, he developed various psychological theories which are quite interesting even in relation to this present audience. He developed what he called the "F" scale. ("F" was F for Fascism.) This is a personality test which under a different name we still use quite widely. It's a test for the authoritarian personality, to see how fascistic you are in relation to trigger words.

Many of these ideas have fed through into the doctrine which is now called political correctness, but they've morphed and changed over time: rigidity in relation to prior assumption, ability to follow a leader without question, undue respect for authority (dialectically related to the idea that you want to exercise authority yourself—a sort of love-hate relationship to the police), and this sort of thing.

And Adorno ticks all of these boxes. So he's very obsessed with the micro side which, on the whole, Marxist theory—which loves grand architectures of theory and great spasms of language for its own sake—usually neglects.

Marx himself of course was a combination. *Capital* is full of endless detail about the suffering of the poor in capitalist societies. One of the reasons many Western idealists were attracted to it in the early part of the 20th century was because, of course, for every new development there were many victims. Marx, if you read *Capital,* there's endless sections of it. Crushed children in machines, people suffering in the early stages of industrialization, but the irony, it could almost be William Cobbett! And yet it's linked to the idea of an enormous theory that can transform the nature of reality.

For human good? Well, the problem with *all* Marxist theory is that it's counter-propositional in relation to what we are, what all races are, what humanity is, and all mankind is as a whole. We're based on nature; we have our being in that substructure. We are not as Leftist ideas would have us.

One of the reasons for the extraordinary rapacity of communist terror is, I think, a sense of disappointment, on a cosmic level!

When you get into power you realize that human beings are partly avaricious, partly sexual, partly acquisitive, partly territorial, partly communal, partly group-identifying—everything that your theory said that they weren't! And there's a strong element of concealed—and not so concealed in the regime phase—misanthropy in communism, that if humanity can't be redeemed in that way we'll fall on them anyway. It's almost a secularization of the idea of sin. "They've disappointed us and so they'll suffer" and maybe through the infliction of various agonies like Procrustes' bed; the man lies on the bed and his arms are over the side and his feet are over the bottom, and you think, "I've got to get him to fit the bed, so you cut off the feet and you cut off the hands." Pol Pot says, the leaders of the Derg, Mengistu Haile Mariam in Ethiopia, says: "Look! Our body fits the bed," but it's limbless! And that's how you've made it fit!

Now Adorno wrote a whole series of books, *Negative Dialectics, Minima Moralia, Aesthetic Theory* which is an enormous book, this thick, 800 pages; it's on Routledge & Kegan Paul.

He was a pessimist, Adorno: all the photos used on the Routledge editions of his books show him with one hand over one side of his face dwelling upon the pain and misery of humanity. He believed, in a strange way—that has echoes of cultural conservatism to it, paradoxically—that the masses are totally brutalized and dehumanized by capitalist ideology.

He believed that everything has been sucked into the spectacle of mass culture, to such a degree that there is no freedom for the masses at all. Of course he never thought "Do we even want to be free?" That's a question that is off-limits essentially.

"Everyone can be free; everyone can be rational; everyone can be equal." To say otherwise is to render yourself a beast and a demon. A reactionary, outside of the doctrine of progress and enlightenment. So remember that!

His first book was called *The Dialectic of Enlightenment*, which he wrote with Horkheimer, and which is an interesting thesis, because like a true Marxist he goes right back to the roots and one of the paradoxes is that although liberalism has embraced a lot of soft Marxism, this is a ferocious critique of liberalism! *The Dialectic of Enlightenment* is now an attack on the Enlightenment! He ferociously lambasts these liberal theorists for their reactionary nature, their desire to exploit man in the name of capitalist progress, their desire to dominate nature. Adorno believed that fascism was a *natural* reaction against capitalistic exploitation and the desire liberals, *liberals,* had to exploit man and nature.

Adorno is so far to the Left that liberals are the enemy! Never forget that for a true communist the liberals are the scum, and the middling ones, to whom you will give enough latitude, you will give enough rope to, before you hang them. I think Lenin in *One Step Forward, Two Steps Back* said of all these social democrats and so on: "We allow them their time. We allow them the time on the stage to weaken the Right, to weaken religious beliefs to open the way *for us*. And when we're there, then we hang them, *we hang them, and we enjoy it,* because they are *worse* than the bourgeoisie! Because they are traitors to the class in history, and we will deal with them with an utter ruthlessness that we won't even treat reactionaries with."

That's the *real* Leninism talking, but Adorno doesn't like that sort of talk at all, because although he's not a humanist he does believe in the Alsatia of forgotten possibilities. Don't forget, for a Western Marxist—and this theory's called Western Marxism or Euro-communism as it became—the Soviet experience has been a disaster.

I once had a conversation with E. J. Hobsbawm who was the Marxist professor at Birkbeck, the extramural and evening college of London University, and he said, in private of course; "Well as a member of the Communist Party of Great Britain I would never have admitted this, but the entire Soviet experiment has been deleterious!" You know, 20 million dead, 50 million dead, multiple wars, dictatorship? It's been "deleterious." As he reaches for another drink, you know. He said, "All it achieved was the socialization of the means of production; it's not enough, it's not enough!" you know.

And yet when the *coup* happened against Gorbachev, he supported the coupsters; he supported the *coup d'état* for reasons of what he called "revolutionary conservatism," you should hold what you have. Even if it's totally broken.

Hobsbawm's interesting, because Neil Kinnock was a close personal friend of his, and there's always been an interconnection not between communism and elements of the Labour leadership, certainly in the Cold War period, but between Marxism and the Labour leadership and other leaders who are regarded as more liberal, more social democratic, more moderate.

At the beginning of the 20th century "social democrat" *meant* Marxist. By the end of the 20th century they were people who were aligned with George Bush I and were Atlanticists. Denis Healey begins in the Communist Party youth wing, ends up a Right-wing social democrat and Atlanticist supporting the Vietnam War! Something Wilson, slightly intelligently, kept us out of, but the Australians fought on our behalf.

So there's a strange element to which Marxism is "alright," at least when it's considered to be a theoretical add-on to Center-Left disputes. Claire Short's a descendant now in the modern Labour party and is advocating a hung Parliament even as Left Whip in the House of Commons, but when the Soviet Union went down she was asked "Is communism dead?" by some *Independent*-type journalist, and she said "Communism may be dead [she probably said, 'in the West'], but Marxism isn't!"

And this idea that the theory can be obtained, retained, rebranded, and recycled, even though the hardcore vanguard politics has gone down, is something that most of the Left still believes.

One of the reasons Liberalism's triumphed in this society is the mental wetness, the irresolve, fear, and funk of conservatism morally and intellectually and ideologically. And I don't just mean naked, middle-class self-interest and the sort of slightly impoverished range of politics based around that, which is the core of all Center-Right parties. What I mean is conservatism philosophically and intellectually, unlike the moderate Left that's always looked to the far Left for its energy, for its theory, for its radicalism. They repudiate bits they don't like (particularly the harsher bits), but they're, "Come in brother, come in comrade." They take it into themselves.

Conservatives, even of the Professor Roger Scruton and Maurice Cowling type, there is a permafrost between them and the far Right and radical Right ideas. This means, theoretically and mentally, they've cut part of their own body off. Whatever their much more moderate political views are, they will *not* take the energy which exists to one side of them. Always in thinking—which is one of the reasons intellectuals often make bad politicians! Thinking goes to the margin of the prospect of a thought. Politics often has to deal with great masses of people, with what they can understand and appreciate, with short attention spans, with people who've got a hundred other things to do. Politics is even, in society, a minority sport amongst a minority sport!

People who hate each other but are political, often have more in common psychologically than the anonymous mass of people who don't give a damn how they're governed as long as there's bread on the plate the day after next. And because conservatism has cut itself off from racio-biological, from elitist, from Nietzschean, from radical views—because they regard them in almost a satanic light, *they couldn't fight back* against liberalism, because they had *no mental ammunition!*

And because conservatism is an anti-intellectual attitude anyway, often philistine, often atheoretical, when a *Marxist* version of Center-Leftism comes along, they increasingly laughed at it, scorned it, accepted it a bit, accepted it a bit, moved to the side, said they were against it, pushed away an egregious bit, accepted a bit. Then another generation would accept a bit more. Then another generation would accept a bit more.

The average Tory in the 1960s would have regarded race as a fact of social existence. Now you'll be expelled from the modern Tory party for saying that. That's 50, 40 years! *It's nothing.* Half an adult lifetime! And that's because of what's up here, particularly amongst relatively sort of unintelligent people, up to a point. But there are *many* intelligent people in the Tory party. But it is because of the Second World War and its aftermath, and the *fear*, the *self-loathing*, and *self-hatred* in many relatively normal "conservative" people who are the mainstream in any society.

In any society you have to have a mass of people who are a bit stuck, a bit boring, a bit uncreative because they are the bedrock. They're not going to be exceptional, but you can't have that in any social order. One of the delusions of Marxism is that everything could be different. Trotsky wrote an extraordinary essay in the early 1920s when the Soviet regime had just been created and was caked in blood. He wrote this essay saying, "When we've achieved pure socialism there'll be a Wagner, yes a Wagner! There'll be a Shakespeare, there'll be a Byron on every corner. *Everyone* can be liberated to be free and creative. But now? *The Struggle!*" And we've stood in our little Bolshevik peaked, flat caps on pyramids of skulls, which is what they were!

Lenin was an extraordinary man in some ways, because in the 1921 Congress, he had a secret speech to the congress which wasn't revealed until the Soviet Union came down. The interesting thing about communists is, because they believe they are the wave of the future, they write down everything they do. And they write down all their massacres as well!

The massacre of the Polish officer corps in the Katyn Forest for example, which was ordered by the Politburo, and they all signed it! Stalin signed it. Khrushchev was next: "Yes, I'm signing!" And they *all* signed it, and this was revealed after the breakdown.

Because they believed that they were the wave of the future, and an atrocity is important. It's not something you should be ashamed of, because you are aiming for the betterment and progress of the whole of humanity. You have to be *proud* to wade in the blood of reaction in order to achieve the future which is socialism. They called it the "yawning heights." The "yawning heights of Socialism." There's a very satirical, negative, anti-Soviet novel called *The Yawning Heights* written by a working-class university professor of philosophy called Aleksandr Zinoviev who hated the system by the time of its end, because everything creates its reverse you see.

Communism has affected and mutilated the world to an extraordinary degree which most people in the West who believe they were on the winning side in the Cold War haven't even really begun to understand.

Communism has also, in a Marxist sense, affected their own societies *extraordinarily radically* whilst appearing to have completely lost in the terms of fringe-Leftist sects and groups.

Adorno wrote in *Minima Moralia* that "After Auschwitz there can be no poetry." He believed that after this seminal event there could be nothing but sackcloth and ashes forever. And somebody once said to him, "Well that's a pessimistic position," which is ultimately *conservative*. Conservatives don't believe life can be perfect because *man* isn't, and therefore utopianism is an impossibility.

Leftists say, "Oh we reject all forms of progress," and the two sort of square up to each other in political terms. Don't forget I'm talking about the philosophies, not the sordid little compromises of parties that in the Western world are virtually indistinguishable from each other. Now Marxism believed almost with post-religious ardor—as it shot religious people!—that everything could be *changed*, everything could be reworked, that man himself could be reworked.

One of the most fanatical postulates is hostility to all biological notions of man and all notions of prior inequality. The idea that, in the end even human rights jargon will always disappoint, because there are always beautiful people and ugly people. There's always unintelligent people (and there's many of them), and there's always very intelligent people and always a range in between. There's always people of great physical power and people who are weaklings.

A very Left-wing socialist friend of mine from years ago said "The trouble with you" (he was speaking to me) "is you're against human fairness; you're against being 'fair.'" And I said, "Go to a maternity ward, go to a maternity ward, and one's born without an arm, or without an eye. Others are born hale and hearty. Some are intelligent and will never have a moment's disease in their lives. Others are crippled from the very beginning. And you talk to me about fairness?"

And he said, "Maybe it's not like it should be, but we must strive to make it so!" And I said, "Well, why don't you just *accept* the plenitude of that which is created?" And he said, "No, that's too passive! We must work on it to change it, to make it better!"

Now most people, in their hearts, in this society believe that making things more equal makes them better. I don't. I believe making them more *unequal* makes them better (which means you're monstrous in contemporary terms). Because the greater the space between people, the greater the prospect of transcendence and the greater the prospect of overleaping the present, means you can actually not evolve physically but mentally and spiritually into something else. If there's nothing above you, there's nothing to aspire to; there's just endless stuff beneath you. But I'm an elitist.

No contemporary, even Right-wing conservative politician, will admit that their party actually stands for inequality. Even in capitalism, which has endless inequalities of outcome doesn't it? That's why you have two big classes. *Of course* you believe in inequality! But the Majors and the Camerons and the Hagues of this world, the Duncan Smiths of this world, they talk about liberty . . . "liberty," and they talk about "freedom," and they talk about "choice."

Choice, choice of schools, choice of race, choice of gender, choice of where you go to buy stuff, and so on. "Choice!" But oh, if you choose one option you deny another! If you *radically* choose one thing, you disprivilege another variant. All life, even at the moment of small decisions *teems* with the bias towards inequality, discrimination.

I believe in discrimination. *Discrimination is a moral good and a moral law!* It's an aristocratic spirituality. Of course you discriminate. You discriminate over who's your enemy and who's your friend. You don't treat people all as the *same* except in some universal ninnydom which only exists in the minds of people who'd like human nature to be different from what it is.

People become more Right-wing as they get older, on the whole. Even within Leftist systems, people actually do get more metaphysically conservative as they get older. Why is that? Because death approaches, reality approaches. They can't live with these deluded, nonsensical views about human life, which is based on inequality and glory and difference. History's been made by a small group on behalf of and in the name of the groups from which they themselves derive their energy and purpose.

Marxism is false in almost every area of life; that men and

women are interchangeable (false); that the family is an enemy construction of man when it's the basis of human dignity in all groups. That economic activity between human beings is always a form of oppression when in actual fact almost everybody at one level or another gets something out of it otherwise it couldn't subsist in the first place. That man is nicer than he is, when human nature is dualist. Human beings are kind and nasty. They're avaricious, but they have a capacity for self-sacrifice. They're endlessly cowardly and lying, but they also have a penchant for courage and glory. That's what we *are!*

The great religions actually have always *known* what we are. They shift utopianism and the desire that we could be different from what we are, to another world. But, the Leftist pseudo-religions of modernity have brought it down to this level and tried to counter-propositionally achieve it through violence and political struggle. And the reason that it's got bloodier and bloodier, until in the end they become sickened of it themselves, the emergence within the Soviet Bloc of neo-liberals like Gorbachev who realized the whole system was a fraud, and it didn't work, and they could hardly produce anything economically, and you went to the West, and you went back home, and people were struggling to get razor blades and bits of cheese and bits of soap and so on, and you thought to yourself "*This* is a Superpower? We slaughtered tens of millions for this?"

And in a sense I think that the fact that he wouldn't defend the structure as it shuddered, because you can't reform a structure like that, it has to go down, and he sort of managed its descent, really, if you look retrospectively on what he did. He's *hated* in Russia now, hated because he took away the security of ordinary people, and that generation particularly, their life expectancy went from about 76 to about 53 because they lost *everything!* When capitalism came in, they hadn't even been educated to write a check! It was sheer terror for them, because they'd never had to survive economically at an individual level, and that generation just sort of died off as a gangster capitalism came in, because they had no lead-up time.

That's the great tragedy of Russian destiny, that every system has been imposed in a slab-sided and ferocious way with no softening of the edges. One sort of plate has replaced another one. Just as Marx wanted! Not the idea of gradual reform, the Blairs and Browns of this world, but total, utter, transfiguring change which will completely revolutionize the nature of man.

One point which is never dwelt upon, and there's an enormous amount of work on communism now, because it's now in the past, people can debate its details openly: the Jewish nature of communism. That is never, ever discussed and indeed is completely off-limits in nearly all academic discourse.

The truth is that nearly always half of the major core intellectuals in all Communist groups are Jews or partly Jews, nearly always half of the Central Committee or the Executive Council, the Revolutionary Vanguard or whatever it calls itself; the rest is made up of bohemian revolutionary gentiles who are totally hate-filled and despairing and hostile to their own society, and it's a medley of these two groups essentially. Outsider/insider groups to tear it down, tear it down—in the name of love of course, *in the name of love* – but as you tear it down you can catapult yourself from the fringe to the center.

It's the Gerry Healy speech, you know in the Workers Revolutionary Party of the past, the most fanatical Marxist-Leninist group probably in British post war history. There's others. There's Tariq Ali's International Marxist Group. There are various incarnations of the Trotskyist tradition which began in the '30's with the Balham Group in South London of the Communist Party of Great Britain and then grew up as a separate tendency.

One of the things that is, of course, interesting is that when they were more powerful, 30 years ago, and if they had known of this meeting, there would be a riot outside. Not just a bit of pushing and shoving, but an *absolute* riot. The pathological hatred of the radical Right by the *Trotskyist* Marxist-Leninist Left needs to be looked at, and there are several reasons for this. Partly they are the most connected to international revolution; they are the most committed to the idea that we have no groups;

"One race, the human race!" One race, the human race, and those who doubt it go under! *Reactionaries!* Who can't be brooked, whose ideas are a menace to humanity! Because you see, ideas are important for these people, it's not just "Oh you've got an idea." You get two English intellectuals: "You've got an idea. I have an idea. It's cricket you know. We debate, one wins the other loses, we draw, we embrace." No! Ideas are life and death and are the basis of struggle and *meaning*, you see? Because meaning for them is in the "praxis" they call it, the moment of achieved struggle and recognition of truth in ideology.

Now a Marxist intellectual called Malcolm Evans is a Marxist deconstructionist (he told me with extreme pride). I said, "So you believe in the complete destruction of all Western cultural norms and the replacement of it by a foreign ideology?" And he said, "You're only saying that to me because you're a bourgeois reactionary of the most *hateful* sort." Because he once said to me, "The bourgeois goes through life with common sense, the Marxist with his theory; theory *is* truth!" And I said, "And you put to death those who don't agree with your theory?" He said, "You're putting words in my mouth."

But the irony is that these people who believed in this current of theory were near the top in nearly all of our universities between about 1930 and 1980 plus, even in the United States. The University of Texas—can you imagine a more redneck state than Texas?—the University of Texas' Economics Department was *Marxist*. This is the state of the Bushes and so on. They had achieved an ascendancy in parts of the academic world, part of the mental thinking within Western society, which is difficult for many people to understand.

And conservatism was so weak-kneed in these institutions, and it was terrorized by Trotskyist mobs as well, it virtually disappeared.

I knew a chap who was the head of sociology at the Polytechnic of North London for a period, an Irish chap. He was just a conservative really, a Right-wing conservative. O'Keefe, I think his name was. And every term he moved his office, because there would be a brick, from the Socialist Workers, through the window. But he knew it was coming. And I said to him, "Why do you put up with it?" He said, "Well, why should I give in to these people?" So he had a little bit of spirit.

But for every one like him, a hundred gave up, a hundred went along with it, a hundred resigned. They sort of went into internal exile within their own institutions. And don't forget we're talking about conservatives; we're talking about people who are well to the Left of anyone here; so if *they* haven't got a chance, what do you think the sort of opinions that are canvassed by this group have? Because, since the Second World War, the sort of opinions this group deals with have been outlawed in all institutions of higher education.

I once addressed a BNP meeting, a bloke put up his hand and said, "You've swallowed a dictionary, mate, haven't you? What's it all about then?" And I said, "Look, I'm putting forward ideas to you which have been banned, in the auditoriums where they should be heard, for 60 years!" He said, "Oh alright, fair play mate."

But there's a degree to which that's what this group[1] *really is for*, because the reason that we have the society that we have *is* due to large scale economic and cultural forces, admittedly to a degree, but it's also due to the mindset that accepts them before they've physically happened.

Now Marxism, in a sense, advocates two contradictory things. But it believes its contradiction holds together in struggle. It believes everything is economically determined, and yet if you theorize about the way in which it's determined enough you can actually change the nature of the determination.

There was a theorist called Antonio Gramsci at the beginning of the 20th century who was in the Italian Communist Party ranks who split the idea of the superstructure—culture, society, the arts, intellect, media—from the base, economics. Then Marxism can go completely cultural and just swim around. Not linked to proletarian movements, not linked to trade union politics, not linked to working class political struggle as defined by the far Left.

Marx was quite funny about the working class actually, because he said, "When I meet these German trade unionists, I like them less," because they were stroppy individuals who'd contradict "Professor" Marx, as he insisted on being called. Don't forget he was giving the proles their theory. The structural rela-

---

[1] The New Right (London)

tionship between the intellectual master and the working class followers was quite apparent.

And Marx fancied himself as a politician not just a theorist, because he founded a group called the International Working Men's Association which is the First International. Communists talk about "Internationals": First, Second, Third, Fourth. The Trotskyist one's the Fourth, tiny little Trotskyist "four men in a kiosk" groups who'd "struggle" about which one represented the Fourth International, which was out in Mexico.

But of course a Stalinist agent killed Trotsky by penetrating his brain with an ice pick through the skull. Ramón Mercador, I think his name was, and he crept into his study and *stabbed him through the skull.* Anarchists to this day wear T-shirts saying "ICE-PICK A TROT!" because you know anarchists just love being offensive to everyone, even on their own side. And as the spike penetrated his brain, Trotsky's last words were his hysterical Ashkenazic shriek, in which he said, "You've been sent by him, *him!, HIM!*" (namely Stalin). And he had! And he had! He went out in the light and in the dark, one could say.

I once had a walk round one of these areas where they have these plaques, you know these blue plaques, and if somebody famous lived in the house there's a white writing. And I was with a Right-wing intellectual called Bill Hopkins at the time, and we looked up at this house where Engels had lived. "Friedrich Engels" it said, and the dates, "Economic Theorist." That's a bit tame isn't it? "Economic theorist?" I thought. You have to consider in the "percussion of ideologies," Nietzsche said, "the idea has an effect *after* the stone is thrown."

Consider the destructive impact these individuals have had on our civilization, and "economic theorist" doesn't cut it, does it? Perhaps you could scrub that out and say "The Destroyer of a World" The destroyer of a world, and that's largely what Marxist-Leninist ideology amounted to, the destruction of the norms of pre-existent Western civilization. Done in its name, done as a revolutionary detritus, brought to power by tamed theorists and political criminals who saw their way to a main chance. And it's dominated the thinking of our peoples in one form or another to such a degree that if you meet somebody in the arts now who's a fluffy liberal, and they say "Ooh, all races are equal; all men are equal; anyone who says otherwise is a reactionary beast; I'm for aid to Africa; I'm for saving the planet," they are mouthing the tenth rate approximation to this theory.

The hardcore theory would *appall them!* Ten stages back: Frantz Fanon saying whites should be killed, because they incarnate the guilt of the oppressive, imperialist, capitalist classes, which is based on Lenin's book in 1916 called *Imperialism,* whereby you have to explain the fact that socialism hasn't come about. That capitalism hasn't led organically to socialism, imperialism, and the defamations of the persons of color by (although he didn't call it this) "the White Economic Colossus," which is *still* the justification for many Third World radical groups even now.

This mixture of sentimentality, high theory, a Jewish desire for power, an extreme misanthropy which has used—because it's secularized and has no objectivist moral basis—any means to bring itself in, has almost at times brought our entire culture and civilization almost to the point of disaster.

Their armies dominated a half of Europe until relatively recently. Tens of millions of white people grew up under their structures, lying, evading the truth, just surviving. If you did Marxism-Leninism in Warsaw when I was at school in the '70s, *it* wasn't a joke! You didn't write sort of ironic, quizzical, and deconstructive ideas about the Founding Fathers. *You knew* that it was a secular religion, and you toed the line or things would happen to you, a file would go to the secret police about you.

In Romania, in Bulgaria, in Hungary, in East Germany . . . Dissidents would go to the shops in East Germany, and there'd be *eight* Stasi behind them in a car, an *amazing* degree of surveillance. Why? Because you need to impose dialectical purity on the masses. Because if they are allowed their own way, they'll just drink, fornicate, consume, and do what they want. You have to hold them to the mark, even by terror, and you have to build a wall around your country to keep people in! The classical thing is you build a wall to keep enemies *out* don't you? You don't keep them *in*.

Now, in closing, I'd like to say that there's been an extraordinary cowardice amongst Western intellectuals in the adoption of these sorts of views.

Robert Conquest, who was a minor poet in Hampstead, used to go to all these salons in the '40's and '50's. *And this is Hampstead!* Ultra-rich, creamy bourgeois types, many of whom have never suffered anything in their lives, and many of them were Stalinists at this time, never mind Trotsky, or never mind the revolutionary alternative, but *actual* Stalinists, people who'd read hagiographies (and there's plenty of them) written to Stalin: "Oh Great Leader, we are not worthy to kiss the feet of the son of the real proletariat." All this sort of stuff. People laugh at it now, but in those societies then, it wasn't a laughing matter

And Conquest was revolted about this and wrote two sort of revisionist books *The Great Terror* and *The Harvest of Sorrow* about the Ukrainian famine as a response to that. He also wrote the *Lenin* book in the Fontana Modern Masters, and although he got facts wrong, he was a pioneer in rolling back the mystagoguery of that sort of thing.

Don't forget that when Sartre was told there were camps in the Soviet Bloc he said, "Ohhhh! . . . but they're based upon love!" Based upon love, and that makes it alright of course. This is the idea that you torture them on their graves, you know, we're doing it to redeem the soul of man. But they don't believe man has a soul, so that's a bit problematic.

The one thing I would think, looking back on Marxism after 150 years in all of its variants, is the *extraordinary* cowardice of some of the most privileged people in Western societies who would not stand up to this type of theory, which is how it always begins, and didn't realize that in the end it would *destroy everything they loved* and everything they wanted.

You even see it in Oxford recently don't you? David Irving and Nick Griffin. Griffin's not a pal of mine, you know. But Irving and Griffin are there at the Oxford Union. They're speaking for *us* really, whatever we may think about them as individuals. The mob is outside seething, you know, *maaaad staring eyes!* All the rest. Smaller than in the past, but still there though! If they could, they'd get in and *tear them to pieces!* And they'd burn down the library as well. They really would. And yet, the ninnies at their Oxford tables will say the day afterwards, "Terrible riot y'know! These people Irving and Griffin coming along and provoking these people, bringing this mayhem and this mess into our lovely little Oxford streets, these . . . monsters!"

Where in actual fact, the theory of the mob is the street version of what their ideas would be in power, and these people would have *no* status. And what they really believe in culturally and spiritually—sensitivity, the Western way, listening to alternative arguments, basing things on empirical knowledge—they'd be out the window!

And they've gone along with this out of corruption and being almost too pleasant for their own good, being too comfortable, and flirting like an adult teenager with ideas of rebellion that are half-disbelieved in as they brook them, and not thinking that they will be used, and used again and again and again to basically destroy nearly all of us. And it's because they haven't realized this that—in a slightly softer version—we're in the plight that we're in.

But everything has its eras, and these ideas are breaking down, and I'll leave you with the fact that recently there has been an attempt in France to revive Sartre's reputation. Sartre was an Existentialist and a Marxist. He wanted to bring together two enormous areas of theory. He wrote a book called *The Critique of Dialectical Reason*. He could only write volume 1. It's 750 pages. It's in New Left Books, and it's a real, real ripper of a read! New Left Books produce it. He wrote it on amphetamines, high in jazz cafés, speeding away like this.

He was going to try and find a humanist justification for Stalinism. Yes he was! That was going to be volume 2, but he could never get the theory right, and volume 2 never appeared.[2] And at the end of his life Sartre and his common law wife De Beauvoir joined a Maoist group, *Maoist group.* These are Western intellectuals, don't forget, joined a *Maoist* group and sat with all these Chinese in these little garages. He edited

---

[2] *The Critique of Dialectical Reason*, vol. 2, *The Intelligibility of History*, was published posthumously in 1985 in French and in English translation in 1991.

a paper at the end called *The People's Fist*[3] or something like that, you know . . . "the people's fist." He's *totally persona non grata* in contemporary France, intellectually.

They had a big exhibition recently, at the Sorbonne, the big Bourbourg Centre, these sorts of things. And no-one went! *And no-one went!* And that is *genuinely interesting*. So people thought—because Sartre's famous existential line is "Hell is other people"—maybe people thought as they *didn't* attend those galleries, "Hell is Jean-Paul Sartre's theories!"

Thank you very much!

Counter-Currents/*North American New Right*
May 9, 2012

---

[3] *La lutte du people*

Revisionism:
Hard & Soft, Left & Right*

Now this talk which I'm going to give on Revisionism, Left and Right, hard and soft, could be construed in the future as a dangerous talk, because the Chancellor of contemporary Federal Germany would like to extend, as a particular remit of the constitution/treaty which is being negotiated at the present time, the idea that revisionist laws—or more accurately, *anti*-revisionist laws—that exist in certain Continental societies which have allegedly "known Fascism" at a particular period, be extended to this society and to all other EU access states, including a great wave of Eastern European countries who of course have acceded to the Union in recent years.

Now, one of the ways round this of course is to speak methodologically and in such a way as you talk *about* an area, and you interpret what people have said, and you put forward what very mainstream and counter-propositional and non-revisionist historians and others have said. And if you keep it within that box and within that framework, to be frank, you will be "alright." Don't forget, my father's generation was told they'd fought in the Second World War for freedom of speech. And now we have to attenuate what we say before we even get down to saying it, so that we will not fall liable to particular laws that haven't even been introduced yet.

Now the concept of Revisionism: there are several different meanings.

One comes from Marxist-Leninist theory. Whenever you have within communism, say Georgi Plekhanov teaching Lenin quite a bit of the Marxism that he actually knew and some of its materialist theory. When you then had later on a reinterpretation of theory, either for reasons of brutal state power or statecraft or genuine ideological split, it was called a revision. You

---

* A transcript by Davied E. Clarke of Jonathan Bowden's speech at the 12th meeting of the New Right in London on November 3, 2007.

were revising the prior theory, and it is true that certain Right-wing writers, academics, fringe academics, people who will have been expelled from the academies, and so on have used the term "revisionism" as a counter-propositional term, as an "enemy" term. They've shot an arrow back at former political and ideological opponents by using this term.

There's also, as the President of Iran[1] said quite recently in a German magazine, a genuine element within historiography—which is the *writing* of history, history as texts over time ramifying with each other—whereby different interpretations are revised over time and statements which were considered normative and absolute and beyond comparison later get changed and attenuated and repositioned and looked at in a different light.

Before I get on to the most controversial areas of Revisionism let's just have a few, more minor and less emotionally charged examples.

Sir Winston Churchill: In the 1940s, '50s, and '60s, biographies which were not hagiographies, in other words biographies which weren't enormous tributes to the man's internal and external excellence, would *not* have been permitted. He was in some ways a secular sort of sacral figure. When these revisionist biographers—Ben Pimlott a little bit on the Left, John Charmley on the Center-Right to Right as a dissentient Cambridge don, and David Irving's two volumes known as *Churchill's War*—when these books occurred, they occurred in an era when Churchill was already dipping down. Charmley's biography has Graham Sutherland's portrait of Churchill on the front, which of course the Churchill family destroyed because they didn't like that particular image of him.

So to revise something is to change the cultural shift, is to change the way in which something has been perceived that otherwise was uncritically received.

There are many examples. One key one in recent Anglo-Irish historiography is Cromwell and the massacres in Wexford and Drogheda. He was believed to have massacred, with the

---

[1] Mahmoud Ahmadinejad

English New Model Army, two whole Irish towns, and Irish people have been taught this for centuries. Indeed in popular Irish culture the word "Cromwell" is worse than the "c" word in traditional usage because he killed *everybody* in those towns and all the women and all the children and all the animals!

Now there was a book published by Tom Reilly, a Trinity College Dublin university professor (similar to an Oxbridge level professor over here), called *Cromwell: An Honourable Enemy* and building on the partially revisionist essay by Thomas Carlyle about Cromwell in the 19th century which forced, particularly within Protestant discourse, a re-evaluation of our only military dictator in English/British history. The idea began to creep forward. There's a little echo of it even in Churchill's *History of the English-Speaking Peoples,* where there's a little bit of congratulations to Cromwell for being at least a man of will, of honor, of courage, and of decision, even though he was in turn a hateful regicide. So Cromwell has been revisited and has been turned around and has been revived.

It now appears that in Wexford and Drogheda, the Catholic parishional and diocesan records state that nearly everybody in that area who lived *before* his army passed through lived *after* his army passed through. That the number of people killed may have been a thousand combatants who were slaughtered at the high point of a battle when they themselves had surrendered and probably put up the white flag to draw people in before they used arms, which in most forms of war does result in such an event.

That event occurred in the context of Protestants being massacred in 1641. It's taken *four centuries.* And this is just historical events between different peoples *in these islands,* for a slightly more judicious, a slightly more rounded, a less emotive, and more temperate view of massacres and events which are believed to have occurred, to be rewritten and entered into mainstream historical record.

Now when you're dealing with events like the First World War and the Second World War, which are *climaxes,* which were the sort of the industrialization of the principle of death in relation to the First World War; many who went through that experience saw a sort of factory-type killing established in battlefields in Europe, whereby the surface of the Earth became lunar and looked like the surface of the moon. Millions of men slaughtered each other in mud and filth and barbed wire. These were extraordinarily savage events, almost sort of revolutions in consciousness for the generation that went through them. Therefore, even to have revised views about the circumstances that led to that war has been very controversial.

One of the earliest American revisionists was Harry Elmer Barnes, and he really concentrated on the First World War and the currents that led to it, both at a micro level, looking at the *Lusitania* sinking, and at a macro level, looking at the power politics that came out of that war and that many believe led to the Second World War, because many do see the second war as a postscript to the first. Many see it actually almost beginning in a stage one before war is actually announced in '39 to '40, because it was partly unfinished business and we were partly into a cycle. Much of the hedonism of the '20s in Europe, and much of the despair of the Depression in the '30s in Europe, was that generation sensing an enormous revisitation of the bloodbath was coming.

Most of the writers and intellectuals during that period realized they were living between two explosions and between two wars. We in 2007 are living in the after effects of the Second European Civil War, which is really what the Second World War in Europe amounted to. And the First World War was the First European Civil War.

There is a dissentient notion within political history that the American Civil War, which of course is different and distinct, has echoes of some of the conflicts that will follow. The use of mass artillery and early machine guns of a sort against massed forms of cavalry and infantry, leading to massacre on one side and a very defensive warfare on the other. And the fact that you have two regimes: a white racialist, aristocratic, slave-owning regime against an industrial, liberal, bourgeois regime which preaches radical democracy, which tries to lead us on the other side to a degree, which puts a client government into the defeated South after it's all over. There *are* echoes. But this is inevitable because in cycles of war and history you will have echoes before, and you will have echoes afterwards.

Even the Boer War and its origins in 1899 through 1902 between ourselves (the British) and the Afrikaners has been revised and looked at again, even by liberals. But that is a war about which the controversial heat and the gas flare of intensity is much lower down.

When you're dealing with much more incisive and explosive matters these things are much nearer the edge. And it's *not* "talk"! You'll lose your career; you'll lose your reputation; you'll lose your respect; you'll be put in prison for having certain counter-propositional views about historical events.

In several major European societies at least 10,000 people, in one category or another, have been arraigned for these "crimes" of thought, including many major historians. Many historians, if you read them today, know that this is a minefield they will not go near.

If you take a very contemporaneous book like Richard Overy's history of Hitler's and Stalin's regimes[2] (as he calls them), the Soviet death total and the Soviet camps he's infinitely cautious with. He's prepared to draw an enormous amount of criminological and empirical evidence to prove that the Stalinist genocide *maybe* claimed a quarter of the lives that somebody like Robert Conquest writing in the '50s and '60s with *The Great Terror* and *The Harvest of Sorrow* said. And he's *extremely* careful and very judicious; very, very mainstream; very, very obliging to fact or presumed fact. Don't forget many of the KGB archives have been opened up since 1990.

But when he comes to the Germans in the Second World War, there is a gap, and there is a statement whereby he said, "Some of what I'm going to say in this section *may* be refuted by future research." And then he goes on to give a new version of the official version of the issue that most generations of schoolchildren have been indoctrinated with now for 40 to 50 to 60 years.

---

[2] Richard Overy, *The Dictators: Hitler's Germany, Stalin's Russia* (New York: W. W. Norton, 2004).

In the town that I live in, a selection of sixth formers from all schools were recently taken on an Auschwitz tour paid for by the local authority and its taxpayers to prove the evil of racism, to prove that voting for certain tendencies is regarded as *a priori* illegitimate and immoral, and also to look at a crime against humanity leading to the need for universal constructions of law and of morality.

And leading to trials whereby political leaders in conflicts that have little to do with what happened in Europe and beyond between '39 and '45 of the last century, can themselves be arraigned! The trial and death of Saddam Hussein involving procedures very close to the Nuremberg ones, very close to a similar ideology that was applied to post-war Yugoslavia, very close to an ideology that was applied to some of the fallen militarist leaders from Imperial Japan, very close to trials that people have wanted to enact but have held back.

Now, what's happened in modernity is that the ability to kill large numbers of people has become an ideological weapon on all sides. During the Cold War, one part of the human race learnt a view of history. Few people know that there was a massacre of communists in Indonesia in the middle 1960s. I've met an Australian who saw a pyramid of bodies on one side of an airport in that society. Whereas other crimes would be on the media almost every other night. And the reason for this is that one of the legitimizations of human rights and civil rights rhetoric is the belief that certain tendencies are evil and unregenerate and that other tendencies "make mistakes" and "have excesses" and "commit blunders" or are "not opportune."

Even in relation to the Iraq War 2 there is a mass debate within our contemporary establishment. *The Lancet,* which is the journal of our doctors, has said (methodologically) that 670,000 Iraqis, and more, have perished since the invasion, and Blair and Bush say, "It's a lie! We refute their figures, we refute the methodology upon which those figures are based. The actual figure is 150 to 170,000."

Why would they bother about that?

They bother about it because in the war of position and the crucible of political struggle *the numbers matter* and are of *cru-*

cial importance, because they enable you to demonize one side and extol another. They enable you to excuse one thing as deviation or error (subject to revisionism of one sort or another). Or you actually say that one tendency, by virtue of these actions, is beyond even what it is to be political, is a species of Satanism, is that which you have nothing to do with.

One of the reasons we have a Left-wing society, a liberal society, is partly because conservatism, that which is supposed to "conserve," is *brain-dead* in the West, and is terrified, and is afraid. But one of the reasons it's afraid is because of this area of secular demonology. Because when you have to think in an illiberal way you will "go over there." You will *have* to go "over there." You will have to touch certain thinkers who actually are in that proximity, and that is *demonic*, and you have to remain in the Center. And if you remain in the Center, you *can't* oppose the liberal Left. You can't oppose the world as it now is inside Western societies. We're now in the position that we're invading other societies to impose what exists here (or variants of same) on them!

Of course there are a lot of people inside the West who do not agree with the dispensation that exists here.

Now, Germany was divided at the end of the Second World War into two occupation regimes. In contemporary history and journalistic writing the Eastern regime of Walter Ulbricht and Erich Honecker was in some ways described as it was, a country that built a wall to keep its citizenry *in* and *shot* them if they got over the barbed wire in an attempt to get over that wall

The Western Zone though, was never said to be "occupied." It had been "freed." It had been "liberated" by Western power and liberal jurisprudence, French, British, and American. We had set up a zone there that later became the Federal Republic of Western Germany. Since then, the German political elite and beyond it—Central European political elites—have been terrified of any reversal in the demonic fortunes of the parties that fought the wars that brought them to power. Any change, any shift, any relativism even, any minor factual amendment (which always will happen in history) becomes decisive.

In the First World War, Lloyd George and others invented a

large strand of German atrocity story which was revealed in 1928 in the House of Lords. This is the idea that the Germans committed bestial atrocities in Belgium; the Germans ran around with babies on spikes; they committed atrocities against prisoners that were outside of the European consciousness and form of civility. It was later realized that it was complete propaganda, although in a society with a mass media that was far less refined and pervasive than it is now. You go out there and look at that screen out there, it's enormous![3] It covers the *whole room* ideologically and sort of in terms of its system of signs.

Now media understanding was much less cynical in 1914–1918. There's a degree to which a large number of white people were stimulated by propagandistic elites to loathe and detest each other and to kill not just hundreds of thousands but *millions* of each other right across Europe. In accordance with actually predated forms of alliance politics which in an era of mechanized and mass politics meant less and less.

Now the First World War's dipped down, there's hardly anyone left. But the Second World War is still alive and still real in human consciousness today.

Mussolini and Franco have largely been historicized. Their dictatorial regimes, their traditionalist, European, socially authoritarian governments have largely entered into a process that acclimatizes them to the memory of Caesar, never mind Cromwell and Napoleon. They are seen as regrettable but *normal* European dictatorships.

The National Socialist one is not and remains in a sort of shadow, *outside*. And while we have the present dispensation that we have in Europe, that will have to be so. So you have to understand that what appears to be historical research *is* historical and *is* research. It isn't about historical research as power perceives it.

If somebody says that Zionist terrorists blew up a hotel in Jerusalem in 1948, and Menachem Begin said, "There was a

---

[3] Referring, apparently, to a big-screen television in the adjacent room

warning, but no-one else heard it." That's one view of history. Zionist militants say to this day that MI6 had its headquarters in that hotel, and therefore it was a "legitimate act of *struggle.*" Struggle! And those are two perspectives. But that is for historians and for minor debate and for articles in *The Times* and *The Jewish Chronicle.*

What happened in the middle of Europe in the 20th century is *cardinal* to certainly a definition of white or Caucasian identity today.

One of the many reasons why our people find it so difficult to assert themselves—even to think about the prospect that they might!—is because of these events and how they've been interpreted. Because, as soon as they say "This is the English flag behind; this is the British flag, the Swedish flag; this is the German flag": "No! No! He's got the English flag! He's gone over there!"

You are entering into proximity to moral danger, to what some philosophers call "moral hazard." You're tiptoeing towards what the first thing a liberal journalist will ask you. I was once representative of an organization called "Western Goals" (it was a Cold War organization). The second question the journalist asked me on mainstream media was, "What's your view of the Holocaust?"

That's the second issue, because they actually had—and he had it on his paper there—two lines. One is, "Treat them like a negative barrister. They're hostile to your case, and you rag them and you try and take them down." That's the *first* mental proposition for the interviewer.

The second is: "National Socialism—*Shoah.*" Get them squirming on that, and what they've got to say about what Enoch Powell said, or what they've got to say about the European Union, or what they've got to say about contemporary crime is of no significance at all, because *you have them there!* In the pit, squirming! And that pit is pre-programmed. It's preprogrammed! And quite deliberately so. It's irony piled upon irony, because, of course, many of the people who use these weapons partly don't care about the truth itself, indeed deeply, often cynically have *no* interest in it at all! It is a weapon that's used, a grenade; it's a spear that is used.

Now a series of historians, often privately funded, often researching themselves, often people beyond even fringe academic life, have published a series of books since Maurice Bardèche in the late 1940s, questioning the veracity of some of these events, including people who've used other names which are not their own. Whether or not Alain de Benoist ever published a particular revisionist article using another name, he has never admitted to it. He has never said he didn't do it. No-one knows, because you have to understand that this was extreme and deep thought criminality.

An intellectual rather similar to Bardèche was executed by the French Resistance and its occupation/liberation authorities in France just after the war: Robert Brasillach. So there is a degree to which certain people have paid with their lives for having certain ideas or living through them.

The French film director Truffaut knew Lucien Rebatet very well, because certain fascist theorists in France were obsessed with cinema; because that is mass ideology and mass visualization; if you have an authoritarian view of society you will want to communicate not with just the small elite but with the masses; you communicate with the elite *before* you communicate with the mass. And Truffaut once said, *vis-à-vis* his friendship with this old French National Socialist—which is what Rebatet was, he was *beyond* the Vichyite!—nevertheless he said, "You can respect men who are put to death for daring to adumbrate an idea."[4]

This is in the land of Voltaire, don't forget, where ideas are supposed to be free and set us free in pursuit of the truth.

Now, a range of writers, normally they're in the United States. Why in the United States? Because they at least have (strangely) the covering of First Amendment rights and can publish freely, which is why an enormous amount of this material of course has come back; it's come back into Europe; it's come back even beyond Europe into the Arab and Muslim

---

[4] Rebatet was not put to death. Bowden seems to be referring to Brasillach here.

world in relation to the Israeli-Palestinian conflict. It's come back from often German Americans or expatriate Germans in America doing this sort of thing.

Tony Hancock said to me years ago, "What should happen to this material?"—by which he meant revisionist material—and I said, "Well, the internet will solve all that for you, but one way to do it, just one of many, is to give it to the Muslim world. Because it will then come back into the West in a way which does not seem congruent with the radical Right within the West. That's one of the ways in order to do this."

Now many of these revisionist historians of course *are* historians, who do not agree with each other and have different lines. Paul Rassinier is a social democrat of a sort who was actually imprisoned in a camp himself. Others may well be dissentient Jews like Friedrich Berg and Alexander Baron and others. Others are radical neo-fascists and ultra-conservatives. Others are Germans who believe that the use of the *Shoah* is a form of racism against them, that it is used to demonize German people and people of German ancestry all over the world.

The interesting thing about these "crimes" and the memory and the historical narrative through which they are institutionalized, is that they began affecting a particular nation-state and its warrior elite at a particular time. Then it extended to some of the allied nationalities. Then it extended out to (reflexively) the nationalities of people who destroyed that country! Now if somebody who's English asserts themselves in an ethnic manner, with a little bit too much militancy, they will be accused of spiritually being aligned to those forces, when they are descended from men who flew planes that obliterated the cities of that government.

What has happened is that it has become a generic form of thought criminality which extends out to almost all Caucasians, and then beyond, including in the victor and successor states! So it's become a generalized negative propaganda against *all of us* stretching from Iceland to Australia. No-one is immune from the taint of this retrospective "criminality."

So it's been used as an extraordinarily effective thought weapon and ideological buttress. And in societies where you can't read Arthur Butz or Robert Faurisson or Michael Hoffman or Paul Rassinier or Wilhelm Stäglich or Maslow[5] or Walter Sanning or Jürgen Graf or Germar Rudolf or Carlo Mattogno or any of these people. The irony is that people actually know what they say. The *Daily Telegraph* had a poll about four years ago in which they said—to the average Briton, this is the average Radio Four Briton:

"Do you believe the *Shoah* occurred?"

"Yes."

"Do you believe that the numbers that are used in contemporary historical record are right?"

"No!"

That is interesting. That is Joe Public, who've had nothing but one view, are prepared to accept that the figures are exaggerated, which of course if you put it in a certain way will get you imprisoned in certain contemporary Western societies. The irony is that because we have a conflict between state law and *power* and the desire to *crush dissent* and historical research, all sorts of little people, nerdy academics—people who don't look both ways before they cross—get smashed down in the middle, because it's a doctrine and an ideology of *power* against *power* in terms of memory.

If you're a German citizen and you say what the Israeli state says occurred, you can be imprisoned!

This is a fact, because Yad Vashem says that the number of victims for the *Shoah* is a half of the number that you're supposed to use. Therefore we have a situation that European countries will imprison their nationals for saying what the Israeli President can say openly!

But that's because *it's about power.* It's not *about* truth! The view is that the significant proportion of the European population believe that the post-war settlement was unjust, that it was victor's justice, that the government in 1948—although Adenauer may have genuine sides to him and was broadly speaking

---

[5] First name unknown. Bowden includes "Maslow" in a list of revisionist authors in his novel *Louisiana Half-Face* (London: The Spinning Top Club, 2010), p. 83.

conservative in difficult circumstances—nevertheless his regime was a partly illegitimate one. That there is unfinished business there, that America's domination of half of the Continent was a different version of Soviet domination of the other half of the Continent. That the endless laws of memory, and trace of memory, are an endless vilification of German people and people of Germanic ancestry.

During the 1970s and '80s there was an enormous split in Germany between the generations, and there was an enormous amount of intergenerational hatred, and far-Left terrorism grew out of that: a rebellion against everything German, a rebellion against everything that had gone before, a destruction and a hostility towards everything that was prior. You had very great oddities, though because some of these revolutionary Left groups ended up fighting against Israel with the Palestinians: fanatically anti-Zionist but would kill anyone for a scintilla of what they deemed anti-Semitism. So you get these strange combinations as you always do within a crucible of history.

But nevertheless, the extraordinary damage psychologically and sort of intestinally, that was done to modern Germany by the self-hatred and loathing that has been institutionalized there as a result of the discourse of the *Shoah,* is incalculable.

The Jewish-American novelist Norman Mailer said that the *real* victims of the Second World War were the Germans. A revolutionary statement, and in many ways a truthful one. What he means by that is that the people have been partly spiritually destroyed, morally destroyed.

Because before you take a structure down, you take it down spiritually and morally and in terms of its ethical sense of itself. You take down that which is above the top consciousness of the rational mind. You take down that which leads to a morally efficacious sense of self. If you grew up believing that you're descended from murderers and your nationality is worthless, and the most extreme form that your nationality took has no value—and even the communist states have an element of that—you will end up with a self-loathing population as Benoist has described it, which characterizes a large number of

Western individuals at the present time.

It's a sort of moral and psychological form of cancer, and almost everybody who doesn't like the changes in Western societies has had this moment. Almost everybody who's thought "I might in the 1970s vote National Front . . ."

"*No you don't!*"

"What do you mean?"

"*No you don't!*"

Because you're going to be linked to a trajectory that links you to this, and a lot of Caucasian people feel, "Oh my God, you know, to sort of assert myself in a minor and nationalist way, I will be re-routing my sensibility through what is presented as 'the dungeon'; the sort of Fred and Rosemary West writ large."

Your average Western person says, "*No!* No I'm not going there. I'm not going *there*. A bit of conservatism's alright. But I'm *not* going there!" And this means that we are, or have been left partly mentally defenseless in relation to many of the changes which have occurred. It's a sort of secular version of a fall, in a way, and there is within contemporary liberalism the belief that there's a denied God that needs a Devil, an extraordinary parallelism in the use of this idea.

People who hold these sorts of ideas, these sorts of historians including Serge Thion, who's a Leftist, including Noam Chomsky who wrote an introduction to Faurisson's book saying he should be given at least freedom of speech, for which he was vilified by neo-conservative lobbies in the United States. Everybody who's gone into this area faces demonization. Not just white people either. Anyone who touches this area faces it, and it's created a sort of paralysis and a double reflex in our entire population.

It means that the most Right-wing view that's allowed in our society is virtually President Bush and those around him. That's where you can go and remain within the spectrum of the non-demonic within secular modernity. You go outside that, you are morally *other*.

And it is not nonsense that I'm speaking. Almost every self-conscious generation that's come up since the war has this moment, irrespective of education, of class, and of everything else. There's this moment when people will say, "You're one of them, and it leads to that, and I don't want to know!"

And the problem is that we as a European civility will gradually disappear, because the generations that fought in that particular war and came after will disappear, but the memory and the ideological reinterpretation of these events will not.

Blair was asked in 1999 why the Second World War was fought, and he said it was to protect the Jewish race from extermination. Which is an extraordinary remark and an extraordinarily illiterate remark! This is what you get. Because many Western politicians never inform their population about normative historical truth, an enormous number of people are totally miseducated now.

The fact that the Second World War resulted from a confluence of parallel institutions of power, and the idea that great powers in Europe balanced stable alliances with each other, so that Germany could have one area but not another, and Britain would give guarantee to another state in order to invade, which in the minds of some of the people who made these decisions was the cause of war.

It's all out of the window with Blair. Blair views the whole of that war—and the present intellectual clerisy and academic and intellectual life; turn on the media that isn't sport over there and they *all* agree with this view—this war was fought from the retrospective outcome of ovens at its end. It had nothing to do with rivalry between states, nothing to do with ideological conflict! It had to do with some of the victims of that particular conflict and its aftermath.

So why has this event become so crucial?

It's become so crucial because it justifies the post-war age.

It justifies Western multiculturalism. It justifies Western multi-racialism. It justifies mass immigration by virtue of reverse. It justifies forms of liberal and attenuated European integration, because separate nationalism is a bad thing. Therefore you integrate to overcome the memory and legacy of events which have occurred. This isn't theory. No-one's interested in the European Union, let alone most Europeans, but there is a degree to which whenever they get a chance to vote on these things, a certain mania of consciousness intrudes.

We had a referendum recently in two Continental countries that were before then thought to be very pro-EU. One politician from one of those countries went to stand in the demarcated fields of Auschwitz and said on mass European and world television if people vote "No" in this very minor, methodological referendum/poll they are "voting for the *Shoah*; they are voting for *this!*" He later revised—a bit of revisionism on the spot—he later "revised" that sort of remark. Jack Straw said that the rejection of those treaties "would be a moral disaster for Europe." He later said that he'd said no such thing or meant something completely different. Because a vote before it happens is crucial, and then afterwards you think, "Well, who cares about that?"

So there's a degree to which the post-war world is based upon this. And one of the most crucial reasons for this is the domination of the whole of the Western self-conception by the United States, and the domination of Mid-East politics by Israel and Israel's conception of itself in relation to the United States, and America's conception of its own self-interest as almost being aligned with Israel to the degree that maybe there is a little bit of separation, maybe there is a distinct chink of light between the contemporary American nationalist/neo-imperialists and Zionism. But it is so fine a difference and you have radical Protestantism as the cultural discourse in the background that forces—even if there *was* any difference—a virtual merger between the two.

And this means that European countries, whether they like it or not, in the First and the Second Gulf Wars, were dragged along to fight essentially an Israeli war pursued by American power, whether they wanted to or not. And all the muteness and the partial semi-surrender, and the very weak and rather corrupt French president daring to stand up to the United States and its colossal power, with Germany hiding, *literally hiding*—contemporary Germany—behind the French, was an attempt at a minor neutralism and which is an attempt *not* to go along with that.

Britain? We're in with America, and we go where they go. And any war or adventure they want, we go in as well. We've spent six-and-a-half billion of our cash in Iraq. We've lost 200 men. We've achieved absolutely nothing! *Absolutely nothing*. And we have done so because in 1956 we attempted a very minor independent move with the Israelis and with the French and earned American disapproval. And that was a very cold burst. And the British establishment doesn't like cold bursts. And American power faced internally within the West is awesome, even though they have very little idea what to do with it.

And yet, in a strange way, they do know exactly what they're doing, and what they're doing is imposing the logic of an attenuated French Revolution, of the American Revolution, on the whole planet. Equality, indeterminacy, aspiritualism, materialism, the right to shop, the right to vote (parts of it are the same), human rights, civil rights, Israel always safe. This is the agenda that's being pushed all over the world in Africa, in Asia, in the Middle East, in Central and Latin America, which they virtually regard as a dominion and an extension of their own state power, from the Monroe Doctrine onwards.

Now, this means that when you tack against certain historical verities, even in relation to numbers, you are pushing against the nature of the modern world as it's become, as it's been constructed. So in a way you are chipping away at the foundations of an enormous edifice.

An element of the emotion around these issues is semi-religious! There are many people who regard blasphemy in relation to this orthodoxy in the way that atheism would have been treated in this country before 1800. It is: you are *outside* if you posit this. And this is a crucial thing that Right-wing and Europeanist discourse has to confront and has to, in a sense, overcome. The past won't do it. To just say, "Time will pass, a century will pass. In 40 years from now it's a century from me to them! People will forget."

No! Because these things will be put before them *always* and present and forever and a day. They'll even be used against assertion by the new Russia, a country which can only be fitted into the schema in a sort of strange way, but a power that fought might and main against fascism and has achieved an element of national sense of itself under communism in that war. *It* has to go along with the feelings of guilt and moral reparation as well, certainly if it's ever to join the rest of the West in a wholehearted way. And if you are perceived as a country that links at all with the ideas of the regimes that fell in flames and have been demonized by trial, *even* if you fought against them in the past, you are part of that trajectory of guilt and that solidarity of lost innocence.

Now, the figures that were adumbrated immediately after the war of seven-and-a-half million have come down to six, have come down to four-and-a-half according to Norman Stone. Raul Hilberg, for instance, would push that much further down. So we have a sort of collapse in some of the paraphernalia of this particular historical narrative. But what's really happened is that the political use of this has partly separated off from revisionism and counter-revisionism, because it's become an ideological arrow, bludgeon, weapon, independent of the facts.

So there is a degree to which, even if there is a sort of conceptual shift—like your computer goes down, "clunk" and then you reboot it, and it comes up again—and Western ideology in the next 50 years, from the top down, recomposes itself to say, "Well there was an error about these figures, and there was Communist post-war exaggeration particularly from Poland, and we're now revising it all for you, maybe for a lesser figure."

But the impact of the *moral statement* will in a sense be the same or different. Indeed, to say that because the figure may well be less, that less of a moral crime is imputed, will be made to be worse than the prior discourse, because it's not really about those who suffered and those who died and those who didn't in a particular way. It's about who rules the West, and who rules Britain, and who rules the United States, and what the future of the world will be.

At the moment we have an enormous "clash of civilizations" as it's called, and much of the Western world is now convulsed by the idea that we are pitched headlong into an antithetical struggle with the Islamic world. You only have to turn on the news broadcast to see that. And many ordinary Westerners internalize this and cannot at all understand, in many ways, what is going on. Has communism been replaced by a new bloc in secular Western terms that we need to oppose?

But in actual fact, of course, although cultures and civilizations will clash and will often clash violently with each other, the reason for these wars and the reason for this contestation began in 1945, began in 1939, began in 1914 and is a continuation of these processes that may even predate that. We are always in a situation whereby if we were to chart an independent course we would have to overthrow American foreign policy in the last 50 years.

I was once asked on a platform for a party[6] that I used to be a member of—that changed its opinions about some of these matters several years ago—what my view of Israel was, and I said—and everyone else on the platform had refuted what I'd said *before I'd said it*, which is an interesting conceit—and I said, "Israel is a terrorist state, and is not a morally legitimate one."

Horror! But he's posh, and he's got a bow tie on, so we'll let him say it. But there was moral horror. And this is a group that is regarded as fascistic, don't forget. This is a group that is regarded as a far-Right group by the media. *The Guardian* would say they've just changed their lines to accommodate themselves to new realities. It's just cynicism.

In actual fact it's not quite that actually. It's cynicism and other things as well, all combined. But, there's a degree to which we will be dragged into war after war in relation to the Third World, in relation to American power politics over the Gulf and their need for oil, but also we will be systemically dragged in to the radical *and increasingly radical* consequences of the post-war dispensation. The fact that in a way the governments and opportunities of white people in Europe that were occupied twice over after 1945 by communism and American capitalism and by a particular world view which is *not* a

---

[6] The British National Party

European one, and that the occupation of the West was subtler and deeper and more invasive and more destructive than the occupation of the East.

Communism killed and chopped off the arms and behaved like you're on a Procrustean bed. "You want more sympathy? We'll cut another finger off!"

But American domination was subtler, more deconstructive. It's broken down people in the West far more than people, though physically savage, were broken in the East, because it's destroyed elements of their self-respect. Peter Hain was asked recently, "What has Western civilization achieved?" He said, "Nothing! . . . Nothing at all!"

He said "Nothing at all"!

"These are the people," he said with his finger in the air, "these are the people," he was then negotiating the peace deal in Northern Ireland, "these are the people who gave us Stalin," interesting as he's a Leftist, "Stalin and Hitler, these are the people who gave us that!"

It's interesting isn't it? This is his *own* civilization as he allegedly perceives it, and all we've done is that!

We've created *no* millennial civilization. There have been *no* libraries. There's been no classical or neo-classical sculpture. There's been no Beethoven. There's just death and pillage and authoritarianism. This is allegedly what we are responsible for. And this is a man in *our* government! As though we're beasts without mind and without wit and without intelligence.

There's an irony here. When somebody's uncultured, when somebody's boorish or doesn't know anything about art and those kind of things, they're called a philistine. There are certain archaeologists who have actually dug down and looked at the Philistine culture. And the Philistine culture, such as it was, was not quite as barren, not quite as stupid, not quite as archaic as one might suppose, or their enemies supposed. And there's an important lesson there, and that is that civilization and barbarism—often in a Western, Faustian context—are interwoven with each other.

We believe in the ferocious remaking of reality, moment by moment and layer by layer. Our previous speaker partly touched on some of the dynamics in our very complicated, fluid, but also hard civilization. When you ask a contemporary liberal what do they believe, they don't really know, and they fear that if they authenticate themselves they will be revisiting the after-effects of the *Shoah*. That's the truth. That *is* the mental construction that people face. It's almost tendentious, if somebody says a bit too militantly, "I like the music of Richard Wagner!" That implication is only just under the surface. And it's only just under the surface of being under the surface if you say Beethoven and Mozart instead of Wagner. It's there! *Any* white self-assertion is regarded as an act of semi-criminality now, and it is because we cannot face certain facts, certain misreading of facts.

Let's have a few facts. Hundreds of thousands of Germans who were pushed out of Slavic countries they'd been in for centuries, decimation of German cities by British terror bombing (let's face it), total destruction of those cities. A friend of mine called Bill Hopkins once told me that if you went to Hamburg—and I believe he was in the RAF there in '48—the stench in summer of all the bodies under the buildings was unbearable, unbearable in the height of summer.

Let's have a few other facts: massacres of large numbers of white Russian prisoners who fought on the Axis side because they had become "enemies of the people." When we decamped them back to Yugoslavia, and they went before people's courts to receive the summary justice of the masses.

The large number of death squads who roamed French towns and villages after the Liberation with white sort of things on their sleeves and they said, "We're with the Free Forces of the French Interior." And you had a book by Charles Maurras on your shelf, and they drag you out, and shoot you in the back of the head, and put your body in a ditch. "Purification" it was called, the purging of those who had collaborated in a corps, against the interests of the French masses and humanity, and so on and so on.

You see there are facts and *facts*. And there are those that are used one way and those that are used another. When America bombed Serbian positions in the 1990s, they said they were doing it to "stop ethnic cleansing." But Israel is based on ethnic cleansing. So one standard for one and one standard for another.

But that's life, and that's *power,* and that's the reality and the vortex of power. What we have to do is to understand that things have been used against us for ideological reasons, irrespective of the facts, and only when we have the courage to do that will we revive.

So it's really only when a leader of revivalist opinion is asked, "Well what's your view of the *Shoah* then?"

And they say, "We've stepped over that."

"What do you mean you've 'stepped over' that? Are you *minimizing its importance to humanity?"*

You say, "We are minimizing its importance to *our* form of humanity!"

At the present the United States Congress is trying to push through a sort of moral "statement," if you like, and they're always very keen on this, saying the Turks committed genocide against the Armenians at the end of the Great War. This is causing great contravention, because they need Turkish support given the situation in northern Iraq. As we speak, the Turks have massed a large part of their army on the north Kurdish border to invade, to attack a Marxist group that's attacking Turkish territory.

The Turkish state has put out what would be regarded as revisionist ideology for most of the 20th century actually. You can get it from quite a lot of Turkish embassies and so on. And yet they also would contextualize much of the violence: as many Turks died as Armenians, different groups were involved in the slaughter, marches by one were met by hostility and massacres by another.

When Saddam Hussein was arraigned and tried, he was tried for gassing a Kurdish village. But don't forget they were fighting a war which was called by some a First World War-type war often with gas, which was used by both sides in the Great War in the West of course. The Kurds fought on both sides simultaneously. The Iranians and the Iraqis *both* used gas. In the vortex of a war and the context of such struggle, to abstract one line of events and one series of interpretations and to arraign those who are responsible as criminals before humanity—a bit like Mafia leaders who are to be strung up on butcher's hooks—this is part of the discourse of *power*, not of history. But history is *about power*, and that's the situation that we find ourselves in!

So I do advise people, before these books are banned and before various people fish around under their beds looking for this book: "Sanning? What on Earth's that? And why has it got such a cheap cover?" "What's inside it?" And this sort of thing. Well this book called *The Hoax of the Twentieth Century* or another book called *Auschwitz: A Judge Looks at the Evidence*. Or some of the ones that Germar Rudolf's presently incarcerated for are up-to-date versions of some of these things.

One of the interesting counter-methodologies is that as the death totals in the most notorious camp of all have gone down and down and down, the burden of guilt/proof has been shifted to other camps (many of which don't even exist now). Because you *have* to keep the primary figure, because propagandistically the great fear and the great threat is that it will be destroyed.

I'll end with one quote.

There is a minor political historian who was at the University of Bath in the West Country of England. And he wrote a book about Fascism in the last ten years.[7] And he was asked about Revisionism, and he was asked particularly about Holocaust Day and the *Shoah* and its use in schools, and its use in primary schools, as a weapon of . . . as a "means of moral instruction."

And he said: "I'm worried about it."

And the researcher said, "You're worried? Why are you worried?"

And he said, "There're two problems with it. One, there's too many Muslims in British schools, and some of them will stand up and say 'I don't believe in it,' and then the propagan-

---

[7] Roger Eatwell, *Fascism: A History* (London: Chatto & Windus, 1995).

distic effect dips with white children." And the second thing, he said, is, "There are too many lies that have been told about it after the war, too many lies, and it's becoming *dangerous* propagandistically!"

And this chap said, "Well if that's the case, what do we do?"

He said, "Ah, ah, ah! I've got an answer. What we do is we conflate that in *with all other crimes,* so we have a 'Genocide Day' to deny the self-affirmation of *all groups!*"

Because ultimately, you see, the logic that applies to us will apply to everyone. Because identity, if it leads to the consequence through history of massacre, will affect *all* groups. So all groups partially de-scale or de-escalate *all* of their rival and competing identities. So we have One World for us all. That is in some ways what is proposed.

That is why, although radical Right people are thought by others to be full of hate against other groups and so on, it's actually a philosophical position of extreme conservatism: about structures from the past and how they relate to where we are now, and also how we can live on this planet together *without* losing identity which gives life meaning. Because without it, there is no context for art or beauty or philosophy or science or knowledge or progress of *any* sort. Because if somebody says to you "Who are you and what are you?" and you have no answer, all civilization will have come to an end.

Right-wing views are about difference, they're about inequality, they're about distinction, and they're about meaning. So I advise you to have a look at a few of these texts on the internet before Mrs. Merkel drags you away!

Thank you very much.

Counter-Currents/*North American New Right*
May 10, 2012

CREDO:
A NIETZSCHEAN TESTAMENT*

I think ideas are inborn, and you're attracted, if you have any, toward certain systems of thinking and sensibility and response. From a very young age, I was always fascinated about meaning and purpose and philosophy and those elements of religion which impinge on real matters.

And very early in life I was attracted to vitalist, authoritarian, and individualist ideas. And in my late teens I came across Friedrich Nietzsche's writings in the 28-volume, Karl Schlecta edition. Now those ideas predate my interest in them, because I was drawn towards them in a particular way.

As we look around us in this society now, our people have an absence of belief. They're very technically sophisticated. We still as a civilization bestride much of the rest of the world, like a sort of empty technological colossus. But if you peer inside, as to what we are supposed to believe, and account for, and what we think our destiny is individually and as a group, there's a zero; there's a nothingness; there's a blank space for many people.

A hundred years ago, Christianity was an overarching system in our society, for those who went along with it socially, for those who believed in it in a deep core way. It's now virtually—apart from small minorities—invisible. It's extraordinary how a faith system that can shape a civilization in part for a millennium-and-a-half to two millennia, can disappear. Those who say that certain ideas and ideals are impossible should look at what's happened to many of our belief systems.

A hundred years ago we had an elite. We actually had a government. We really haven't had a government in this country, pretty much, for about 100 years. Not an elite that knows what it wants and understands its mission in life, and that will hand on

---

* A transcript by Michael Polignano of a speech at the 11th New Right meeting in London on September 8, 2007. The original title of the talk was "The Art and Philosophy of Jonathan Bowden."

to people after it, and that comes out groups that exist before it. We're ruled by essentially a commercial elite, not an intellectual elite or a military elite or even a political one, but a commercial, profit-and-loss one.

And things have slid to such a degree now that if asked what does it mean to be British, probably about 8 million of our people will say Posh and Becks. That's what it means for many people inundated by the tube and its vapid nonsense.

Now there are many complicated reasons why much of what Western and white people used to believe in has gone down in the last century.

Nietzsche prophesied that the collapse of Christianity, for many people—even though he welcomed it personally—would be a disaster for them. Why so? Because it gave a structure and a meaning and an identity. A death without a context beyond it has no meaning. It's meat before you. I believe that we're hardwired for belief, philosophical and religious, that we have to have it as a species and as a group. Look at the number of people who go completely to pieces when there is nothing outside beyond them to live for beyond instantaneous things right in front of them.

In France they teach philosophy from the age of six. For the last couple of hundred years in the Anglo-Saxon and Anglophone world there's been hostility to theory. There's been a hostility to abstraction. There's been a complete reaction against a thinker called Thomas Hobbes, who in many ways prefigures many events on the Continent in the last century, many many centuries before. We had an extremely violent and convulsive political and dynastic revolution during the Cromwellian interregnum, and since then it should appear that we have a quiescence in this society. Yes, we've had radical movements. But the last major political movement to occur was the forming of a party by the trade unions in 1900, which grew into the Labour Party after the Labour Representation Committee.

But the idea that nothing can ever happen in Britain and that we are asleep is false. English life is often depoliticized, yes, but culturally English life has always been quite vital, quite violent underneath the surface, quite emotional. In our Renaissance, which is really the Elizabethan period, we were renowned all over Europe for being vital, for being scientifically oriented, for having our minds completely open towards the future. We were regarded as an aggressive and a powerful group that was coming of age. We created the greatest interconnected set of theater that the world had seen at that time since the Greeks.

We have lost our dynamism as a people: mentally and in every other way. Our people are still quite strong when it comes to the fist and a bit of pushing and shoving. But what's up here[1] is lacking. A thug is not a soldier, and a soldier is not a warrior. And it's the strength which exists up here which is the thing that we have to cultivate. I believe that strength comes from *belief*, in things which are philosophically grounded and appear real to you.

One response that a critic would give to what I've just said, mentally speaking, is that it's so individualized now and so broken-down and everybody sort of makes it up as they go along—that's called heuristic thinking, technically—and if everyone does make it up as they go along how will you ever have an organic culture again?

But I think this is to misunderstand Western society, and Western thought. When Blair says, when he used to be premier until couple of months ago, when Blair said that tolerance and equality and forbearance and humanism are our virtues, he was talking about, and turning against us, a tiny strand of our own civility which is part of our nature. English and British people often don't like to impose their ideas on others, often will avoid conflict until it becomes actively necessary. Many of these characteristics have been turned on us and used against us.

There's also a subtext to this country in the last four to five hundred years, and a lot of our Puritans and our obsessives and our fanatics and our extremists went abroad to found the United States. That's where our Puritans went. Now many of them were Gradgrinds, and the New Model Army banned Shakespeare in Newcastle, and flogged actors who dared to perform it. This is England's greatest writer of course. So there's a sort of Taliban

[1] In the head.

self-destructivity to that type of Puritanism. But we could do with an element if not a Puritanism, then of asceticism, of belief, and of asking foundational questions of what life is about.

To me this is what Right-wing politics is really about. The issues that people campaign on at the level of the street are not incidentals. They are the expression of what's happened when you are ruled by liberal ideas. We've been ruled by liberal ideas for many centuries, but in their most acute form in the last 50 years. Liberal ideas say that men and women are the same and are interchangeable, that war is morally bad, that all races are the same and should all live together. That a population just exists, that a country is just a zone, just an economic area, that everything's based on rationalism and materialism and is purely a calculation of economic self-interest.

Now there'll be millions of our people who say, "What's this chap talking about? This is all abstraction." Go out there on the street, and you see the example of the society that is based on these sorts of ideas.

Everybody's mouthing somebody else's ideas. Even Brown and Blair and the others. They are coming out with, in their own way, their tenth-rate way, certain of the ideologies that they knew when they were at Edinburgh or Oxford or wherever. Because everybody speaks—unless they are a universal genius who takes hold of reality and reshapes it as a cosmos of themselves—everyone uses ideas that precede them and to which they are attracted. Even to say, "I haven't got any ideas, and it's all load of nonsense," is an idea. Everything is ideological. Every BBC news broadcast is totally ideological, and is in some respects a soft form of communism, which is what liberalism is.

The last speaker today is a man called Tomislav Sunić, and his book *Homo americanus,* is about the American role in the world. And of course America is the model for much of the development that is going on in every continent and in every group on earth. America is the model. He said that, and don't forget he's a Croatian, and Eastern Europeans have *lived* under communism. Middle-class Left-wing students in 1960s used to hold their fist in the air and *talk* about communism, but these people actually had to *live under it.* And that is a totally different formulation, in every respect. What was a protest against mummy and daddy, and a desire to smoke a bit of pot and do what you wanted, led to concentration camps and slavery and dysgenics and death in certain Eastern European societies. What was just the mantras of adult babies out of their cots in the West was terrorism in the East, and that's what people don't understand.

But in that book he said something very revealing. He said that communism kills the body, but liberalism rots the soul. And that's exactly the case.

We face a situation in the West, where, paradoxically, spiritually we're in a far worse state than the people who lived under communism. And this is one of the great ironies, because amongst its manias and the rest of it, communism *froze* things. It froze things glacially for 50 years in many respects. And much of the decay, the voluntarist decay, much of which we've imposed ourselves, because of ideas that successive generations of our leaders have adopted from themselves and from others, didn't occur to the same degree in the East: the idea of self-denigration, that patriotism is the worst evil on Earth, that patriotism is one stop from genocide, that your own group is always the worst group. This hadn't been institutionalized and internalized quite to the same degree. It's perverse that peace and plenty can produce more decadence and decay than hardline Puritanism, artistic philistinism, queuing, and terror. But that's what's happened!

And in the East, of course, they now have the dilemma of Westernization. And that's joining us, because these are universal processes, and they won't stop at the boundary between the old East and West Germany.

I was born in 1962. At the beginning of the 20th century, this country ruled large stretches of the world. We're still relatively a *normatively* powerful country. The statistics say we're between the fourth and the 20th most significant country on earth. But you also know, on all sorts of registers as you look around, that we don't believe in anything anymore, that we're in chaos, that a large number of our people are miseducated to the degree they hardly even know who they are. That patriotism, although it still exists in the blood and bone and in the consciousness of many people, has been partially indoctrinated out of many. That people look behind them before they make an incorrect remark, even if they're in a wood! Even if they're by themselves, they still look around! Because all these things are mental. They're in the mind.

Five percent of all groups rule their own groups. And 80% always conform to the ruling ideology. If somebody says, "He's a demon you know. He's in one of those far Right parties. He's in the National Front." That's what they always say, because that's the generic term amongst apolitical people for all Right-wing groups, even though the BNP is by far the biggest group and has had by far as the greatest degree of electoral success, "It's all the NF really." And the mass attitude towards all this is "It's dangerous and threatening!" It's being a Catholic under high Protestantism. It's something that's a threat, and the masses are like this, and they always have been.

In Eastern Europe the present regimes would have you believe that the dissidents were loved. I tell you it's a fact that under Soviet tyranny, if you saw Anatoly Sharansky, if you saw Andrei Sakharov walking towards you, you'd say "Oh my God!" And you did everything to pretend that he was an unperson, that he didn't exist, that you weren't in the street with him. There could be a man in a watchtower watching you. Now everyone comes and says, "Oh, we agreed with you all along."

And in this society liberalism has learned how to rule in a far more sophisticated way. Towards the end of the quasi-Stalinist state in Czechoslovakia, secret policeman were looking under people's beds for abstract paintings and jazz music and this sort of nonsense. The West allows people to dissent, just to think in their own little boxes, and don't give a damn. Doesn't bother to ban books because 40% of the population can't read them anyway. This is how liberalism rules. It doesn't allow the privilege of dissent, because it disprivileges dissenting ideas. And if people can't think, and those ideas aren't worth anything anyway, it's invisible. And therefore you don't even need to "persecute." You can put economic pressure on people, so you got a choice to be sort of decanted from bourgeois life if you manifest in public certain types of opinion. That's one of the pressures that's put on people. That's done deliberately to stop people who have education forming in the head, forming a brain, forming an elite with the fist. And that's done quite deliberately, so that the leaders will be choked off.

If you go to the university—and Blair and Brown say everybody should go to university—at the University of Slough straight up the Thames Valley, there are 28,000 students, and they give courses in golf and tourism and hairdressing. It's just mass training for a postindustrial society, for sort of semi-robotic nerds to do repetitive tasks in trained environments where they've been timed and watched all the time.

Now, because I believe it's thought which characterizes our race and our group more than anything else, I think thinking is cardinal for many people.

When the events of 1968 occurred, there were convulsive riots all across the Western world by Left-wing Western youth. They can raise hundreds of thousands in the streets, and in the key events in Paris and elsewhere, there were a million in the street. There were also very large riots in the United States on many campuses. Western people have always been convulsed by ideals and by ideas. The idea that it's all in the past, that Francis Fukuyama said that history is ended, and then 9/11 happened. History never ends, and things go on and repeat themselves and come back again, at times even more violently than before.

What our people are crying out for isn't really a religion or a belief system, it's a form of mental strengthening in and of themselves, to overcome the disprivileging mechanisms that don't allow them to think and also allow them to reconnect with core areas of identity.

I'm not a Christian. And I never was. Although I went to a Catholic school, and they educated me very well. And almost every book in that library was by a dead white European male. And almost everything the one learnt culturally—from the rather gory sort of Grünewald-type crucifixion as you went in, to the Dalí on the wall, the reverse crucifixion scene, in reverse perspective from above, that was next to the assembly point, and to everything else—everything was European. And that's why people become Catholics. Did you notice many parents become interested when their child's about ten? And that's because they want to get them into these schools. Why do they want to get them into the schools? Because they retain the structure and the discipline. You don't leave when you're 16 and don't even know what your name is, you can't read or write, you speak like a Jamaican gangster, you have no respect for what you are and what you could become.

Now you hear about youth crime, and you hear a lot about the uncontrollability of many people in society. They're not controlled because there's no control up *here*.

One of the cardinal weaknesses of the contemporary West is the feminization of all areas of life. Masculinity is a sacred thing, and yet it's been demonized and disprivileged in the Western world, regarded as just an excuse for brutality. Masculinity is about self-control. It's about respect and power that's ventilated when it's *necessary* to use it. The only way in which you would cure many of the problems that presently exist with elements of lumpen and criminality at all levels of life is to reintroduce national service, with *maximum harshness* in the initial period.

And a few would die because, they'd be too obese to get through those tunnels, and over those walls with serrated glass, with people screaming at them in an unpleasant accent. But you would need to do that. And the reason isn't physical; the reason is psychological. Some of our Marines cried when the Revolutionary Guard in the Gulf took their iPods off them. This is where we've declined! This is the Green Berets! These are the Royal Marines! The Revolutionary Guard in Iran, the Quds brigade, which is the elite brigade which reports directly to the supreme leader, Ayatollah Khamenei, couldn't believe it when they saw that sort of thing. The post-imperial British truly have a tremble in the lip. But these things in the end are cultural, and philosophical, and psychological.

Now our civilization has had many religions and many dispensations of thought. But one of the things that we have forgotten is that open-mindedness to the future and respect for evidence does not mean woolliness and an absence of *certitude* in what we are.

There's a thinker who existed two-and-a-half thousand years ago called Heraclitus, and my type of thinking is his linear descendant. He's a Presocratic; he's a Sophist; he begins right at the beginning of Western thought, when we actually write down what we think. He wrote a book on nature which Aristotle glossed, and which has survived in fragments.

What did he believe?

He believed that everything is a form of energy. "Fire" he called it; we would call it "energy" today. That it exists in all forms of organic and inorganic matter. That thought and the sentience of nature is what we are. Nature has become sentient in us, which means we must incarnate natural law as a principle of being. It's called becoming in my philosophy. The Right, even if you don't use that term, stands for nature and for that which is given.

What does that mean?

It means conflict is natural, and good. It means domination is natural, and good. It means that what you have to do in order to survive, is natural, and good. It means that we should not begin every sentence by apologizing for our past or apologizing for who we are.

Tony Blair made several interconnected apologies when he was Premier, but he didn't apologize for being Premier. He apologized for the Irish famine. I've got Irish blood, but I'm not interested in apologies for the Irish famine. He apologized for the *Shoah*. He apologized for slavery. He apologized for almost everything going. These apologies are meaningless, as some of the groups that they were targeted on had the courage to say. It's just temporizing sympathy.

In my philosophy sympathy multiplies misery. And if somebody's in pain in front of you, you give them some options. And if they can't get through it, suicide's always an option.

Now, what does Nietzsche believe? He believes that strength is moral glory. That courage is the highest form of morality. That life is hierarchical. That everything's elitist. There's a hierarchy in each individual. And a hierarchy in every group of individuals. There's a hierarchy between groups of individuals. Inequality is what Right-wing ideas really mean.

Right-wing ideas aren't just a bit of flag-waving and baiting a few Muslims. Right-wing ideas are spiritually about *inequality*. The Left loves *equality*. It believes we're all the same. We must be treated the same. And they believe that as a morality. As a *moral good* which will be *imposed*.

Under communism, Pol Pot shot everyone who'd read a book that he didn't approve of. Why did he do that? Because he wanted everyone to be the same, and everyone to think in the same way. Asiatics have a formal description. It's called the tall poppy syndrome. They look at the plants. They decide one's a bit out of kilter. It's standing higher than the others, so you snip it down, so all are the same.

Pol Pot's not his real name by the way. It's a joke name; it means "political potential." When he was very young, Maoists wrote down, "This man has political potential." "Pol Pot." And that's where he took it from. This man is a terroristic psychopath. But when he took over his society with a teenage militia high on drugs, and almost everything had been blitzed and was defenseless, he put into practice in a cardinal way, what many of these Western idiots in the '60s with their fists in the air have been proposing. He sat in Paris, in salons listening to Kristeva, listening to Sartre, listening to De Beauvoir. And he imposed it implacably like the cretin he was. The family is immoral. Shoot all the village priests that got people married. Shoot people who are bit too keen on marriage. Shoot everyone who's read books about marriage. Shoot everybody who ever said marriage is a good thing. That's quite a pile of bodies, and you haven't started yet.

That is communism in its rawest and its crudest form. It's a sort of morality of bestiality, essentially. And it can't even impose equality, because in the communist societies of yesteryear, the elite will have its own shops, and its own channels, and they will have their own corrupt systems to keep their children out of military service, and so on. Just like Clinton's America, or Vietnam America before it. Every elite in that sense will recompose, despite the stigma.

Inequality is the truth. Because nature is unjust, but also fair in its injustice. Because there's always a balance. People who are very gifted in one area will have grotesque weaknesses in another. People who are strong in one area will be weak in another. People who are at the bottom within a hierarchy have a role and have a place in a naturally ordered society. And will be looked after, because patriotism really is the only socialism. That's why the Right appeals to *all* parties. And to *all groups* within a culture. Because *all* have a place.

Now, I believe that in the Greek civilization, a peasant woman could kneel before an idol, and could have a totally literalist—it's called metaphysically objectivist—view of the religion. She believes in it *absolutely*. A fundamentalist in contemporary terms. And you can go right through the culture to extremely sophisticated intellectuals, some of whom were agnostics and atheists who supported religion—yes they did!

Charles Maurras was believed to be an atheist, but he led a Catholic fundamentalist movement in France. Why? Because if you are Right-wing, you don't want to tear civilization down just because you privately can't believe. You understand the discourse of mass social becoming. What does a wedding mean? What does a death mean? What does the birth of a child mean? Unless there's something beyond it? What does a war mean? Just killing for money? Unless there's another dimension to it

We are reduced: as white people first, and just as humans second. But we have to understand that belief is not a narrowness. Belief is an understanding that there are truths outside nature, and outside the contingent universe that's in front of us, that are absolute. The Left-wing view that it's all relative, or we make it up as we go along, is false.

Nietzsche believes that we test ourselves here now in relation to what's going on before us. And the more primordial we are, the more we live in accordance with what we might become, the more we *link* with those concepts which are eternal and that exist outside us.

So what appears with half an eye closed to be an atheistic, a secular, and a modern system, if you switch around and look at it from another perspective, is actually a *form* for traditional ideas of the most radical, the most far-reaching, the most reactionary, and most archaic and primordial sort *to come back*. To come back from the past.

What the New Right on the Continent in the last 40 years has been is the reworking of certain ideas, including certain ideas associated with fascism, and their reworking so that they *come back*, into modernity, where we are now.

If you look at mass and popular culture, the heroic is still alive. It's still alive in junk films, in comic books, in forms that culturally elitist society and intellectuals disprivilege.

Why the heroic treated at that level? Because liberalism can't deal with the heroic. It doesn't have a space for it in its ideology, so it decants it.

Nothing can be destroyed. Liberals think that they've destroyed the ideas in this room, but they haven't. They've just displaced them into other areas. And they've found new ways to come up, and new syntheses that emerge.

Much of popular culture involves the celebration of men—iconographically, in films and so on—who are authoritarian, who are hierarchical, who are elitist. How many cinema posters have you seen with the man alone with a gun staring off into the distance? It's the primordial American myth.

These are men who think "fascistically." And they fight against fascism. They fight *against* authoritarian ideas of what the West once was and can be. This is always the trick: that they will use the ideology of the Marine Corps to fight for a liberal, a humanist, and a democratic purpose. That's the trick. In every film, in every television program, in every comic, in every simple novel, in everything that the masses consume that isn't purely about sex or sport, the heroic is there. And they always fight for liberal causes, and their enemies are always grinning Japanese generals, or Nazis. Used again, and again, and again, as a stereotype, of a stereotype, of a stereotype, to impose the idea that that which is core, primal, Indo-European, is *morally wrong*.

I must have spoken, in the four years I was in the British National Party, at 100 events, 120 events, 150 events, if you add everything together. Now, I've never mentioned this topic, which I'm going to talk briefly about now. And this is the topic known as the *Shoah*.

Now all my life, this has been used as a weapon. All my life.

Against any self-assertion by us.

Whenever the most mild and broken-backed Tory starts to think, "Immigration has gone a little too far," the finger will *go down*. And he will fall on the ground, and say, "Oh no, oh no, I may have made a minor complaint before I was going to leave office, but don't drag me in that particular direction."

And of course, many of the people who use this as a weapon don't give a damn either way. It's a weapon they can use. And it *shuts people up*, instantaneously. And it does so because it impinges, at quite a deep level, on what white and European people think about morality.

And this is a deep problem. And it's a problem that all Right-wing politics since the Second World War, which was in reality a Second European Civil War, the European equivalent of the American Civil War in some ways in the century before, of which in a very complicated way it's both an attenuation and reverse reflex.

But this issue is very, very deep. And very complicated and important. And goes beyond methodologies about the figures for the number of purported victims involved. Many Western people feel that, because it is generally a given in the society and culture that they're in, that variants of our group have committed atrocities, that our civilization is therefore rendered worthless, almost in its entirety.

Except when it apologizes before it even states that it has a right to exist. So every time Wagner is played on Radio Three there will be, *there will be*, a sort of 30-second health warning, like on a packet of cigarettes. It's as literal as that! And because it's an ideology. It's got to. It imposes itself. Ideologies want to impose themselves, like liquid finds its own level in a tank.

If I was running the BBC, it would be slightly different from what's on tonight. In fact those dumb people working at the BBC at the moment would hang themselves in their studios at the thought.

There is a degree to which the issue of the *Shoah* is very cardinal, because it has caused intergenerational hatred, particularly in Germany and elsewhere. It has caused degree of self-hatred among our own people, something that de Benoist, the French

New Right theoretician from France, talks about a great deal.

And this is the worst type of denigration, because denigration that comes from without is rain that bounces off, and can be withstood: you can put up an umbrella and get rid of it. But that which comes from *inside* is much more corrosive, much more deconstructive, much more disabling. And one of the reasons why this issue, as if this is the only event of brigandage that has ever occurred, but nevertheless, relativism, deep down, isn't enough.

When the IRA committed an atrocity they said, "Never mind ours, look at the British! Look at the Loyalists!" And people said, "What about this, what you've done?" They said, "No, no, no, look what *they've* done."

Deep down, philosophically, that's not good enough. The problem we have, is if you are very Christian or post-Christian in your morality—where there's a total dualism of good and evil—and if you think and have been indoctrinated at school from a very early age that our group has committed some monstrous evil, you are "endwarfed," to invent a word. You are semi-humiliated, from the start.

When you begin to assert yourself you suddenly begin to remember, "Oh, I need to apologize before I do." And that's not just a strange intellectual concept. *Millions* do that all the time.

They say, "I'm not this, but . . ."

They say, "I don't want to make an extremist remark, but . . ."

They say, "Well, I don't really wish to go into the area of self-assertion, but . . ."

And the reason for all that garbage is because of this shadow. Or those that relate to it, in the background. And if you knock down one, another will emerge.

Every black group in the United States wants a holocaust museum about slavery in their own cities. That's the next thing. And they say to their congressman, "We want our museum!" "Well, I don't . . ." "If you want our votes, you're going to get us our museum."

It's as straight as that. Each group claims status for strength through victimhood. That's what we face. "I can be strong because I've suffered, and I'm going to get back because I've been weak in the past. And my strength is revenge, and I'm morally entitled." And lots of our people think, we were the primary and primordial and dominant group on Earth, for quite a long time, and now we're losing it, in almost every area.

Oswald Spengler wrote *Decline of the West* after the Great War, which of course was a dysgenic war, which had a considerably destructive impact upon Western leadership, at every level. But as you look around you sense the decline, and if you have a decline and you have a desire to assert yourself to arrest the decline, and you have to apologize to yourself about even having the idea of assertion to arrest decline, you're not going to get anywhere, are you?

And that's what this weapon is.

Now, my view is the following. I'm technically a pagan. And pagans believe that creation and destruction go together. That love is fury. That whatever occurred, and whatever occurs, we don't have to apologize. We step over what exists.

There's a concept in my philosophy which is called "self-overbecoming." Where you take things which exist at a lower level, that you feel uncomfortable with, and you sublimate them, you throw them forward, you ventilate them. You take that which you don't like, and you transmute it alchemically, psychologically, and intellectually, and you change it.

And you step forward and say, "No!" to past humiliations, to past indoctrination and degradation of the German people, who are *cardinal* to the European identity. Both because of their cultural and linguistic specificity, and also because of the fact that they were over half of the European Continent. If they have to apologize every day of the week, for being what they are, our group as a whole can never assert itself.

And my view is that when this is viewed as an issue: there are relativist dodges, and there are things you can say. The deputy chairman of the party that I was in[2] was asked about the *Shoah* on a Channel Four program. And he said "Well, which '*Shoah*' are you referring to? Are you talking about the communist holocausts, many of which were inspired by Jewish

---

[2] Simon Darby of the British National Party

ideas?"

Silence. A very radical statement for a contemporary BNP leader. Silence. Silence.

But of course, that's a clever answer, and it's a political answer, and it's a relativist answer.

But my view is I would say, "We've overcome all of these events." And we will stride on to *new* forms of glory. *New* forms of that which is implacable. We can rebuild cities again! Every German city was completely destroyed. It was like Grozny in Chechnya now: nothing at all!

I have a friend of mine who is a well-known Right-wing intellectual. He's almost 80 now. His name is Bill Hopkins. After the war he served in Hamburg, and during the summer in about 1948 when he was in the RAF, he said all the British troops used to go often outside the city, because the stench was so bad, because of all the bodies under the buildings that hadn't been reached, that hadn't been dragged out, or hadn't been put into lime pits.

But everything has been rebuilt. Because everything *can be* rebuilt, and built beyond what even existed in the past. So if somebody says to you, "You're descended from brigands." Which is in a sense, individually, what that sort of contrary ideology is. You say, "I'm not going to bother about brigands and who did what to whom. I've overcome that!"

"Oh well, I don't like the sound of that. That's a bit illiberal."

And I'd just say, you just say, "Liberalism is moral syphilis. And I'm stepping over it."

"Well, I don't like the sound of that! You sound like a bit of a fascist to me!"

And I'd say, "There's nothing wrong with fascism. Nothing wrong with fascism at all!"

Everyone now adopts a reverse semiotic and runs against what they actually think, in order to convince people who don't agree with them anyway. Because democracy—and I'm not a democrat. I'm not a democrat. When I supported the challenge in the party that I used to be in, I did it for various reasons, but to encourage greater democracy wasn't necessarily one of them.

But, authoritarianism has to have morality with it! Those who make an absolute claim and who don't live up to the nature of that claim, or don't even begin to live up to the nature of it, can't advocate authority. Mosley, for example, was regarded as above the movements that he led, and therefore there was a degree of absolute respect: even if people disagreed with him totally on Europeanization and various other things. Because of the respect he had, as a man. And if you are to lead Right-wing movements, you have to have that degree of character. Character is integral to that type of authority. It would be so in a military commander, never mind a political one. If it's not there you can't make authoritarian pledges and carry on in that sort of way, because you're just involved in the grubby game, which consists of Labour-Liberal-Tory and different versions of the same thing.

To make an absolute claim and not live up to it is worse than being in New Labour. Because they don't pretend, even though people have been fooled.

So my view is that we must return again to certain sets of ideas which suit *us*, that are cardinal for *us*, that are metaphysically objective and subjective, that see the flux and warp and weft of life, and its complicatedness, but know there are *absolute standards* upon which things are based.

If we can't overcome the weapons which are used against us, we will disappear. These are the facts. And therefore we have to do so in our own minds.

Every other group that's ever existed in human history has not had the albatross around it, that it only remembers as a form of guilt and expiation, and as a Moloch before sacrifices must be made, their own moments of grief and of slaughter and of ferocity. They configured the world in another way.

When the Greeks sacked a city in internal warfare, everyone would be enslaved. But they did not remember, when their bards sang of their victories, that they had denied the human rights of other Greek city-states.

No people can survive if it incorporates as a mental substructure an anti-heroic myth about itself.

This is why war is largely fought in the mind in the modern world. When Iraq was invaded and that regime was taken down, the precedents for everything which occurred had been done earlier in the 20th century. De-Baathafication, removal of the Army—but allowing them to keep their weapons; bad move, the Americans have learned the error of that, subsequently—the removal of the top of the civil service, trials for those involved, their moral degradation and expiation: hanging, in public, put on YouTube so the world can see it! A degradation of these *villains,* not foreign statesmen to which we were opposed and against in this war, but *villains, criminals,* that we must *demonize* and *destroy!*

Why is it done? Because it destroyed them morally, in the mind. And Iraqis think, "Well, Saddam was the one who did such-and-such. Why would you say that, Abdul? "Well, I've seen it on the telly." That's what 80% of people are like. These extraordinary reversals because this is a mass age. In the past countries were ruled by elites. You shot up an elite and put another elite in place. Now the masses are allegedly in charge, you have to indoctrinate the masses. You have to stimulate them to *fury*: your enemies aren't human, they're *beasts.*

Beasts!

Milošević: beast, human rights abuser, genocidalist. Saddam: our man in the Gulf for years, now a demon, a *demon!* An anti-Zionist, ferocious apostate, and so on. But most of the chemicals that he used in the three-way war—Kurds, Iranians, and Iraqis, fought on the First World War level—companies in Berlin, Germany, and France, in Russia, in Belgium, in Britain, and in North America provided that. The gas was used by the Iranians as well, and the Kurds fought on both sides. Now that is the complicatedness that people don't want to see.

And it's also applicable to all groups. An American colonel in Fallujah will be fighting in his own mind, physically, in a courageous way. At the level of him on the ground with the sand around it, and the flies in his eyes. He's not thinking about grand theory. He's thinking about getting through that tour of duty and getting back to the wife and the kids in Maryland or something. That's the level. We always have to understand that individual white Americans have absolutely *no control* over their elites, just as we have *no control* over ours. Because they've gone to a global level. And they think they've left us behind. They think England and Britain is a puddle, and they can step out of it to universality.

Well we can't step out of it to universality, because if you're not rooted in something, you don't come from anywhere, there are no roots that go down into the earth, then you can be moved about like a weed which has very weak roots and just rips out. And somebody stronger will rip you out.

So my goal, really, in all these Right-wing partisan groups I've been in, in one way or another, for the last 15 years is to preach inequality.

"Did you hear that? He says people are unequal." People are unequal: 75% of it's genetic and biological. Partly criminality's biological; predispositions to drug addictions are biological; intelligence is biological; beauty is biological; ferocity or a predisposition to it is biological; intellect is biological. You can do a bit, but you're born to be which you are, and we should celebrate what we were born to be. Because we have created 90% of value in modernity.

I am a modernist in many ways because I believe we created a modern world that has been taken away from what it could have been. The modern and that which preceded it are not necessarily in complete opposition. If people with our sorts of values ruled modernity, everything about the society would be, at one level the same, and in every other respect completely different. People would still drive contemporary cars; there'd still be jets; and there'd still be supercomputers, and so on. But the texture and the nature of life would be different in every respect.

How so?

Firstly, cultures would be mono-ethnic. Secondly, there would be a respect for the past glories of our civilization. Thirdly, we would not preface every attempt to be strong by saying "I'm sorry, I'm sorry for what we have done."

We're not sorry!

And we've stepped over the prospect of being sorry.

Menachem Begin in his autobiography, which is called—is it called *My Struggle*?—it's called *My Life*.

He was asked about the massacres of Palestinian villages, which was certainly instituted by his paramilitary group. And he said, "The sun comes up and goes down. It was necessary. We lived, we struggled, and they have died. Israel!" And we have to do the same. We have to do the same.

I once spoke at a BNP meeting, and this chap came up to me and said, "You're a bit Right-wing, aren't you?" He said, "I used to be in the Labour Party."

I said, "That's all right."

And he said, "Don't you think this party is a bit too nationalistic?"

And I said, "Well, what, do you object to these flags?"

And he said, "Well, I'm just being honest."

And I said, "Okay." He's willing to stand, and this sort of thing. I said, "Why does it upset you?"

And he said, "Well, wouldn't it be better if we presented ourselves as the victims?" I don't want to caricature the bloke too much. He said, "I'm obsessed by the case of the red squirrel." And I gave him a very strange look.

But what he meant, what he wanted to configure, was that we are the victims. And the problem with that is that it's what everyone else does. And it can be done, because there are many white victims in this society now, in the way that it's going. But if you concentrate on pain and defeat, you will breed resentment. And I believe that resentment and pity are the things to be avoided.

Stoicism should be our way. Courage should be our way. When somebody pushes you, you push them back. When somebody's false to you, you're false to them. When somebody's friendly to you, you are to them. You fight for your own country, and your own group, and your own culture, and your own civilization, at your own level, and in your own way. And when somebody says, "Apologize for this, or that" you say: "No. I regret nothing." As a French singer once said, "I regret nothing."[3]

And it's a good answer! I have no regrets.

One's life is a bullet that goes through screens. You hit your final screen, and you're dead. What happens after, none of us know. There's either a spiritual world, as all the cardinal and

[3] Edith Piaf, "Non, je ne regrette rien"

metaphysically objectivist religions of every type for every culture and every group say there is, or there's not.

In my philosophy, the energy that's in us goes out into everything which exists. That there is an end after the end, but it's not finite or conscious. That's what I think.

That's why believe in cremation. Because I believe in fire, and the glory of fire. I remember when my mother was cremated. If anyone's ever been to a cremation, there's a bit of ghastly simpering and this sort of thing, and they have a curtain because they don't want you to see the fire. Because it's a furnace, an absolute inferno.

And I said to the Vicar, "Look, I'll even give you some money. I want to see the fire." And he went "Ahh, ahh, ahh . . . Pardon?" "I'm a pagan. I want to see the fire." He said, "Good lord, are you one of those?" I thought he was going to say he'd take 20 quid more. But no.

And I was allowed to stand near the coffin as it went in. And it's just a blazing furnace. It opens, the sort of ecumenical and multi-dimensional curtain that they have over it, which has a peacock and various multi-faith figures on it, goes up.

And you see this wall of flame. This amazing wall of flame, that's like the inside of a sun. And you see this oblong box go into it. And the flame finds every line, and every plane, and every sort of mathematical conceit in the box. And soon it's completely aflame. And then the gate comes down.

And I believe that's what life's like. I believe that's what happens when a sun forms, when a galaxy forms, when one ends, when a life begins, and when a life ends. That for me is life. Fire, energy, glory, and thinking.

Thinking is the important thing. Being white isn't enough. Being English isn't enough. Being British isn't enough. Know what you are! In this book to read about your own culture is a revolutionary act. People are taught to rebel at school and hate our high culture, hate our folk culture—it's all boring.

I heard a Manchester Club leader who I vaguely knew earlier in my life who died recently. And he was in charge of Factory Records. Very Left-wing. That's why he produced bands called New Order and Joy Division, to make money out of it.

He said, "I didn't like '80s New Romantic music," and the Radio Five jockey said to him, "Why is that?" And he said "Because it's too white." Too white! Because its bass wasn't black enough, he said.

Now, if you have these sorts of ideas you will mentally perish over time, and you will physically perish as well over time.

But you have to know about our own forms to be able to deny the postulation of these people who would deny them. Knowledge is *power*. Listen to high music, go into the National Gallery. It's free. You can stay hours in there. Look at what we've produced as a group.

This is what the Muslims teach their people. To be totally proud of what you are in your own confirmation of identity. Because identity is divine. It's just like that fire that consumed the box when I was younger.

Nietzsche's philosophy isn't for everybody. It's too harsh and too forbidding for many people. But it is a way of thinking which is reflexive and absolute. It's a way of thinking which is primordial and extraordinarily Western. It's a way of thinking that enables people *to be religious*, in the sense of the sacredness of life, but also to be open to fact, and to evidence, and to science. It combines those things that lead to glory. And express themselves through tenderness and ferocity.

I urge all white people in this era to look into the mirror and to ask themselves, "What do you know about what you are?" And if you don't know enough, put your hand on that mirror, and move towards greater knowledge of what you can become.

We're all going to die. Make use of that time which remains.

Greatness is in the mind and in the fist. The glory of our tribe is not behind us. We can be great again. But the first thing that we have to do is to say, "I walk towards the tunnel, and I'm on my own, and I'm not afraid. And I have no regrets."

Thank you very much!

Counter-Currents/*North American New Right*
May 23, 2012

HANS-JÜRGEN SYBERBERG:
LENI RIEFENSTAHL'S HEIR?*

This 14th talk of mine is about a filmmaker called Hans-Jürgen Syberberg, who's not a household name, it has to be said, even within contemporary Germany. But if there was a title for this talk behind me, as there sometimes is at our meetings, the title would have been "Hans-Jürgen Syberberg: Leni Riefenstahl's Heir?" Because there is a degree to which in these talks I always try to find figures occasionally who are contemporaneous, who are alive and amongst us now, who are in this most difficult of eras, this most liberal, most democratic, most egalitarian of eras, the eras that are in every sense post-modern and after the crash, perceived in every possible way, of 1945 and thereafter.

Syberberg is a filmmaker who is possibly at this moment in time one of, if not *the*, loneliest cultural figures in the modern unified Federal Republic. He's most famous for a film called *Hitler: Ein Film aus Deutschland* released in 1978 which lasts seven-and-a-quarter hours. Seven-and-a-quarter hours! I saw it when I was 19 at the National Film Theatre, and it's one of those things where . . . Richard Nixon once said you needed a cast-iron behind to read law, but you really needed some vitamin C anyway to watch this film for seven hours, just physically. Because when you come out after having sat for that length of time you really are sort of rigid.

He's an East German, essentially, and he was born in 1935 of minor aristocratic and upper-class parentage. He lived in Rostock until 1945. He was too young to have gone through, or have had to go through, the de-Nazification process as a focused individual. But, of course, he went through everything that happened later, and indeed, experienced the beginnings of the communist statelet in the occupied East.

---

* A transcript by V. S. of a speech given at the 14th New Right meeting in London on April 5, 2008.

Syberberg was always—and is, because he's still alive although very elderly now—a controversialist, in every sense. When he came West there was a large reception for him from the cultural apparatus of the new federal West German state, and he made some equivocal remarks about the communist regimes of Ulbricht and Honecker. He talked about the fact that it's one of the first countries to build a wall to keep its people in. "But at the same time," he said, "they've managed to teach nearly all of us to read and write, which you over here in the west post-war don't seem to quite master." There was a slight pulling in of the welcome carpet, and people realized that Syberberg was in a sense a man who said what he liked, and that isn't liked in contemporary Germany or most other countries.

He began with a thesis on Friedrich Dürrenmatt and the absurd, which seemed to chart him out for a regular academic, non-artistic career. But he always had a yearning for total art, for the total art form of Wagner's vintage of the late 19th century: the *Gesamtkunstwerk*. But the idea of a total form that combines all others: speech, poetic higher speech, song, dance, movement, the visual image of the human and nature and the two together, of narrative story, of action and drama, and so on.

And when you think about it, film and the use of film, particularly by radical and authoritarian governments of the 20th century, is the total artwork for this era, as Leni Riefenstahl knew and discovered and made use of, which is why she became the greatest female filmmaker of the 20th century, the most vilified (if you turn it around) cultural propagandist as she was seen in that era—forbidden to make films in the post-war era.

Interestingly, a couple of years ago Mel Gibson was asked about her in the enormous brouhaha of controversy that blew up around his film *The Passion of the Christ*. He said that he would have given her a few tens of millions, because he's got that sort of money now, to make some of the films that she wanted to make—although she did make *Tiefland*—post-war. This is because the amount of money that you need to start up production costs for films is so great prior to digital cameras coming on-stream in the last five to eight years (HD cameras and so on) that for small but very large amounts of capital you can be completely stymied. Most films before the internet, if you can't disseminate them, it's almost the vanity form of all vanity forms, and that's what faced her after the war.

Syberberg's career began with two very short films made in 1965 and 1966 respectively. One thing that he did is after the destruction . . . because although if you go to Germany today much of it looks like a poster tourist card, but that's because everything has been lovingly rebuilt because it was smashed not just a little bit but to pieces, to atoms so that one brick hardly remained on another. North, south, east, and west Allied bombing, primarily British bombing, smashed city after city after city, so there was nothing left. Nothing left. Every urban area was like Grozny in Chechnya now, where I believe even after the present clique have been in for quite a few years one street in the center has been rebuilt.

He wanted to go back to many of the great actors and actresses who were then nearing the ends of their lives in the '60s and put them on the screen for the last time. Sort of an addendum, a memorial, a thank you note. These were all short films shot on quite primitive equipment. Black and white.

The first one was called *Romy Schneider: Anatomy of a Face.* Rather unusual. A film about a woman's face. It's a film about this great German actress beauty from the past. The theatrical bone structure was still there. The whole film is essentially about her face. It's rather interesting, isn't it? Because there are certain modern theories about the contemporary face—its weakness and its flabbiness and its absence of structure. And that's what he's hinting at in that. There's somebody who people here know in a small little group or sect, and she was called the Countess, and she was once asked about the modern face, and she made remarks like that. People were appalled.

But what Syberberg's doing by that very small idea is he's indicating that people didn't always necessarily look as the way they do today, and the sensibilities that they articulate is not that which says that 1945 is a year zero for us all and that there's nothing before, and we've all reinvented ourselves subsequently, and we're all post-modern and reflexive and think every possible thought at every other possible instant. In other words, there's something maybe classical that prefigures value.

But it's a short film and didn't get too much attention.

In 1966, he dealt with Fritz Kortner who was a very well-known actor, particularly of Shakespearean drama in Germany. He was very elderly then. This is just scenes of him rehearsing, almost a radio film in a strange sort of way. He's going through the motions. His great performance in German theater was his Shylock, and Syberberg has him possibly in his last ever performance, because the point of film, as these elderly actors realized, is it memorializes them. Who remembers these people now, if there isn't the film there of them?

Kortner's an old man who's quite clearly suffering with various illnesses that will take him away a year or two after filming in '66. But he gets him to articulate this superhuman/inhuman scream of revenge: Shylock's desire for revenge against the Gentile world. A sort of primal scream.

Remember in the '60s there was that cult called Primal Scream? You could go into your unconscious and draw it all out. Get rid of it through a big scream. That cult didn't last. But it's been replaced by something else.

Nevertheless, Kortner gives this scream in this film . . . and then it ends. That's another little vignette of what's coming later on in Syberberg's career. At this moment he was just dismissed as a mildly academic eccentric making some odd revivalist films about previous German cultural figures. Inoffensive stuff.

As we move on, the obsession with the Romantic movement in the 19th century and the *völkisch* movement in the 19th century and their visual art and some of their religious ideas and their overlap into the *Wandervogel* movement of the 19th century where large numbers of youths would move around the countryside; it's almost like an alternative society movement much of which prefigured German involvement in the Foreign Legion, in paramilitary organizations, in the enormous volunteering across the German-speaking parts of Central Europe for the Kaiser's army in 1914 and thereafter. It's quite clear that this is the era of culture that Syberberg wishes to concentrate on.

He did another famous documentary on Winifred Wagner, which caused enormous problems for the Bayreuth Festival and enormous problems for her family, because he kept the microphone on after the interviewers had left, but he did it with her consent because the microphone's in front of her. And she talks and she talks and she talks, and then after a certain gap she starts talking about Adolf Hitler. And she talked about Adolf Hitler for four hours without a break, and quite a lot of this found its way into what would then be the final cut of the film. The family went utterly berserk when this film was distributed, and Syberberg was black-balled. He was never allowed to attend the festival again.

It was a scandal to a degree, although the scandal was slightly undercut by the fact that he was regarded as a revealer of something that had been widely known anyway; in other words, that she was extremely sympathetic, but also that Hitler had once told her that Wagnerism was his religion, or the nearest that he ever came to one.

Hitler cost £100,000 to make in 1977 prior to its release in '78. You can get it on the internet. It takes *ages* to download, because it's seven hours, and therefore most people just give up, but it is there up on the internet.

The BBC partly financed it, which is truly extraordinary in certain respects, but this is because of the disjunction between Western German culture and the rest of the West, even the rest of the NATO West, of which West Germany was indisputably a part, at that time. And not just East Germany, not just the Germany that existed before the collapse and destruction, but the difference between say the Anglophone world within the West and Germany proper, however defined in the multiple ways I've just delineated. So, from the English BBC sort of viewpoint the Germans were living an unmastered past. No one would talk about this material. Here is a man who's prepared to make a virtually 8-hour film about it! Therefore, give him some money: £50,000. Quite a lot of money in the 1970s, but not an unbelievable amount for a state broadcaster.

It's true that in the '70s very few people would deal with *any* of this material at all. Indeed, he was so short of actors that in the final sequence, the fourth quarter—because it's divided into four pillars, four sections of which *We Children of Hell* is the fourth one—puppets appear. When somebody asked him why he used puppets he said, "Well, I'd run out of actors."

The thing about this film is that it's quite visually extraordinary because it's based in one set. If you've ever seen Derek Jarman's film, *Caravaggio,* which is in Latin, it's set in one set, which of course means that from a cost basis, you can keep costs to an absolute minimum, and you can also perhaps film for a month, seal it up, and three months later you come back, and in some respect everything's still *in situ*.

Henri Langlois, the French set designer, had a lot to do with the set, because it's noticeable that a lot of back projection is used, because it's a very theatrical film. For a long time, it was treated as an essentially avant-garde and modernistic film, because it's not narrative based. It's episodic. It's slightly Mannerist. It superficially appears to be very anti-, whereas its real crime is neutrality about matters that you can't be neutral about. Not in the contemporary or post-modern Federal Republic.

Aesthetically, Syberberg's in love not with a particular government between '33 and '45 but with the aesthetics from which it originated. He's a sort of Germanic race-soul artist really, of that sort of yearning, transcendental, and instrumental spirituality which you sense the Germans as possibly the primary, central, originating European character reference possesses. He wants to go to those areas that contemporary Germany has cast as off-limits to most of its artists and writers since the war.

Why is this important? It's important because, as Ezra Pound said, genuine creators are the antennae of their entire populations. If you want to find a contemporary art, art in the broadest of senses—I mean creation that has a social dimension—in a society that's deracinated or broken-down or self-questioning, doubts everything about itself, doubts everything about its past, which is why it doubts its present moment, and so on, you'll find the sort of art that's epitomized by something like the Turner Prize. Whereas if you look at the sort of art that he's dealing with, you see a more communitarian, more organic, more restorationist art. Art that's closer to representational fantasy in the mind and beyond it.

Dream is extraordinarily important to Syberberg, because he believes that in a sense the real truths are deeper than reason, which is why he is a quasi-religious artist, whatever his actual statements about religion may be.

We know quite a bit about his actual views. Something which many artists don't put on record either because they don't have them in a formal way or because if they do they reveal too much, and it's difficult to get funding and this and that. Because he wrote a book in 1990 called *On the Misfortunes and Fortunes of Art in Germany after the Last War.*[1] Now, this is a remarkable book, but we need to discuss *Hitler* in detail before we come on to it.

The film stars an actor called Heinz Schubert. It also stars Syberberg himself in the fourth quadrant and his own daughter, various puppets, and minor figures. The first section deals with Hitler's personality cult. The second section deals with *völkisch* romanticism in the 19th century. The third section deals with the *Shoah,* particularly as it's seen from Himmler's perspective. The fourth section deals with the aftermath and the generation who feels it with incredible acuteness because Syberberg's generation mentally comes of age in the immediate aftermath of these events. So, for them, the year zero for Germany is the beginning of adult consciousness with an occupied society that's divided hemispherically in accordance with the two world blocs and hyper-powers that then exist.

There is a collection of short stories written by a young German who died relatively soon after the war called Wolfgang Borchert which Calder published in the 1960s which is *Germany in the Ruins,* something like that. It's largely the stories

---

[1] Hans-Jürgen Syberberg, *Vom Unglück und Glück der Kunst in Deutschland nach dem letzten Kriege* (Munich: Matthes & Seitz, 1990).

of people scampering about, surviving living in cellars, shooting rats. There's no water. There's no electricity. During these three years between '45 and '48, at least two million Germans died because there was very little food. Parts of the Morgenthau Plan were implemented in certain sections of American zones of occupation. Other American commanders were completely opposed to that plan and subverted it. So, it was a mixed picture. But, nevertheless, at least—according to the contemporary German historical record—two million Germans perished during that time. Nearly always the people liberals say they care most about: the weakest, the illest, the oldest, women, children, the infirm, and so forth.

Syberberg's mental space of reference, if you like, in terms of maturation, his immediate pre-adult to adult beginnings, is there, and yet he is an anti-realist and a luscious Romantic of the most extreme and German type in a way that almost strikes the slightly ironic attitude that the English always partly have to things as very Teutonic, almost overbearingly serious. The *seriousness* of it. Sort of pietistic romance.

At the end of his career, his last major fictional film was of Wagner's opera *Parsifal* with an extraordinary performance as the female lead, Kundry, in that opera.

But back to *Hitler*. The first section involves all sorts of scenes—some taken from circus and vaudeville, some drawing on Weimar culture, some drawing on what inevitably replaces it, use of dolls, use of sets that are lit in red, use of a lot of flame, use of a lot of sort of occultistic Thule gothic imagery—to create a sort of sensibility about the nature of the German biological Romanticism, really. Quintessentially a Central European artistic sensibility which has been completely voided. Completely voided in the post-war dispensation.

Syberberg has become almost a cultural unperson, although people know he's there, and he lives as an old man in contemporary Germany and so on, because he's gone back into the area that that movement originated from. It's not that, in some ways, that movement is the culmination of that era, but it comes out of it. The dilemma that Syberberg has is he's not a politician. He's not a political partisan. He's a German partisan.

He's a partisan for German culture, and therefore his perspective is you cannot have German artistic culture with this voltaic energy, this storm sense of this sort of condenser battery removed from the circuit. The energy, even to rebel against it, of what it is to be German comes from this vortex. Therefore, to disprivilege it is to cut it out completely.

It's like Elizabethan tragedy without the example of the Greeks in the past or Seneca as a sort of low Roman version that Shakespeare was aware of. You have to have that primary fodder, that primary material. Fuel upon which to feed. If you can't have it, because it's been denied to you in a particular era, then you can't express nationally what you are.

This is the real thesis of this film, which people saw in the '70's and thought, "Eh, interesting critique of the fact Germans won't mention their past by a fringe German director." That's how it was first regarded. That's why the BBC used to show it, insofar as you show things extensively when they're over seven hours. But I remember . . . you know what Christmas day is like when you get sick of your relatives, so you go up to another room and watch the film on BBC Two, and I remember in 1980 watching Syberberg's *Hitler* for seven-and-a-half hours on a grainy black and white set. And you know, it was quite extraordinary in all sorts of ways.

The second section also has a significant, if potted, filmic history of German 19th-century art, of pictorial art, added into the general mixture.

If anyone logs into Syberberg's site . . . He's got several and there's a significant Wikipedia entry concerning him, which details all the controversies that ever engulfed him. The first section is "Syberberg: interesting and provocative German director"; the second section is Syberberg's films; the third section is "Comparison and Criticism"; and the fourth section is "Controversy—The Danger of Anti-Semitism," so you can see the chronology as it sort of goes down. But there's links to his sites and your ability to, if you've got the patience or the machinery to do so, download *Hitler: A Film from Germany*.

One of his more outrageous ideas is that the entire experience to someone who comes culturally of age, who is mentally born if you like, just after it is so extreme, is so devastating, that his way of dealing with it is to internalize it and view it as a film. That's why he calls it *Hitler: A Film from Germany*. So, he actually sees the past as a film.

Now, many people, particularly people who are not particularly artistic, would consider this to be either a *non sequitur* or a disprivileging of reality or the sort of thing that artists do to cope with life or whatever. But in actual fact, for somebody who's such as him and his sensibility, it's because he privileges these things more than anything else that he's prepared to make a film of them because he has an essentially spiritual view of art. He doesn't see it as a money-making exercise or a trivialization or a fake authentification or something to do with one's time between birth and death or an attempt to please others or gain to one's self. He actually sees it as a sort of spiritual and moral transcription.

The third section is very interesting because this is about the *Shoah*, which is totally accepted as a fact in this section of the film, for which there is no apology. This is the interesting thing about it. That it's dealt with in a tone and in a briskness that's almost identical to the way Menachem Begin describes the ethnic cleansing of Palestinians in his autobiography which is called *My Life*, I believe, just like Sir Oswald Mosley's. When asked about these events, Begin said, "We did what we had to. Let there not be talk of morality! There is only the necessity of action and vigor! " That's it. Let 'em talk.

And that's the sort of attitude that you get in that third section. I think that a few worrying bells went off when that section was seen, but because it's not in any sense revisionist or even pre-revisionist. It's again, the view that you get subliminally from that section is that if Germany is to ever have a future, it has to master his view, filmically nonetheless, of the consequences of these events.

In some ways, he's preaching what Nietzsche called self-overcoming, whereby you say "yes" to life, you accept even the most unpleasant things, you absorb them just as you absorb rubbish and trash in a fire. You step over it to other things and to other glories. It's the creative use of destruction or the refusal to be imprisoned by the consequences of the destructive urge seen as part of the human potentiality. In other words, it's a non-dualist view of morals of an explicitly non-Christian viewpoint but not belabored as such.

In the fourth section, *We Children of Hell,* he talks about—with his daughter and Heinz Schubert who remains ubiquitous as a varied sort of presence and trickster wearing multiple hats and playing multiple parts, including Himmler, throughout the film—the legacy of what it means to be German in the modern world. The interesting thing is that this film deals very bluntly and very explicitly with the fact that for almost everyone outside Germany since 1945 whenever a German is presented to them they have an almost implacable urge to ask them about these events.

I remember I was at some party or something when I was about 18, and some German students turned up, and various people made a beeline for them, and the first thing that they were really asked of any substance—beyond how they were and what the weather was—was "What's your view of what happened between 1933 and 1945?" And, of course, most contemporary Germans want to make money; they want to get away from as much of that as possible; they want to redefine the nature of who and what they are, and so on. They don't really want to discuss it.

Syberberg's in a sense going straight for that heart of darkness in Conrad's sense of the term. He's going straight there, without equivocation, but artistically. Because he knows that if you don't in a sense bring this material to the surface art in post-war Germany—in other words, morally truthful creativity—is impossible.

You see this in many careers, actually. Look at the famous Leftist to Green novelist Günter Grass, who, seen as an anti-, seen as a sort of Center-Left stalwart of the Adenauer post-war government and so on. Then it's suddenly revealed, it was right at the end of his cultural trajectory, almost the last book, that he served for a fraction of time when he was a youth (he had no choice) in the Waffen-SS and how this almost led to a perspectival altering, not just of one book or one incident when he was a late teenager, but of his whole career.

In other words, truly the unmastered past. Because, bluntly, this is what Syberberg has been dealing with since the very beginning—not the end, when it's sort of looked back on when you've written a shelf-load of books to prepare for the moment, but as the first step to dealing with the possibility of the last moment.

The film had a reasonable success and was shown in art cinemas all over the world. It was shown extensively in the United States, where it was seen as an elegy and an indictment. You know, that sort of thing.

Susan Sontag wrote extensively about it. She wrote an essay called "Fascinating Fascism" which is largely based on that film.[2] Philippe Lacoue-Labarthe, the reasonably well-known French critic, also wrote a review of it. It seemed reasonably successful. Far too artistic and obscure for many people. Some of the German is very complicated and the translation terse and so on, although the English-language version isn't too bad, because the BBC got some expert German linguists in, because they half-financed the thing in the first instance.

After *Hitler,* he moved on to do this film of the Wagner opera *Parsifal,* which again is an attempt at what Brecht would call epic theater and also what Wagner had wanted with the idea of total art and high opera, which obviously would have lent itself to the idea of total film, total theater, total art.

Brecht had the concept of epic theater, and Syberberg has always been very pro-Brecht. Not ideologically, but because it's the desire to make great statements that are great German statements. Indeed, his views of Brecht were quite unfashionable once Brecht went East and became almost the sort of privileged puppet-master of the Berlin Ensemble, where they all said they were oppressed and made to do it now, but in actual fact because they loved every minute and he had his own

---

[2] Susan Sontag's "Fascinating Fascism," *The New York Review of Books,* February 6, 1975, primarily discusses Leni Riefenstahl. Syberberg is not mentioned. Her review, "Syberberg's *Hitler,*" appeared in *The New York Review of Books,* February 21, 1980.

chauffeur, private public flat, guards, limousine. You know, the whole works.

Syberberg went to the East and did a film about Brecht and his legacy, because he was a great German. Again, you almost sense that equivocal element in Syberberg as well as the pride of an Easterner as well. Because, as we all know, there is a distinction between the East and West German sensibilities, which has been exaggerated and exacerbated by the fractured nature of their experience in the post-war period. Even politically today, there's a disjunction between the amputated limb of the East that's been put into sort of cryogenic storage and repositioned back on the rest of the trunk.

Syberberg's film of *Parsifal* was a truly extraordinary film. It can be obtained on Amazon and so on for very small amounts of money now. That opera, which essentially preaches not just total art but total redemption through love and the creation of a Germanicized Christianity (a sort of dejudaicied Christianity in many ways), is a chance for Syberberg to luxuriate (his critics would say fetishistically wallow) in Germanicism and in a culture of deep linguistic Romanticism that is outside politics, but types of extreme politics grow from it.

The thing about his type of work is that there is no distinction, as there usually is, between political statements, aesthetic statements, ideological statements, philosophical ones. They're all merged into . . . if not a total attitude towards the world, a sort of *Weltanschauung*, but a total attitude towards art, because for Syberberg art is the world. It's the view that it's more important than creativity at that level. It's more important than life and death, which to most people is just highfaluting nonsense, but Syberberg believes in it with a passion, and this has made him—particularly with the material that he wishes to deal with—very, very unfashionable.

After about 1990, he found it increasingly difficult, certainly in the Federal Republic, to raise money to make films. Possibly, he'd come to the end of his trajectory. Made a film about Karl May. Made a film about the Wagner family. Made a film about Ludwig II. Made a film of Wagner's opera *Parsifal*. Made his enormous film *Hitler*. Did the shorter films when he was younger.

He was in a philosophical, narrative-based, and yet largely linguistic film where people discuss their ideas, including some famous elderly German actors, called *The Ister*, which was made in 2004, and he has a producer role in that and a performance role as one of the philosophical spokesmen.

Since then he's done not very much, or been allowed to do too much, in film, which always costs money if you're going to have it disseminated with any public prominence beyond the internet.

He published this book, however, in 1990, which I've already referred to, called *On the Misfortunes and Fortunes of Art in Germany after the Last War*. This created an enormous "culture war," as they're called, in Germany at the time. It's largely forgotten now, but not by quite some of its protagonists. Many people who were associated with Syberberg until then dropped him after that, and he became a little bit of an unperson.

In this book, he says that contemporary Germany is essentially culturally rotten and has destroyed itself and is self-hating, and—ironically, in relation to everything connected with the past—is philo-Semitic. Excessively so. And this was not really good for him, I think.

I remember Michael Walker of *Scorpion* magazine, who I think had become a German citizen by then, writing in one issue of that publication that Syberberg better know what he's doing, because the way things are going he won't be making too many films in the future.

Syberberg's politics are less important than the spirituality of the artistry that he represents. As with all extremely visual artists like him, describing what he's done makes a lot more sense if you've actually seen the material. But of course very few people are entirely aware that this material exists, even though probably a lot of that comes up on the internet almost instantaneously in English.

But the reason for this is because people understand what he is doing. He's positioned himself to be the repository of the sort of sensibility, which didn't come to an end in 1945. There are certain forms of German classicism that are not particularly redolent of it. There are certain forms of German medieval art that don't really relate to it. There's something rather trans-German and quasi-Catholic and German in the European sense, in Nietzsche's sense of being European as against German, about him. And there's not very much Protestant in my view about his art aesthetically, for example. But he is the repository of the Romantic *völkisch* sensibility which people know is quintessentially German and yet is largely denied apart from tourism and a few prissy things now. But it is ideologically denied in contemporary Germany.

What's wanted are endless novels of guilt and expiation and anti-Romanticism and Existentialism and writers like Robert Walther, Elias Canetti's *Auto-da-Fé* and this sort of thing. "We've destroyed ourselves, and we've deserved it!" This sort of stuff, endlessly. This is what's wanted. Needed. Required. Expiation before the possibility of a primary statement. Even before the possibility of a primary statement. It's the sort of Angela Merkel, never be proud to say that you're German, without an enormous preliminary screed of apologetics that has to be read out before you can even get to the moment you enunciate in a quiet voice.

Now, the truth is you can't create anything in a culture without that element of fire-in-the-belly and without that element of prior authentication.

After German unification, there were quite a few articles about Syberberg. There was one well-known one by Diedrich Diedrichsen and Peter Chametzky called "Spiritual Reactionaries after German Reunification: Syberberg, Foucault, and Others."[3] Many people, of course, saw a great danger in the nationalisms, as petty and confused though some of them were, that were released when communism was taken off and there was lots of angst building in allegedly quality journals all over the world about the dangers of this and that. So, Syberberg had his moment in his book in 1990.

It's also very important to consider his class position in a

---

[3] Diedrich Diedrichsen, "Spiritual Reactionaries after German Reunification: Syberberg, Foucault, and Others," trans. Peter Chametzky, *October*, vol. 62 (Autumn 1992): 65–83.

strange sort of way in post-war Germany. The sort of Germany he came from—his father managed estates on behalf of other people, partly related to the people who owned them, partly not—that type of class background was destroyed several times over really. Destroyed by the collapse of the Second Empire, finished off by the First War, any savings pretty much decimated by the inflation, which is probably why his father was later managing other people's estates; the Weimar period was sort of an interregnum they just got through; then there was a quasi-authoritarian, semi-militarist government between 1930 and '33; then Hitler's chancellorship thereafter; then the German world seemed to have come to an end with every city and every town in complete steaming rubble and tens of thousands of corpses under the rubble, so that when the sun came up in the summer there was an incredible stink of all the carrion. Because first you had to get all the stone up, then you had to bury them in lime pits and that sort of thing. And this was before you could rebuild, in accordance with what would later be called the German Economic Miracle, that which had been destroyed before. Everything is a sort of simulacrum, a version, a *film*, a virtual version, a virtual reality version of what existed. It's sort of *Thunderbirds*, you know. You blow it up, it's still there. And that's why he sees everything as a film.

The most outrageous thing of all, as Susan Sontag worked out long after she wrote her essay, "Fascinating Fascism," is that maybe he regards the *Shoah* as a film. A film. A film from Germany. A film from Israel. A film from Palestine. A film from Germany. Which, if you like, of course a film is a fiction. But it can be truer than fact and more important than fact, like a great religion is more important than fact because it can move millions of human beings to behave in ways they would never do otherwise. One man with an idea and certainty is worth 50 other men.

So, when you look at the artistic basis and the methodological premises of his cultural practice—as contemporary Marxist cultural studies types would call it—you suddenly see that there's something actually slightly insidious to liberal order. But my view is that it's less conscious than semi-conscious, in my opinion of his work. Because he's somebody whose total focus in life is artistic. In a very German way, he's totalitarian about art, in a way someone like Otto Dix was, for example. It's that desire to not just penetrate to the core in the way that the Elizabethans in our own dramaturgy would like to do, but to actually go to the *limit* of what is possible to say in a given trajectory. And his trajectory would be what Wikipedia calls "the dark side" of German Romanticism.

Is he, or can he at all be, described as Leni Riefenstahl's heir? Firstly, the cinema that she made, the idea of making anything comparable in post-war Germany is utterly unthinkable. It's unthinkable. Therefore, all that could ever be made is to approximate to the sensibility that she shows in her films as much before *Triumph of the Will* and *Olympia*, parts I and II, *Festival of the Peoples*, as they're congruent with these works themselves.

The first films were mountain films and films of extreme Aryan wistfulness in the sort of permafrost of the ice. She was a dancer before then. The last film is about the threnody of the body and opera/operetta and again a return to that which she knew best. When blocked, you go back.

Always with her you sense this yearning and transcendental idealism and desire to attain archetypal perfection visually. She's an extreme visualizer and an extreme feminine visualizer, which is artistically unusual, which is why Hitler chose her to make that film in the teeth of all sorts of party opposition. Goebbels couldn't stand the idea initially that a woman would make the film and was overruled. Because she viewed that movement with the religious eye, essentially speaking, of a female artist, which is why Hitler chose her. Because he wanted it seen in that way. And it's very rare for the male world, if you like, for an extreme version of part of the male world, to be viewed by the female artistic eye from without—with technical ability and genius as well, editorially and so forth.

This, I feel, is the comparison that can be made between Syberberg and her. But with him, likewise, there's a technical search of perfection given monetary and budgetary limitations. And there's also a yearning idealism, which exists in many cultures, but I often quintessentially associate with Germanic forms of art and with the German sensibility without which—north, south, east, or west—there can't really be a center.

It's not that we're all Germans really, although English people are primarily Germanic, but nevertheless, it's that they're the core to the European identity, which can have many outer chambers but without the core, doesn't exist.

Despite the fact that we technically fought against them savagely two times in the 20th century, that is actually less important, in my view, than the spiritual damage which has been done to Germany since the Second World War and the degradation of Germany and of things German in casual British parliaments and American as well, and much more subtly and culturally than that at every level: from the mass cultural level, things like graphic novels, to modernist opera and back again. At every level there has been this attitude of not just cynicism or disrespect but deconstruction, and willed and vigorous and sort of emotionally violent deconstruction at that.

Unless contemporary European people can, in the next years that face us, step over that, there will be a hole right in the heart of the European identity. Right in the hull of the Caucasian identity. Because our identity without German culture is essentially unthinkable. Without its art, without its literature, without its music, without its philosophy, without its, at times to the English spirit, ponderous seriousness, without its fanatical attitude towards ideas, that streak of virulence that's part of the Germanic nature and of which now they've been taught to be afraid.

Syberberg's work is an artistic attempt to wrestle with what it is to be German, which, if you think about it, being a German artist or any sort of creator who's not making schlock television just as sort of butter mountains. What he's actually trying to articulate is a vision of life.

There is no nationality in Europe, even in Russia under communism, which is more difficult to bring off or even to deal with than the German identity. Because even the Bolshevik Revolution didn't so disprivilege the very idea of what it was to be Slavic or Russian from the inside out. It destroyed and burned and blew up churches and destroyed artworks. I think every musician that Shostakovich was at the Moscow Conservatory with in one particular year was shot. Every one, on Stalin's orders. And when he asked, through party officials, because you had to be a member of the party of course, why he'd been spared, Stalin said, "Shostakovich can write film music. We need film music. Because we need film. Because with film we can go straight into the mind of the masses!"

There's this Czech novel called *The Engineer of Human Souls* by Josef Škvorecký, and that was a Stalinist term. "We are the engineers of human souls, and we need men who can write the music for the films, where we can go straight into the brains of the masses."

Because with film you can go straight into the front cortex. Because that's what visualization does. Before you hear a sound, before you hear the music, you see the image, an image gone straight into the mind. That's why it is the form of the 20th century. It's where representational art has gone in the 20th century. It's why radical governments have used it in every way.

That's why the Chinese use film extensively with the masses, but also of course in all other cultures—India as well, now coming up economically. In the United States, the whole dream factory has been created since basically the consolidation of the Hollywood studios as an industry perforce in around 1919 prior to creation by some of the artists like D. W. Griffith of United Artists.

It's interesting just as a sideline in American cinema to think of what's happened to D. W. Griffith's films like *Intolerance* and, above all, *Birth of a Nation*, parts I and II. The Golden Globe Awards and certain Hollywood awards up until the early 1990s used to have a D. W. Griffith prize.

Of course, for those who don't know, in *Birth of a Nation* the Klan are the heroes. Not a film that would be made today.

In the early 1990s, certain black nationalists complained, and the D. W. Griffith prize . . . they didn't get rid of it all, because he's crucial to the development of world cinema, with Lillian Gish in his major films and this sort of thing. So, the Shakespeare of American cinema, it's a bit difficult to completely put him in the closet. But by this date in time, 15 years further on, the D. W. Griffith prize is no longer awarded.

That's sort of Hollywood cinema, which over time and at certain times has had certain genuine European features. And yet over time also has changed to the degree that the amount of European sensibility that's left in contemporary Hollywood is very small. The amount of it that was there in 1920, correspondingly, was quite significant. Indeed, there have always been many Hollywoods, and, as Gibson discovered with his film, if you make half-a-billion dollars in personal profit, criticism dries up.

John Wayne opposed racial desegregation. He gave money openly to the Klan in the 1960s. He was such a big star, he was left alone. Because he's a big brand, and you want them. But there's a degree to which the sensibility which he represented, they just made sure it didn't appear on the screen too much. That's how it's done.

Syberberg is not a Right-winger, in my view. He's a conservative nationalist of a mild sort. But he's an aesthetic German. And his real premise is that Germany is in all of us, and without its cultural inheritance as something to use and step beyond, we cannot have a coherent Europeanness. And without that trajectory, it is not possible to survive.

So, I would ask you next time you've got an hour or so on the internet to put Hans-Jürgen Syberberg into Google or one of the other search engines and bring up what you can and see what you make of it. Because he's somebody who is obscure, but he's obscure not because he's no good and not because he needs to be obscure, or has been falsely kept so, but because he's slightly dangerous. And in this era of standardization and of dumbing down and of conformity, there is a great need for those who are prepared to stand up for the inner lives of their own peoples. And he's still alive.

Thank you very much!

Counter-Currents/*North American New Right*
April 23, 2013

HANS-JÜRGEN SYBERBERG — LENI RIEFENSTAHL'S HEIR*

Hans-Jürgen Syberberg, the *enfant terrible* of modern or post-war German cinema, was born in 1935 of vaguely upper class stock. His father owned landed estates in Eastern Germany before the war, and his son lived in Rostock until 1945.

Syberberg's doctoral thesis—very much in the Germanic tradition—concerned the notion of existentialism or the absurd in Dürrenmatt's drama. He himself seems to have been influenced by two vast and yet "monstrous" paradigms: these were Brecht's notion of epic theater and Wagner's idea of the *Gesamtkunstwerk*—the total artwork.

Without doubt, his seminal achievement has to be *Hitler: A Film from Germany* (*Our Hitler*) which appeared in 1978. Although Syberberg was to later furnish a retrospective and documentary feel to his ideas in a non-fiction treatment, *The Ister*, in 2004. It comes across as a companion piece or dialectical counterpoint to the previous work. It's definitely not a *mea culpa*.

Hitler – ein Film aus Deutschland ran to 442 minutes and happened to be co-produced by the BBC (somewhat paradoxically). It starred Heinz Schubert and had no definite plot other than an intriguing series of tableaux. In a different set of circumstances (or primarily dealing with variegated meats) many would have found it *avant-garde* or occult. Its matter proved to be episodic, mannerist, arcane, and dreamlike. Syberberg, its director, made extensive use of rear projection amid an orgy of declamation, dramaturgical feel, and topical onrush. Tropes are

* Originally published on Jonathan Bowden's now defunct website in 2008 or 2009, this brief article repeats many points from Bowden's longer lecture. It is included here because it adds new details and thus rounds out Bowden's portrait of Syberberg. A comparison between the written and spoken versions also illustrates Bowden's compositional techniques.

introduced, not like Nathalie Sarraute, but after the fashion of a flickering magic camera or F. W. Murnau's *Nosferatu* in 1924. (A film which came to be suppressed by the German authorities owing to copyright tiffs.)

The first part deals with the issue of Hitler's personality cult; it's dark, deliberately baroque and romantic in its aesthetic. It is quite clear that Syberberg wishes to plunge headlong into the thicket of what George L. Mosse called *Nazi Culture;* that's to say, the *völkisch* underpinnings of German "irrationalism" in the 19th century. National Socialism emerged out of this heady stew, but contemporary Germany has repudiated it or deliberately buried this memory. It allows itself the backward glance of Elias Canetti's *Auto-da-Fé* when spliced with Henze's agit-prop.

The second part of this monumental piece of cinema (which is almost as long as Gance's silent *Napoléon* from the '20s) explores Houston Stewart Chamberlain's *Foundations of the Nineteenth Century* in every sense.

The film's third section deals with the *Shoah* and Himmler's various attitudes towards it—the latter very much seen in vignette.

Whereas the epic's fourth quartet—signposted as "We Children of Hell"—consists of a personal appearance by Syberberg as the director. This is by no means either solipsist or Hitchcock-like, merely a desire to intrude an authorial and personal insistence. Having done so, he strides around with a large Hitler puppet (ventriloquism originated in Germany) and enters into debates over the bitter harvest of German Romanticism and the plight of artists in the Federal Republic.

What does Hans-Jürgen Syberberg hope to achieve by means of this activity? Well! His enormous filmic canvas sets up a challenge to every known rule of Hollywood cinema. Whereupon the work's visual *Weltanschauung* also happens to be partly French, being strongly influenced by Henri Langlois' set designs. Likewise, the fact that the work's stasis or static vortex involves one location—one set—brings it very close to Derek Jarman's *Caravaggio* in Latin.

Influential critics pontificated about its significance upon arrival, but neither Susan Sontag nor Philippe Lacoue-Labarthe could hammer out definite conclusions. Most of them miss the fact that the clue to this piece lies in its visualization: its medium is truly the message in terms of Marshall McLuhan's hectoring.

For the film's visual language exemplifies its deeply romantic, roseate, ethereal, Germanic race soul, anti-modernist, dreamlike, oneiric, and Wagnerian climacteric. It happens to be deeply fascistic but purely on an auric or eye-sensitive level; at once happening to be lit up by a post-modern mantra. The film comes across as heroic in its anti-heroic indeterminacy.

Superficially—and with the objective part of the mind—Syberberg appears to be opposed to what Moeller van den Bruck called The Third Empire. But not really ... since, if we enter into back-brain subjectivity, then we are dealing with a fantasy or phantasmagoria which mourns the fact of Germany's defeat. What Syberberg is doing literally confuses the rational, practical, and political mind (perforce). For, by virtue of adopting an apodictic structure, he can remain aesthetically entranced while preserving a strict ideological neutrality.

Like the Australian effort *Romper Stomper*, this film is ultimately neutral and neither for or against—at the level of the journalist's page. In reality, such a transgression proves to be deeply blasphemous under Bonn's republic ... if we conceive of Adenauer's construction as a second Weimar.

Moreover, the inner methodology of Syberberg's attitude can be seen in various articles—one in particular, "Spiritual Reactionaries after German Reunification" by Diederichsen and Chametzky, springs to mind. Likewise, Syberberg sought to clear up any confusion with his own polemic—*Vom Unglück und Glück der Kunst in Deutschland nach dem letzten Kriege* (*On the Misfortune and Fortune of Art in Germany after the Last War*, 1990). This contained a strong attack on Bonn's philo-Semitism.

Michael Walker, the editor of *Scorpion* magazine and by then a German citizen, warned that Syberberg faced "unperson" status as a result. For his filmography has little real appeal either on behalf of NDP supporters or contemporary liberals. In this overall regard, his visualization might be considered to be a splicing of Caspar David Friedrich and Houston Stewart Chamberlain. It's not a tabernacle of the ruins, *à la* Wolfgang Borchert's stories about the "year zero" of 1945, but an aesthetic Germanicism which remains cool, cynical, acidic, upper class, and even "subversive."

Hitler: ein Film aus Deutschland appears to be "anti-" on the surface of its discontinuous images; themselves a kaleidoscope of Cranach, Pacher, and Kracauer's overflowing *The Cabinet of Dr. Caligari*. Yet the inner or subconscious mind that directs this movie proves to be spiritually, not factually, revisionist in character.

His earlier cinema history testifies to this. For example, his first effort—*Romy, Anatomy of a Face* (1965)—deliberates on a classic German actress' profile. It is an exercise in phrenology which concentrates on Romy Schneider. Whereas his second example in 1966 deals with the aged actor Fritz Kortner—a star of German theater earlier in the 20th century who specialized in one event: Shylock's eternal scream of vengeance. Syberberg described the rushes for such an epiphany as "superhuman."

You can view *Hitler: ein Film aus Deutschland* for free online at www.syberberg.de.

Counter-Currents/*North American New Right*,
July 5, 2011

Bill Hopkins:
An Anti-Humanist Life*

I'd like to talk about Bill Hopkins, who is obviously not a household name, although he was one of the Angry Young Men in the 1950s, which was one of the major cultural groups—or sort of explosions—that occurred in this society after the Second World War. They weren't a coherent group. They didn't come together. They weren't like the Continental intellectuals who form a group and then publish a manifesto where each of them makes a declaration that achieves some kind of a solemn and combined purpose. They were a disparate group of youngish men who were corralled into the designation of the Angry Young Men by the media in the early 1950s. Indeed, they were one of the first stunts or cultural creations of the post-war mass media, because they all seemed to be against the system of sort of Tory-consensual Britain in the early to mid-1950s.

The most famous of them, of course, was John Osborne, the playwright who wrote *Look Back in Anger*. Technically on the Left, who moved in a sort of crotchety, slightly ultra-Tory and Rightwards direction as he got older and ended up denouncing immigration when he'd actually been a pro-CND[1] progressive at the beginning. So, he has a certain sort of trajectory across the cultural horizon.

Another member of the Angry Young Men who's forgotten now, but he made a very considerable film, was the filmmaker Lindsay Anderson who made a film called *If. . .* , which is an extraordinary film about public school life. He also made a very Left-wing film—because he was a fellow-traveler of the

---

* A transcript by V. S. of a speech by Jonathan Bowden given at the 7th New Right meeting in London on April 8, 2006. The recording and transcription have been circulated under the title "Bill Hopkins and the Angry Young Men."

[1] Campaign for Nuclear Disarmament

Communist Party to a certain extent, but he was also a culturally independent-minded Leftist up to a degree—called *Britannia Hospital*. This was a film from the early 1980s which, because it was released with great fanfare the moment the Falklands War was happening, died a critical and public death almost instantly. This sort of anti-System film from a Leftist perspective went straight down the plug. He had great problems making any films because of the amounts of money that needed to be raised. Indeed, one subtext to all of the Angry Young Men and how they were treated by the society and its culture, was that in the end nearly all of them were broken or pushed to one side or didn't fulfill their potential or partly weren't allowed to fulfill their potential in various ways.

Another member of this group, who disassociated himself pretty quickly from it, was Kingsley Amis. And Kingsley Amis was, as is widely known now, partly through the literary architecture of his son after his father's death, a Communist fellow-traveler and more than a Communist fellow-traveler in his early years. He's another of these ones who has a blue "road to Damascus" conversion and becomes something like an ultra-Tory later in life. You know, he's a progressive Leftist who's against the post-war consensus, and even Attlee's administration, and then switch forward 50 years he's in the Garrick Club drinking whiskey, moaning about immigration, and writing to *The Spectator* saying how dreadful it is. So, there is a sort of progression with a lot of these people.

Another of them was John Braine, who although he wasn't technically in the inner group that was known as angry, young, and male, there was also a degree to which he really was morally part of that group. Came down from the North, of course, wrote *Room at the Top* and all sorts of spin-offs, became a bit of a Surrealist in some ways afterwards, wrote slightly surreal, sort of aesthetically projected novels, *The Vodi* and other things. Nearly all of Braine's work is about the morality and personal philosophy of sexual relations between men and women, in one form or another.

Braine was an old friend of Bill's. Braine was another sort of Communist, who later ended up in the Monday Club on the

Right wing of the Tory Party. I joined the Monday Club when I was 18, and I was later to be expelled from the Monday Club twice (they invited me back and then expelled me again, just for the hell of it); I still keep the '70s clip-on Monday Club tie, the big blue one with "MC" on it which people think is the "Magic Circle," or they think it's "Master of Ceremonies," but it's actually "Monday Club." I keep that because they expelled me twice. John Braine joined the Monday Club and wrote a pamphlet for them called "John Braine: From the Communist Party of Great Britain to the Monday Club, an Essay."[2] So, you see a certain progression with these sorts of people, although some of their opponents and former collaborators, comrades, and associates would doubtless not have perceived it as a progression.

Let's go down the list of other AYM's as they were sometimes called. There was Colin Wilson, and Colin Wilson is interesting in certain respects because Wilson now—despite the many, many millions he's made from writing what might be called popular or middlebrow literature which contains an intellectual element—is despised by the intelligentsia and is despised by the mass culture, even after sort of 400 books translated into nine languages. And yet, he's unbelievably productive. Unbelievably. Almost to a logorrheic degree. It's sort of churned out of him.

Now, when he was younger he was very influenced by Bill and very influenced by his ideas. His first novel, *Ritual in the Dark,* was dedicated to Bill, and although *The Outsider* was written in the British Museum's reading room, but then British Library, when it was based over in the center of Bloomsbury where Karl Marx wrote *Capital,* of course, he used to sleep on Hampstead Heath in the summer (it was a different era then) because Wilson came down from Leicester. One of 9, 10, 11, 12 children from a very poor working-class background, went to work in a bicycle factory when he was 14, had no educational qualifications at all, and genuinely was an outsider which is

---

[2] The actual title was "Goodbye to the Left," *The Spectator,* July 18, 1968.

why his first book was called *The Outsider*.

Angus Wilson, who was then the chief librarian at the British Library, noticed him scribbling every day between the hours when you come in the morning and leave in the evening and said "What are you writing?" He gave him the first draft of *The Outsider*, and he went to a publisher, and indirectly, through Angus Wilson's advice, it was published.

Now, Wilson was taken up by the cultural glitterati of the time, was praised as a new genius by the Sitwells and this sort of thing and then dumped and trashed for his next book as a working-class upstart and *arriviste* who can't write a sentence, and he's exceeded his brief and doesn't know what he's talking about. So, he was brought forward, embraced, and then slapped and sort of disappeared. But didn't disappear to the degree that he didn't write anymore, because he actually became, in Bill's view (and Colin is one of his oldest friends), a compulsive overproducer who's churned out an enormous mass of material. Whereas Bill, when he hit a wall around this time, has produced virtually nothing since that has been widely disseminated. So, you have two contrary reactions.

But if we actually look at Wilson's career, Wilson has been open to the dissemination of far Right views, even though he may not particularly agree with them himself. He wrote for *Lodestar*, which was a sort of literary and mildly theoretical journal that was put out by Jeffrey Hamm, the ex-Mosleyite and continuing Mosleyite for many years. Wilson also defended causes which were ideologically anti-system, illiberal, and very unfashionable.

When somebody using the mild pseudonym Richard Harwood, whose real name is Richard Verrall, wrote a pamphlet called *Did Six Million Really Die?*, Colin Wilson wrote a review, a reasonably neutral review, but a totally unhysterical review, in *Books and Bookmen* which then was probably a much more important publication in that particular era than it is now. This was the *internal* journal within the book industry that was widely used to target particular books and post-manuscripts that would then get mass distribution in the major chains that existed. Now, Wilson said that this is an important thesis and may cause hysteria in certain areas but needs to be looked at. And for this, he alone became a little marked or a little smelly or was considered to have something about him that wasn't quite nice or quite right and this sort of thing.

In my view, this openness to discourse which is unacceptable is partly Bill Hopkins' legacy on Colin Wilson. Colin Wilson wrote, when *The Leap!* or *The Divine and the Decay*, which is Bill's only novel, was reissued in the early 1980s, the Foreword to it. Here it is: Foreword by Colin Wilson. "When this book first appeared," Wilson writes, "in 1957, it was attacked with unprecedented ferocity. Why did it cause such violent reactions?" Now, we'll come on to this in a bit, because we're still going through the Angry Young Men.

Now, the Angry Young Men had lots of hangers-on and lesser people involved. There was also a Scots-Italian writer called Alexander Trocchi who used to write sort of pornographic novels; *Cain's Book* is the most famous. He died with a heroin overdose. He used to meet Bill in Soho and describe his latest fights and this sort of thing, because he was an intellectual who was able mix in the streets and so on.

They came from an era, these people, that's slightly unique in Britain, because we've never had a coherent class intelligentsia in the way that many Continental European societies do. When intellectuals go to salons and this sort of thing, which is very much a Continental thing, although Continental European intellectuals and academics and theorists and people in the media and literati and so on have these things often in London, and you're invited to them sort of by osmosis. People hear you're somebody of interest, often in the most superficial way imaginable, and you're invited into these circles.

I attended one of these sorts of things when I was about 18, and lots of intellectuals were talking about "ordinary people." I don't know what they're talking about. And, of course, I suddenly realize that this is their own class structure. There were intellectuals and the *others* who weren't intellectually minded. And this, of course, is useful because the vast majority of intellectuals, not all by any means, we're dealing with people that are quite contrary in this talk, but the vast majority adopt Left

Humanist, "lovey," Left-liberal, communistic, mildly Marxian ideas. The overwhelming majority do. Often just as lip-service amongst themselves, although there are more hardcore ideologues even than that.

Yet, when you go to these salons, they're talking about intellectuals and ordinary people. So, always the hierarchy exists in the mind, even if the theory is contrary to it, because people raise it again in their own consciousness and speech.

Who else was associated with the Angry Young Men? When in '57 several publishers got together they decided, because of the media controversy, which reached tabloid proportions, although *The Sun* wasn't much of an organ then, the *Daily Mirror* was essentially its sort of Labourish equivalent, and these people were getting headlines: "Osborne Says He Hates Being English," because Osborne announced in a party that he didn't like being English. "I loathe the English!" he said. And therefore, this was . . . so what? A drunken man at a bus stop looks at his reflection and loathes himself and makes a remark, but it's on the front of a tabloid newspaper the day after. He later said he loves being English, but there's a difference of 40 years between the two statements, you know what I mean? But then again, he was an actor, as quite a lot of these people are, in all sorts of wearing of masks and taking them off again in that sort of way.

A publisher called Tom Maschler, who later went on to be head of Penguin UK, in the late '80s and early '90s, thought it would be a wheeze to get all these intellectuals who were *angry* and *young* and *male* to write their manifesto. And he called it *Declaration: A Statement of Intent from the Angry Young Men.* But the first essay's by a woman! Angry Young Female, you know. And she was Doris Lessing, who also a member of the Communist Party at that time, or at least a fellow traveler to the degree that whether or not she was actually in it didn't matter. She was only in it because Maschler was having an affair with her at the time. You see how these things work. But all of the other people who were in the volume were angry, were young, were male, and were generically, up to a point, in this group.

The two that I haven't mentioned who were in this group

who have largely been lost sight of—John Wain's another one who's largely gone down now—were Bill Hopkins and Stuart Holroyd. There's a reason why Bill Hopkins and Stuart Holroyd have partly gone down the memory hole. One is that since the '50s they haven't really published, although everyone has known who they were. And the reason is that they were open to anger and were essentially youthful, but their politics came from a different direction.

Holroyd wrote an essay and even a book, I believe though I haven't read this personally, attacking parliamentary democracy. Attacking parliamentary democracy! Which probably is of all things *the* most heretical thing—certainly in the '50s, when we'd all fought for democracy of course—that you could possibly do! This really was anger and youth and maleness in a cocktail that wasn't particularly liked. And he didn't publish again with a mainstream press beyond his essay in *Declaration*.

And then there was Bill Hopkins. Bill wrote this essay in *Declaration* called "Ways Without a Precedent," which is a Nietzschean sort of manifesto. And he followed it up with this novel, which was reissued in the mid-1980s, called *The Leap!* This was because prospectively it was to be filmed, and this wasn't talk. I mean, there were producers signing contracts and so on. But, in the end, as often with these projects, it came to nothing. The real name of the novel is *The Divine and the Decay*.

This is the original edition actually. I bought it in Hay-on-Wye, where books go to die, for £7, although on the internet they charge up to a £100 for this. It's a bit smelly. At the front it says, "To Jonathan Bowden, a fellow warrior. From Bill Hopkins."

This is an interesting book in all sorts of ways, because this is a book which is a fantasy about a man who essentially gets up in the morning and decides that he wants to be dictator of Britain and how will he go about morally, aesthetically, psychologically, intellectually, and ideologically becoming a man who is worthy to be a dictator of Britain. It's based on the Nietzschean idea that artists of genius should rule, and of course it becomes a little more controversial when you realize that there's one artist in particular who ruled a particular society at a particular time who was very unfashionable and not especially liked in austerity-ridden post-war '50s Britain, who might be compared to the ascetic, white-faced, loose-limbed, and black-haired hero of this particular novel.

It's based upon ideas which are in many ways completely heretical and blasphemous and unacceptable to such a degree as that even many of the partisans of Bill don't ultimately own up to where they end. Because Bill, who's been involved in endless shenanigans and scandals throughout his entire life, has lived about—without hero-worshipping him too much, to be frank—6, 7, 8 lives. The first was as an author.

Bill was born in Cardiff in 1928, but as he'll tell you, "I loathe the Welsh." He doesn't like being Welsh, because he associates Welshness with victimhood, and so he aligns with the English because they're the dominant nation within the United Kingdom. He's like one of these absurd Croats who used to claim that the capital of Serbia was actually in Croatia, you know.

But I know what he means because, being partly Celtic myself, there is at times amongst Celtic people when they gather together a certain whining that we're minorities. I remember Kenneth Griffith, the actor, once said to me, "It's all the English, you know!" He said, "They're like jackboots on our throats." And I said, "Do you really believe that, Kenneth?" And he said, "All my life I've been persecuted by these *people!*" I said, "Why'd you call this house Michael Collins House then, because he's an Irish nationalist?" And he said, "Why, it's all the same, isn't it? Those bloody Germans!" By which he means the English.

It is a sort of rhetorical nonsense that people get out of themselves when they lose to the Welsh at rugby or whatever. But it does exist, and in a society without mass immigration, actually, it would probably be more prominent as a discourse then it would otherwise. And Bill would say to all these Welsh types coming towards him he'd say, "[A rude word] I'm with the English." And they'd go, "Ooh no, no. Dreadful."

Adorno, in his theory of fascist psychology, the F-scale as it's called, has a scale for people who are psychologically fascistically minded. Bill would be off that scale. He'd be so off that scale that the methodology of that scale doesn't actually apply to him, as an individual. One of the prerequisites, according to Theodor Adorno, who was the leading theorist of the Frankfurt group (Western Marxists), says that one of the primary characteristics of "a fascistic mentality" is identification with the violator, which means the victor in any particular consequence. In other words, if you look at the Indian Mutiny, the historically normative happening, you side with the British; you side with the English within the British; you even side with Sikh regiments and people who were aligned with the Raj against other groups; you align with that group that wins.

It's not a very good codex, because everyone would align with Blair, wouldn't they? If they had that sort of view. Because isn't he a winner? Isn't the great peacemaker invading Iraq on a regular basis and making a great mess of it?

But irrespective of all that, this scale would certainly suit Bill, because Bill is an extraordinary example of an intellectual (because he is an intellectual, even an ultra-intellectual) who in his own way is highly sensitive and aesthetic. Just like all the people who are characterized as "loveys," such as in loveys for Labour and so on. But his views are the absolute and totalitarian opposite of those views that convulse the present clerisy.

It's like coming across a dinosaur or strange fossil or something that's a spiritual relic from another era because his is the psychology of another era where the West never apologized, was totally proud of what it was, regarded itself as a preeminent civilization, whatever discourse it felt about itself, without any apology whatsoever. At all. All moments of the day. Without the odd bit of liberal hand-wringing and funk and self-denial.

So, in a way, Bill is a sort of shock therapy for many people. He used to go in the '50s and until the '80s or '90s to these salons in West London. I attended a few of them. Run by Jean Gimpel. Run by other prominent art dealers and critics and BBC executives and other people. And people would say, "Isn't the Rwandan genocide terrible?" And Bill would say, "No. I think there's too many of them anyway." And people would be horrified. Well, it's partly a test, of course. He's doing it because his view is that the liberal Left mind and *Zeitgeist* is based on an easy and bland sympathy, which is universal, that loves all. But for the concrete individual in front of them they don't give a damn, and they'll step over you just like that. What he's doing is he's facing them with some of the psychological architecture of their own undignified position.

His other view, of course, is that Western intellectuality *is based upon conflict* and *is based upon dialectic,* and all these people who say that thought is free, and we will say anything we want, and if we want to have an article in the Venice Biennale which consists of a crucifix in a large tub of urine and it's called *Piss Christ,* and this is an artwork. This is a conceptual, pre-Turner Prize artwork. They wouldn't say the same about Islam, of course, because they don't want to get into that, and also they want to live a bit longer, which is something that can't really be gainsaid can it, really?

But at the same time he is pushing the idea that all this freedom you're talking about, let's unpack this freedom. Let's be Socratic. What is freedom? How far are you prepared to go in order to exclude the possibility of it? What is really a liberal statement where you say, "I will literally die for your right to say anything" while you're holding your hand over the other chap's mouth!? Why not push it a bit *further* and a bit *further*?

And people will say, "Well, that's not a very humanist attitude, Mr. Hopkins!" And he'd say, "Well, I'm not a humanist." And they say, "You're not a humanist!?" And he says, "No. I don't believe human life is worthwhile *just as an entity,* like a slug! And I don't believe that any life is outside of hierarchy of race, of gender, of civilization, of intellect, of beauty, of spiritual preponderance! Everything is hierarchical."

He would make a liberal statement, occasionally. He once said, "But then again, even within the superior race, the difference between the higher man and the lower. It's the difference almost between a near God and a worm!" That's his concession to liberal, multi-ethnic feeling.

Bill reminds me very much of that essay by Evola which is critical of Fascism and National Socialism from the Right, not from the Left and not from the Center. But in a sense it isn't sort of radical enough. Because his view is essentially—rather like one of these iodine tests—that everything is so weak, so broken-down, so syphilitic morally and spiritually, that you really need something acidic that is rebarbarative and is repellent. That will repel it. That will appall it. That will confront it. That will break it. Just as in a way his career was partly broken. But then he had another one.

Bill was in the army after the war in occupied Germany. And his wife Carla is German. He's in Hamburg, and he said during the summer, because they were in the British Occupation Zone, you could hear, feel, and smell the stench of all the corpses under the buildings because all the buildings had been flattened, mostly by British Bomber Command activities.

Bill comes from a long line of actors, and his father was a reasonably famous music hall artiste of the period and before. Think Jimmy Tarbuck. Think those sorts of people. They're well-known in their era, but as soon as they're gone, almost no one remembers them. But they're famous names. Pre-televisual, middlebrow, lower middlebrow British comedy names. His father once lived in The Ritz and had endless hangers-on and lay in a bath with his mouth open with people—fellow Welshman, as Bill would say—pouring out liquor down his mouth, and he ended in Streatham with no money at all, in a bedsit, fiddling with a gas heater.

Because these are radical types, you see? It's all or nothing. You know, one woman, a next, another show, another show. You're rich; you're on the floor. They're radical types. And he grew up in the world of penny-ante carnie and mainstream-to-fringe theater that John Osborne comes out of. Indeed Osborne's very similar in background to Bill because they're both Anglo-Welsh in complicated ways.

The second major play that Laurence Olivier played in as a film based upon that sort of world, *The Entertainer*: that world is incarnated really, that small, slightly enclosed British world of the theater, that great moment of mock-Shakespearean threnody, when the character of the comedian looks at the audience, and there's none of them. They're all gone! Because they're watching telly, you see. It's the '50s. It's a dying world. And he says, "Look at me missies. Look at these eyes. I'm dead behind the eyes!" And that's the moment that the entire world shudders to a halt.

Bill came from that world, and his mother was a sort of music hall beauty who was paid just to walk along the stage and then walk back again with increasingly less clothing on, as various sorts of blokes' eyes and goggles misted up, and that sort of thing. So, he comes from that sort of world. He likes a good show. One thing that he would say to me is that it's all a show. Judges, politicians, royalty: it's all show business, really! They're all *acting*. They're all performing. Blair's performing. The judge who sent Irving down is performing. They're all doing it. It's how things are *run*. It's how things are formatted in front of people who receive power in various circumstances.

The other thing that's very important about him is that his acting, bohemian background is, in a way, unique to England and Britain, *classless*. Because in our very hierarchical society, which of course it obviously still is, although it's been bent around quite a lot and changed in some of its definitions. But in the era he was born into far, far more so than today and 50 years forward, the beginning of the 20th century even more so even to the degree that it was impossible for many people to move really. That bohemian aesthetic strand could go right up and down the society. Because there was one time in his life when Prince Charles—I hope he hasn't kept these letters and diaries—was quite a close friend of Bill's, because he knew all of those people at certain times in his life, because somebody has to.

There's also a degree to which many people used to test themselves against him, because he's a sort of secret figure in some ways in British post-war history. He is the intellectual, he is the thinker who represents the viewpoint that no one ever mentions. But he's there, as a nemesis, as a shadow, as a sort of death's head at the feast in these sorts of parties. The one that people almost sort of test themselves against in argument and dialectic, because it is a position which is disprivileged.

In France after the war, French radical Right-wing intellectuality, of which there was a very large tradition, went underground. And this was after Robert Brasillach was guillotined[3] for treason to the French Republic. Intellectual treason, because he'd done nothing but publish a magazine called *Je suis partout,* and he was guillotined for that, and for his collaboration with Otto Abetz, who was the cultural sort of commanding officer of Germany in France. Contrary to certain things, the Germans' domination of France was in that war very liberal, very mild, extraordinarily civilized actually. But that intellectuality went underground.

In Britain, we've always had a far-Right intellectuality. Henry Williamson, an old friend of Bill's, was one of the people that was going to talked about earlier on, and he represents it. Thomas Carlyle in the 19th century represented it. Wyndham Lewis in the beginning of the 20th century represented it. John Buchan to a certain extent represents elements of it. It's always been there, but it's always slightly denied, slightly obscured. People slightly deny what they are. They put up certain masks to face off against it. They go slightly underground. They have a history of never joining any groups, because that's their one way of being demonized and corralled.

Bill is completely against my involvement in the British National Party, for example. He just says, "You're marching around with a totem of slavery!" He said, "They'll come down on you with their beams, and you'll be there, and they'll say '*Nazi!* There he is!'" And I said, "Well, they've always said that about you, Bill." And he said, "Have they? Have they, indeed?! I have a writ here for the first man who dares."

Now, one of Bill's friends, ironically, in all sorts of ways, because Bill's a complicated man, was the screenplay writer for nearly all of the early films, and they're great films as well, by Michael Powell. And his name, of course, was Emeric Pressburger. He sought Bill out in the 1970s, I think. And Kevin Macdonald, who's a grandchild of Pressburger, wrote a book which has a chapter about Bill in it called something like "The Heart of Intellectual Evil," something like that. "The Heart of

---

[3] He was actually shot by firing squad.

Intellectual Evil."[4] Not the *Heart of Darkness,* Conrad's short novel. He said that Pressburger was a masochist who sought Bill out to be abused and enslaved and whipped and that sort of thing, morally and mentally. He said that Bill was an elitist and an anti-humanist and an anti-Semite.

Bill wrote all sorts of expletives in this 426 pages, and he went down to a lawyer, and the lawyer said for the first part get rid of these expletives, so he cut all that bit out. And he sued Faber, because it was quite a mainstream book, and he sued Macdonald, and that book's never been reissued in paperback. And I said, "Bill . . ." He said, "Yes?" I said, "Everything he said about you is true." He said, "That's not the point! *You must never allow them to say it!*"

He said, "Anyway, I have all sorts of Jewish friends who don't believe Israel should exist." He said, "As to class and elitism, I believe only in the class of *the mind* and of mentality! And all can come from that background and surmount the hurdle of the bourgeoisie!" See, he's always got an answer.

But he would say that's the way of being an intellectual. You've always got an answer for these people. Because in a sense you're fighting a war with them, and you don't just sort of Ceausescu-before-the-guns-at-the-end go down. You put up all sorts of screens, and you engage in all sorts of activities which a sort of traditionalist British author would call "pluck." Not frontal assault. Not the devastation of our young manhood in the First World War, but tunneling under. Going behind. Having a false friendship with somebody, and then collapsing it and going in. I think the present chairman of my party would like that sort of strategy.[5] There's a degree to which these strategies are dividing people against themselves when they're enemies, of not going down in a glorious 7th Cavalry frontal assault type thing, particularly when you're in an isolated position.

---

[4] Kevin Macdonald, *Emeric Pressburger: The Life and Death of a Screenwriter* (London: Faber and Faber, 1994). Hopkins is discussed on pp. 374–75 and 379, but there is no section heading at all.

[5] Nick Griffin of the British National Party

I mentioned French intellectuality earlier. After this novel was published, Bill met Sartre and Camus in Paris. And Sartre had a physical reaction when he met Bill. He went, "Eeerrrrgh! Fascist!" He said, "We fought you in the war!" Bill said, "You didn't do any fighting. You were busy writing a few plays. And anyway, you studied Heidegger in the '30s in Germany when you didn't know anything that was going on, and you were keen on essentialist and primordial and Traditionalist theories, which are close to people like Guénon; Heidegger's secularized them in the 20th century, and they're actually part of the metaphysical system of your most appalling adversaries!" And Sartre says, "We're not getting on."

Camus was there as well, because this was early, and Sartre and Camus ended up hating each other's guts, although Sartre said he liked him after he had a car crash, when of course he was no longer around to receive the plaudit.

Sartre was there. Simone de Beauvoir was there and her other lover at the time, Nelson Algren, who wrote the novel about drug addiction *The Man with the Golden Arm*, was there. Bill used to say Sartre was there reading a Georges Simenon novel, and Algren would be on the job. But they'd all be talking about theory, because they were totally theoretical people.

Sartre's great project was to marry existentialism and Marxism, and he tried it in *Being and Nothingness* and the *Critique of Dialectical Reason*, which is based on Kant. He tried in a sense to come up with a system that would justify Stalinism in the second volume of the *Critique of Dialectical Reason*, but he couldn't finish it, because even he couldn't get through to that dialectical height.

The interesting thing about Bill is that sort of intellectual purity, where he has been in a zone where he has literally met these people and many others like them. Because one thing that comes out is, why is he an outsider? Why are his ideas partly those of a man alone? Well, if you think about it logically, if we had a powerful and proficient and foregrounded and essentialist civilization in the West, his views, possibly with some of the ruthlessness of the rhetoric hived off, would be the mainstream.

And all of these people who say that the mentally ill are sane, and say that white people are guilty forever, and say that criminals are victims of society and say that the only crime is punishment of those who've done one, and all of these ideas which are ultra-Left, anarchistic and culturally Marxian ideas, which are everywhere, which are in the mass media, which are in the tertiary section of education, which are in schools at the intermediate and lower level: these are the hegemonic ideas of this civilization. He is a demon, and these views are central.

There was once a time, of course, when those views were demonic and other. People used to meet in little Bloomsbury circles and have little funny handshakes because, you know, you needed to trust somebody. You liked things which were regarded as deviant and other, and they were in opposition to everything. Opposition to patriotism, opposition to imperialism, opposition to a sense of race, opposition to family, opposition to military service, opposition to the death penalty, opposition to the absence of taking drugs in public, and all this sort of thing.

Virtually all of these things are now in the mainstream, and that which was contrary is now in the reverse and meet in rooms with young men outside with heavy jackets via redirection points and that sort of thing. It's been a complete reversal linguistically, morally, emotionally, psychologically, intellectually. An extraordinary reversal when you realize that the Western superstructure is still hegemonic.

When some little Iraqi's fighting back with his popgun, there's an enormous flying tank coming over the desert sands towards him, which is what these helicopter gunships are, and he's obliterated before he's even got worked out how to get the Gatling gun off the side of his shoulder, the West is *triumphant!*

And yet, its ideas are based upon a moral squeamishness about what some liberal imperialists and globalists are actually doing elsewhere in the world. They've created a dialectical situation where they're against the logic of their own behavior outside this country, and these countries internally go to pieces and fracture to bits under their ideas. So, in the Third World it's a bit of this, but here *we love them all!* And they can all come and replace us in our own island!

Bill used to live in North Kensington in an area called Notting Hill. In the 1950s, of course. And all sorts of things go on in Notting Hill. One of Bill's other lives is he links with various other Right-wing groups. In 1974 or '75, like J. R. R. Tolkien for a year, I believe, he joined the National Front. Bill certainly joined the National Front, because John Tyndall put it on the inside back cover. "I made the inside," Bill said to me. "A famous writer joins National Front." I haven't seen that edition, but I believe there was one. Now, he joined National Front in '74, '75 when there was the possibility of an electoral breakthrough at that time. Henry Williamson told him, "Never join a far-Right group. It ruined my life." There we are. But Bill then left after a while because he didn't think that particular model would work. There's an entrepreneurial side to Bill. A sort of starter-upper and then drop aside as he goes on to his next project.

When he published *The Divine and the Decay*, the reaction to it, that this was a novel that was apologetic of inhumanism, that was against the Enlightenment. It was a novel that was not even appeasing but supporting. A post-collaborationist novel, it was called. It's only a novel, but the idea is that theoretically it is aligning itself with that which we defeated. In fact, there's a book called *The Angry Decade*[6] in which it said that Hopkins is a demonic man that people shouldn't listen to, and he shouldn't be published either. MacGibbon and Kee, who are obscure now but were a tributary . . . Jonathan Cape, is a conference of publishers of which MacGibbon and Kee was one, so it's quite mainstream and then they go to be Penguin as these people buy themselves out and turn the soil over.

He wrote a second novel, which was about the concept of the *Doppelgänger* in German and other literatures, called *Time of Totality*, I think. He said to me, "Is the title too portentous?" And I said, "It never appeared anyway." And Bill said, "It hardly matters, does it?"

---

[6] Kenneth Allsop, *The Angry Decade: A Survey of the Cultural Revolt of the Nineteen-Fifties* (New York: British Book Centre, 1958).

Another thing I'd like to talk about Bill is his spiritual and intellectual views. Bill came from a generation that appears superficially, even in its own propagandistic terms, to be militantly atheistic. And at one level, Bill is a militant atheist. If a Jehovah's Witness came to his door—he wouldn't want to basically; go to the next one.

But in a strange way, as Wilson said in one of his criminological essays commenting on a book by a Bulgarian, I think, called Ira Progoff, who wrote a history of psychology, a discourse which for many people has replaced theology in the 20th century.[7] Psychology began with the idea that God was absent from men's lives. This is my paraphrase of the first line. But as psychological investigation has proceeded during the 19th century, it has come to the conclusion that man is definitely a spiritual being.

And Bill's view, which is always dialectical, is materialistic and/or atheist in one sense. Because Bill is a modern. Bill is not a Perennialist or a Traditionalist. Bill is a Right-wing modernist who accepts modernity, post-Renaissance and later than that. But believes that the modern world can be other than it is. So, if you like, he wants the absolute inverse of the Greg Dyke, Tony Blair world that we now live under and the absolute inverse of all forms of communism that lie to the Left of that. So, he wants a modernity which is based upon *radical, total, and pitiless inequality* as he would say.

Because he loves this fury of language. And this is partly in some ways a Protestant inheritance. If you notice, Paisley, Nietzsche, Kierkegaard: they love this Old Testament language, which partly has a pagan element to it. There's almost a degree to which—it's a sort of line I've invented for my own purposes from the Edda. You can imagine one of the goddesses saying to Odin, "Are you a god of love?" Freya or somebody. And his reply would be, poetically, "No. Fury. Fury is love!" And that's Bill's view really.

But in a sense, love is not enough. Christianity, a religion of

---

[7] Colin Wilson and Patrician Pitman, *The Encyclopedia of Murder* (London: Arthur Barker Limited, 1961), p. 18.

course he's always been opposed to, although he's not opposed to Christian aesthetic culture—it's language, sculpture, buildings, statuary. But he's opposed to the ethics of the religion. Because you cannot build a world, as you're throttling Third Worlders in Iraq and so on, on pity and love. Because you are dishonest at the very core of your being. You can keep the sculpture, but you *must* be correct about your morals. In his view, of course, a crusader would be a pagan with cross on. You had a rhetoric that said it was different.

But if you look at it, it's a key dialectic which is explored in this novel which is about the future of Western Civilization because it involves a relationship between a man and a woman on an island, in other words in a magical realm, where the woman represents, broadly speaking, feminist-leaning, liberal-minded, Christian, and mildly humanist values. That sort of reflexive mixture of liberal humanism backed with a degree of Christianity. As Iris Murdoch, the novelist who knew Bill well, said, "What we need to do is dump Christianity and keep the liberal ethics." Which, of course, is what they've done.

The other character, the demon, Plowart, is will, power, becoming, intensity of religious process, the will to dominate, the will to structure. They have endless arguments about meaning and purpose. Because Plowart says you can't base anything on love solely. Love is energy and contains hatred and destruction within it. But you need to sublimate that and go to another level, because the purpose of life is transcendence.

That is the moral irony which dialectically and intellectually isn't really one at all, whereby a man is perceived as an atheist and even perceives himself as one, writes a novel called *The Divine and the Decay*. Because, of course, in this novel Plowart isn't a human. He's a force. He's coming towards destiny. All the other characters—and because it's a novel that's obscure in a way and hasn't been read by that many people—in the novel are people who are in decay. There's a cripple in this book—it's a disablist work—who in some ways signifies post-war Britain. He lives on Vachau, which is his version of Brecqhou—this tiny little island that the Barclay brothers now live on, irony of ironies—which, rather like Sark, had a feudal structure so he can go from Britain as it is now to a sort of idealized Britain that's narrow and minimalist enough to make intellectual play with.

Because, like all artists, you take reality and you change it, and you transmogrify it. It's Vulcan. You work on the material. You take people. You put things together. You cut bits off. Because art isn't about being humane. There's a strongly objective element to art. The idea that art is a sort of liberal prerequisite when nearly 9 out of 10 artistically-oriented people have liberal ideas is false. A real artist is closer to a surgeon who works upon reality. It's like the coffee table bourgeois view that some of Michelangelo's late sculptures are not nice. Not nice!? Who cares whether it's nice or not! Because it's about *glory and power!* And if you don't like it—this would be Bill's view and mine—*get out of the way!* Get out of the way or be trampled under!

But people say, "Well, that's very inhuman, Mr. Hopkins. What about people who are weak? What about people who want to drink all night? What about people who just want to lie down and have no drive, no push?" He said, "We'll look after them. I need servants. I need slaves. When I walk along, I want people wafting things behind me to take the sunlight off me. In a hierarchical society, everyone has a place, and everyone has a purpose. When they made the great cathedrals, each craftsmen had his place, signed his bit of a gargoyle with his own image, saying, 'I was here.' Now, youth write 'Kilroy was here' or some rude word was here. Then in those cathedrals, they wrote 'somebody contributed to glory.'"

Of course, what he's really saying is that the liberal humanist idea that you can base all of society on the view that we're all educated, that we're all well-balanced, that we're all refined, that we all think out every decision before we make it, that we contract with society as Rousseau said, and bear upon us obligations and responsibilities, the Blair view: obligation, responsibility, the respect agenda. It totally voids biological reality: that some humans are geniuses, that others are subhuman virtually, that others are in the middle, that most people don't give a damn about anything.

Remember the Hollywood film *Twelve Angry Men*? Where

they're deciding a man's fate, and one says, "Come on, I've got a baseball game on the telly. I want to get back for that." And the liberal is outraged! This is a man's life you're talking about! And he says, "Awww, who gives a . . . !" The majority of people in democracies are like this. It's shopping and something else. They shouldn't have, in Bill Hopkins' view, any power, and they shouldn't even have the vote because they don't know anything about anything, at all!

He said what you need to do with a democracy is like in Iran. You structure it before you have one, and you allow people to vote for this Monday Club type and this BNP type and this Third Positionist type and this National Democrat type and this Freedom Party type and so on. They'll all have disputes, and they'll say, "Oh, I hate him," and "He scorned me in this meeting," and that sort of thing. The usual stuff. But in the end, the basis behind it all is patriotic. So it's censored from the very beginning.

If you have a democracy that says all values can trundle forth: My candidate says, "I want to marry children" and that sort of thing. Another candidate says, "A European state? No!" Another candidate says, "All class must be abolished." Another candidate says, "There must be a totally class-based hierarchy." In other words, just a babble of conflicting voices. In the end, you won't have that anarchy. What you'll have is a tendency to the crepuscular middle, whereby in reaction against the possibility of such weird fauna and flora you have a centralization of everything around middlingness, around mediocrity, around that which is unheroic.

If America comes to us and says, "We want you in Iraq." "Well, uh, do we have to?" It's like Wilson in Vietnam, "We don't really want to." "We want you there." "Right away." Because we have an establishment that leans with one wind that comes upon it and then leans with another. It does it culturally. It does it in every other way.

In the National Theatre, I once went to see *The Merchant of Venice* in which one of the characters, Beatrice, gives an apology for the Holocaust at the end. I don't remember that in the play, actually, considering it's 500 years before. Why did they do that? Because somebody on the committee at the National said that there may be a group or a lobby or even an individual, even an obsessive *Guardian* reader, who will object. We need to cover ourselves from the prospect out there that somebody might be offended by introducing something that isn't in the play in the first place so we're safe. *We're safe!* And, of course, they're not safe at all because they're frightened of their own shadow from the very beginning.

There are many, many other examples. There are examples from plays by Marlowe and plays by Webster and this sort of thing from our great period, when Bill would say, "When we were as great as the Greeks, when we had a theatrical culture here that was equivalent to them."

Now, somebody will say, "Oh, Beatrice the heart of my whiteness does go out to you." And he's a Rastafarian. He's sort of gently trying to remember his part. And that is what is called multiracial casting. The idea is that we're all human. We should be blind to these things. It's a universal culture that just happens to be placed on an island off Europe. Da-de-da. You'll be sacked from a mainstream theater if you say, "This play was written in an all-white period." "Really!? Really, is that your view, is it?" "Well, the Jacobean period was an all-white period." "We don't like that time. We don't like that attitude." You see where it goes. It begins there, but it's out there door pretty bloody quickly.

Richard Eyre, I think, was head of the National when many of these things were going on. He now says he was persecuted by Leftists at the National and was holding the line against decadence by doing what he could and that he banned a play by Edward Bond which makes it alright, you know. Because these people are fighting their own wars, of course, bureaucratically and institutionally.

Certainly, the Workers Revolutionary Party was very powerful at that period. Had no power anywhere else. But inside the state arts institutions, because of the influence of the Redgrave family and elsewhere, they had a lot of influence. This is the sort of minority Left elitism that's chiseled out many of the cultural monuments of the society from the inside, that people don't think about. All this croaking about democracy in the street when in actual fact it's sort of vanguard Left elitism of its own sort deep inside these institutions.

They still do it, actually. They still do put on plays like *The Jew of Malta* and so on, but wrapped around with endless excuses and endless procrastination. The latest thing is actually to have a white Othello. So, you don't actually black up the character. Because the play is so irredeemably racist in its language and structure that you admit your guilt and your racism beforehand by having a white actor to foreground your absence of pitilessness and your totalitarian racism. This is the sort of cultural studies beyond Political Correctness view. You basically crucify yourself beforehand, before the show goes on. And then give a fringe white actor a bit of employment in Birmingham Rep or something. It began with a white actor blacked up. Then it began with a black actor. And now it's back to a white actor, because the theories about it and how you deal with it have changed, perceptively. If somebody makes the wrong decision, say, "I thought that old production was not too bad, actually." They're out!

It's a sort of interesting terrorism in a way, intellectual terrorism. Of course, Bill's an intellectual terrorist, but the other way around. Because he responds to all of that with a sort of power and intellectual aggression of his own. One thing I've noticed about very liberal-minded people is that on the whole that spiritually they're very weak. There are hardcore Leftists who are real believers. But the bulk of the liberal vanguard, if you go down from the sort of perceived apex, are very flabby, and as soon as something which is contrary is placed before them they will be a recession and a bit of a retreat. Because it's a force that they haven't heard.

They particularly haven't heard the intellectualization of Right-wing ideas. People would say, "Hopkins, that statement was sexist."

And he said, "Men and women are biologically different. They're for different purposes in life. Everything is based upon biology. But, out of that comes the mind that soars towards spirituality!"

"You're admitting the fundamental nature and essentialism of biological difference."

"Well, I am!"

"Well, that's a sexist statement!"

He said, "I don't care! I'm a totalitarian! I'm sexist."

And they say, "Right," tugging at their collar a bit, "But, but haven't you read Andrea Dworkin?"

"Andrea Dworkin is a fat, ugly, obese, obscene, arrogant, ex-hooker, quasi-lesbian, and Jewish nutter that we shouldn't listen to!"

"But you're a monster! You're a monster!"

He'd say, "Well, I *am* a monster!"

They'd almost have a physical injury.

I met Tony Benn once in some Tory-related thing. And Benn had a physical reaction to the prospect of illiberalism. Somebody in the room said, "Well, I don't like the EU, really." Benn would go, "Oohh!" Almost like a physical shock, which is odd actually because Benn's campaigned against the EU because it's not integrated enough. Because it's just Europe! We need the whole world together! Skinner once said that to me. He said, "You're a Nazi. I can't be on a platform with you." I said, "I'm in the Tories." He said, "Don't give me that. I'm against the EU though, because I want a world proletarian state." Right. But Skinner will come out with it, so there's a streak of honesty there.

But in a way, the use of this sort of psychic and moral terrorism, the facing of it down . . . The fact that Bill after he was blocked, because they wouldn't publish his second novel and so only one appeared, basically. He's written lots of things himself. He's never published them since. I tried to get him to do it, but he won't. You know, pearls before swine and all that.

He then decided, "I need some money." So, he became a millionaire, which of course sounds just like that.

Bill once had a humiliating experience. He was on a tram. There were trams in London then. And the bloke came down the corridor, and he thought, "Oh, I haven't got any money." He's about 28. And it's a long way back to Streatham or Avery or wherever the family home was. The bloke said, "Off." Bill said, "I'm an artist who's trying to further our civilization." The bloke said, "Off. *Off!*" So, he got off and trudged home in the rain.

He said, "I'm an intellectual, and the *Daily Mirror* is throwing mud at me, but I've been shoved off a tram because I haven't got the fare. This is not how things should be." So, he decided, "How do we work this out?" So, he noticed that all these beautiful Georgian houses were being wrecked, and all the fireplaces are being ripped out, and the stairways were being demolished. It's all being chucked in the street. Old Britain? Tat and garbage! Out in the street!

He thought, "Somebody will want to buy this." So, he bought what today would be called a skip, and he went 'round late at night with a few lads who he gave a bit of money to, and he got all of these things that somebody else despised. He realized that in a short while, pre-internet and so on, he could find people who wanted it. Then collectors from the United States used to come over and see him and say, "Oh, I do love that fireplace." And Bill would say, "Thousand quid." "Pardon?" "Thousand quid. You know the meaning of money." And they went, "OK!" That was the start.

Bill is a modernist in many ways because of elements of primitivism and barbarity and fury in it, which essentially accords with his partially demonic nature, and that's just a fact. He's a champion of the movement which in a sense would end modernism by proving some of its antecedents. It's a movement called *art brut*, which technically comes out of André Breton's surrealist movement.

This is a movement where people like Dubuffet, who founded it, would do an outline of a red child with a big eye. "Oh, I like that." Then he'd get some pink paint, and he'd throw it on! And he'd get a big blue roller. "This is really good." Then he'd get a big sponge or maybe some acid or something, and he'd put it on the sponge and chuck it on and have a good scrub 'round. Then he'd stand back and say, "God, a maniac and a child could have done that. *It's marvelous!*" They sell for £85,000 each at Sotheby's. I kid you not. I've been at the auctions when they've been sold.

Bill thought to himself, "This is interesting, isn't it? The art of a maniac. The art of the ultimate outsider. Lunatic! Crepuscular. He hasn't got any arms. He's lying on the ground, but he can paint with his mouth!" So, what do we do? He's part of this movement of sort of anti-artists, which is interesting actually because a significant part of modernism is based upon mental interiority. It's based not on representing that which is outside, which of course cinema has done in the 20th century, but going inside the mind to sexual imagery, to fantasy, to internal discourses, sort of sub-sub-sub-sub-sub-Blake, if you like. And he's made a fortune from this sort of stuff.[8]

Counter-Currents/*North American New Right*
July 26, 2013

---

[8] The last sentence, "And he's not even that fashionable because there are elements of modernism that . . ." breaks off because the tape ran out.

Remembering Bill Hopkins, 1928–2011

A great man is dead.

Bill Hopkins (1928–2011), one of Britain's most estimable Right-wing intellectuals, died on Thursday, May 6, of heart and kidney failure in a north London hospital. He was born into a Welsh theatrical family in 1928. His father was the music hall *artiste* Ted Hopkins while his mother happened to be the theatrical beauty Violette Broderick.

Bill enjoyed six or seven adventurous lives or stages, but he first came to prominence as one of the Angry Young Men in the 1950s. This was a media designation for a polyglot grouping of writers and intellectuals who had little in common save a certain radicalism of tone (the alleged anger) and the fact that they were all of the rising or post-war generation. The group included Ken Tynan, Lindsay Anderson, Kingsley Amis (who refused any membership of this group), Colin Wilson, Stuart Holroyd, John Osborne, John Wain, Bill Hopkins, and a few others . . .

Although largely a media creation, the Angry Young Men did sustain an interconnected series of works and a volume of personal essays or manifestos known as *Declaration*. Bill's contribution was a novel called *The Divine and the Decay* which was published in November 1957 along with his revolutionary essay, "Ways Without a Precedent." The novel was republished by a small house called Deverell and Birdsey in 1984 as *The Leap!* pursuant to a film adaptation that never eventuated. *The Divine and the Decay* now fetches high prices from used book dealers, whereas *The Leap!* can occasionally be found on Amazon.

The novel is relatively difficult to describe in that it is not widely known (not a condemnation) but it features a young fanatic (Peter Plowart) who wishes to become Prime Minister of Britain and his self-imposed exile in the Channel Islands. The work is highly memorable given its strongly filmic and visual flavor—as well as the melodramatic characterization of the cripple Lumas, the estranged Mrs Lumas, her lover the tomato grower Lachanell, the policeman who pursues Plowart (Purchamp) and numerous other characters such as Bourcey (his Party manager) and an itinerant tatterdemalion.

The centerpiece of the book are the intellectual debates that take place between Plowart (who represents an amoral and pagan spirit) and the modern Christianity of Claremont Capothy, the dowager or grand dame of the island. The book exploits the anomalous status of the Channel Islands—the only part of Britain to be occupied by the Germans during the Second World War. The island where Plowart is ensconced turns out to be Brechau (Vachau in the novel), whereas its feudal social structure is based on Sark. There was no democracy—and certainly no motor cars on Sark—until the middle of the last century. A sort of feudal paternalism without the National Health Service or the BBC prevailed on this tiny backwater.

All of this feeds into a picaresque novel of great power—where Lumas epitomizes Britain's present status as a bankrupt Third World country beholden to American power and with seemingly little will of its own. Other groups will obviously find time to feed upon such a carcass. If anyone can pick up a neglected copy of this novel then they are in for a *frisson* or thrill, by virtue of the fact that it's literally a *terra incognita* or a forgotten masterpiece.

What else can be said about Bill Hopkins? The most significant thing about him was his character—at once resourceful, da(e)monic, wide-ranging, and extremely imaginative. One of Bill's most remarkable attributes was his commitment to radical forms of modernism, such as *art brut* or outsider art towards the end of his life. This had to do with the classic 20th-century impulse to make the world again, to make it anew, or to effect a sudden and total change in perception.

The Modernist project failed overall—yet men like Bill Hopkins believed in the future rather than the past . . . and this is something that is relatively rare given his political partiality. Loyalty was another staple with Bill. Given his wide range of meeting guests and acquaintances, from Prince Charles to Jean-

Paul Sartre, many publishers wanted a revelatory autobiography where "the dirt would be dished," and yet Bill always refused because he deemed it to be dishonorable and disloyal to many of the people he had known.

After his bohemian and intellectual life in the '50s and early '60s, Bill became an antiques dealer and earned himself a substantial fortune by the time of his death in May 2011. He was probably technically a millionaire by the time of his demise.

A decided elitist and anti-humanist, Bill was a sort of elixir or *sine qua non* for many liberal intellectuals during the mid-century. One recalls Lady Snow's (Pamela Hansford Johnson's) book about evil which definitely emerged from many conservations that C. P. Snow and his wife had with Bill in which he would have been cast in the role of Mephistopheles. Indeed, the range of people that he'd known was truly voluminous, including Kingsley Amis, Francis Bacon, Iain Sinclair, Heathcote Williams, Lucien Freud, Emeric Pressburger, and Derek Jarman.

Above all, I think that Bill Hopkins convinced me—when we met in the early- to mid-1990s—that anything was possible, the world could be made again, and that, contrary to nearly all present orthodoxies, the Right is actually the side of civilization. It just has to learn to live up to it once again . . . that's all!

Bill Hopkins is survived by his German-born wife, Carla, and a very valuable collection of original artworks, antiques, and *objets d'art*. He died just short of his 83rd birthday.

Counter-Currents/*North American New Right*
June 7, 2011

Bill Hopkins'
The Divine & the Decay

Bill Hopkins was one of the "Angry Young Men" group of writers who emerged in the 1950s. He was the most prominent of the "Outsiders" trio amongst the "Angry Young Men"—a groupuscule which consisted of himself, Colin Wilson, and Stuart Holroyd.

His most outstanding contribution was a *succès de scandale* with the novel, *The Divine and the Decay,* published by MacGibbon & Kee in 1957—and his artistic credo, "Ways Without a Precedent," contained in *Declaration,* the manifesto of the "Angry Young Men."

Doris Lessing, in the second volume of her literary autobiography, *Walking in the Shade,* says that Bill Hopkins revealed a great talent at this time. She also goes on to mistakenly declare that he died tragically young! His greatest achievement remains *The Divine and the Decay.*

The Leap! (a.k.a. *The Divine and the Decay*) is largely forgotten today—yet when it appeared in the late 1950s it produced an absolute furore in the press; a *cause célèbre* which was almost unprecedented at the time. As an anonymous author, who wrote a foreword to the book's deluxe second edition, put it: "an abscess seemed to have been punctured in the general culture."

He goes on to say that anyone who wishes to analyze the nature of contemporary literary censorship—no longer about explicit mentions of sex (of erotica *per se*) but now primarily to do with "incorrect" political thoughts—should spend a couple of hours in the Colindale Newspaper Library in North London (the country's largest repository of ephemeral non-fiction) surveying the literary press's response to this novel.

The book is essentially a consideration of philosophical ideas. It deals with an ideological viewpoint, an aesthetic response to political reality, laid out in the form of a traditional narrative—i.e., a book with a beginning, a middle, and an end. In a sense it is similar to a range of politicized fictions that occurred in the early 1950s across the Channel, such as Sartre's *Roads to Freedom* trilogy and Camus' existentialist *tour de force, The Outsider*. But the irony about this novel is that although it takes a relatively "traditional" form it is, in actuality, a complete moral reversal of the Left-existential works mentioned above.

In his anatomization of the culture of the 1950s, *The Angry Decade*, Kenneth Allsop describes this work as both unregenerate and morally "evil." He basically declares that it is a loathsome product which should have been banned—although, like all true liberals of his ilk, Allsop could not bring himself openly to advocate the censorship that he seeks for this book (somewhat inevitably).

The work in question deals with the psychological origins of a dynamic leader (a veteran "Outsider"). It depicts the spiritual trajectory of a "British Caesar" on his way to complete power—or what is conceived as such. If you like, it is a version of Hermann Hesse's *The Glass Bead Game* played with human eyeballs!

It denotes the "amoral" power-curve of Peter Plowart—at least after he has succeeded in "murdering" the chairman of the New Britain League (the latter his vehicle to obtain supreme power): and furthermore, once he has successfully taken refuge on an almost deserted island called Vachau, which is depicted as a small outcrop off the Channel Islands.

In actual fact this island does not exist; it is purely imaginary. It is merely used for the purposes of narrative-drive, even though it may be based on the Anglo-French outpost of the Barclay brothers, Brechou, a tiny isle off Sark. On his arrival in Vachau, Plowart comes across various human types (or archetypes) against which he tests his will and his future view of the world. These correspondents—i.e., characters in a dramatic dialogue, all contained in the form of a novel—represent a Christian and "female" perspective (Clermont); a weakened, male, humanist viewpoint (ultimately speaking) (Lumas); and the drunken sensualist, the man addicted to fleshly pleasures (Lachanell).

Plowart is a man obsessed by the nature of his own destiny, irrespective of all other things such as human warmth and comfort (for example). He is a perfect paradigm of the dictatorial urge (the "Will to Power"). Moreover he resembles a novelist's version of the young Saddam Hussein (as it were) set in England around the middle of the century. (We should remember that Saddam Hussein had set upon his course at an early age. Indeed he first came to prominence, as a mere stripling of 17, when he tried to machine-gun the Premier of Iraq.)

Plowart is made of a similar human material. For he is a man who believes—in a purely Nietzschean sense—that the "Will to Power" is the basis of all existence (whether civil or otherwise) and that human beings only learn anything through their ability to transgress thresholds of pain. In many respects Plowart appears in this theoretical novel to be a mediaeval figure, almost a mystic, a man who wishes to go beyond what presently exists: but always with a totally different morality to that of liberal-humanism (quiescent or otherwise).

This is why Allsop—together with other journalists of similar views—reacted so violently against this novel: in that it completely contradicted their own beliefs, based as they were on *soi-disant* Enlightenment values. For, in all honesty, Plowart does not believe in the right to life, in humanist ethics, in opposition to slavery, in the belief that the weak are morally best, that women are superior to men, that sentimentality is a form of grace, that corporal punishment is wrong, that human beings are racially equal, that people do not wish to be dominated, that destruction is "evil" (as a principle of life) and that human freedom is anything other than a conceit to be used by those of a higher power. In other words, Plowart is an "inhumanist," an antihumanist—although not in a crude political sense. (Even this is not entirely true for Hopkins does not dwell on political matters straightforwardly—or in any other way—with the exception of a few vague phrases about the populist New Britain League.)

When we describe Hopkins' character in this manner we mean—at least ethically speaking—that he is a mythical being who is closer to the spirit of Aleister Crowley than the contemporary Archbishop of Canterbury: at least as was depicted in Crowley's novels such as *The Moonchild* and *The Diary of a Drug Fiend*.

For Plowart is—in a purely normative manner—a "left-hand occultist" or social magician: an "amoralist" and an anti-Christian; a new Assyrian; a man who believes in a religion older than Christianity, when the latter is controversially dismissed as a humanist creed, the weak-kneed religion of those unfit for life. In spirit, however, this is closer to the Plato of *The Laws*—rather than the lucidity of *The Republic*. In any event, it is a "sadic" faith (a doctrine beyond liberal-humanist and Christian morality) which sees war as the crucible of human meaning: and conflict/death as a state of "liberation" in relation to preconceived notions of being.

For Plowart preaches a "pessimistic" ideology of force and challenge. He believes in the manipulation of mass emotion (i.e., the use of contemporary fear and sentiment) primarily through the persuasive utilization of superior cultural energy. Basically, then, he stands for the values that animated European revolutionary regimes from the 1920s to the 1940s—i.e., the "dictatorships" that were defeated by Britain and her Allies in the last war.

Hence the fact that there was such a furious reaction to this novel—i.e., to a metapolitical inquiry; a philosophical speculation—undertaken in 1957, which was after all only a few years after the war itself had ended. But these events have now passed into history. In this respect Colin Wilson misunderstands the book in his otherwise interesting introduction to the novel's second edition in the 1980s—particularly when he speaks of it as a mystical travelogue. For, in actuality, this novel is an exercise in psychohistory before it has been written. It is a fusion of Dennis Wheatley's *The Devil Rides Out* (its Sabbatesque revelations) with an imaginary autobiography—an auto-hagiography, even—of the young Enoch Powell.

In this sense Bill Hopkins's *The Divine and the Decay*—his greatest literary achievement—stands revealed as a *Bildungsroman* of the anti-Left; a premonitory explosion; a lightning-flash which reveals a *terra incognita*; an intrusion into the *Zeitgeist*; a "storm of steel" against liberal evasion.

Counter-Currents/North American New Right
June 7, 2011

WESTERN CIVILIZATION:
A BULLET THROUGH STEEL*

Being asked to speak about European civilization is like being asked to throw an enormous spool of string into the future, and to try and grasp it as it goes away from you.

What do you talk about? Do you talk about the art? Do you talk about the architecture? Do you talk about the science? Do you talk about the history of various nation-states on the European Continent? Do you talk about what white people have achieved when they've gone abroad into the other continents of the world?

Do you talk about politics in a more narrow way? Or do talk about metapolitics, in other words, the ideas, the philosophy, the culture and history as they impact upon a high level of consciousness and as these gradually feed down into lower-level, more intermediate, more street-political sorts of formulations?

What I've decided to do is to be optimistic, in relation to some of the pessimism that we've heard from various speakers this afternoon. And to look at what European culture and civilization has achieved.

Now, it's such a broad canvas that I'm going to look at two works, that are tragic works. One is a tragedy by Aeschylus called *Agamemnon,* and another is a tragedy by Shakespeare called *King Lear.* And the reason I've picked these out, is because during the course of the 20th century there have been various travesties of these tragedies produced by the Left. I think in particular of Steven Berkoff's version of *Agamemnon,* and I think in particular of the Marxist playwright Edward Bond's version of *King Lear,* which was called *Lear.*

Those who know *Lear* will remember that it involves a blinding scene when Gloucester is blinded by Cornwall, in the

---

* A transcript by Michael Polignano of a speech given in London on November 5, 2011, at the third meeting of the IONA group, which stands for Isles of the North Atlantic.

middle of the play, in Act III, I believe. But in order to mechanize this in a more materialistic way, Edward Bond has a machine: a machine that removes eyeballs, as a complaint against capitalist violence and against violence *per se*.

Just to fill in a little bit of a paraphrase here, Bond is a Marxist playwright. Marxist playwrights took over the British stage and British theater in the 1960s, '70s, and '80s, particularly influenced by Brecht's idea of epic theater. Bond produced a Left-wing version of *Lear*, in which Lear is a mad king who of course gives his territory away to scheming sons, in this case, scheming daughters in two of the cases in Shakespeare's drama.

Lear suffers terribly for this at different levels, and is brought to a form of realization as to his own folly, the nature of kingship, and many moral causative factors about life, by virtue of the suffering that's imposed upon him because of his primordial mistake. When you have a kingdom, you never divide it, because you are inviting civil war into your own self, if you're a monarch, and into your own territory, regardless of anything.

Bond is quite unusual, because Bond is obsessed with the issue of violence. And like a lot of playwrights and filmmakers who are opposed to violence, his entire work consists of violence. All the time. Mayhem, rapes, gouging out of eyes, autopsies on the stage. Mock autopsies, of course, with plenty of blood: watery red liquid and bits of sponge moving about which indicate that they're sort of fillets of steak drawn from the human body. Because in a sense Bond is a materialist, and things have to be kept at a material level even when he's dealing with classic drama.

One of the great difficulties of the contemporary Left—certainly, if we go back over the last 30 to 40 years—has been to deal with Stalinism. Why did their project of universal human emancipation end up with Stalinism, in every sense? Why did it fail, catastrophically, even in its own terms? Why did a doctrine of radical human rights where all would love and all would congeal and all would come together in the fastness of our days, end up with the Gulag? This is something that is very, very difficult to answer.

Jean-Paul Sartre, the Left-wing intellectual in France, ended up as a Maoist towards the end of his life, with Simone de Beauvoir. He attempted to answer it in an enormous philosophical work, called *The Critique of Dialectical Reason*, based on Kant's volume of several centuries before. Sartre was trying to synthesize existentialism and Marxism as two of the great currents of intellectual thought in the 20th century.

But when he got to Stalinism, and when he got to the attempt to explain the internal dialectic and convolutions of the Soviet Union post-Lenin's death, and after the defeat of Trotsky and his Left opposition faction in the Party in 1928, he hit a brick wall. He couldn't go any further. The second volume of *The Critique* couldn't be written, because in a sense it's unanswerable even in the terms of his own theory.[1]

Bond believes that violence is irrational and proceeds from bourgeois man and the context of capitalist competition. But the problem with this, as in the problem with all Marxism, is there is a complete voiding of the biological realities of life.

Man—men and women, in all groups—are 80% inherited, at least, 80% generic, 80% genetic, 80% hereditarian. And the socialized element, the naturalizing, normative element, where we're reared through parents, the psychology of the relationship that we have with them, where we're culturalized through education and behaviorism in a society: that's 20%. And even that is ecology, which is a species of biology. Everybody knows ecology is a subject area within biology.

It's almost as if the 20% which is actually given by naturalization—that which is nurture rather than nature to use old-fashioned formulations from the 1960s—is actually part and parcel of nature itself. Because what sets us up and primes us to be naturalized as human beings if not nature itself?

So there's an easy answer to Sartre and to Bond, and to other people of this sort who pretend that there is a deeply complex and invidious set of reasons as to why the Left-wing pro-

---

[1] The second volume was written but not published during Sartre's lifetime. It was published posthumously in 1985.

jects ended up in the way that they did.

It's now a canard, it's now a sort of species of rhetoric, that Stalin's Soviet Union was one of the worst regimes that's ever existed in human history. I recently re-read *Nineteen Eighty-Four* by George Orwell, which is a satire upon the Hampstead Left of his day, and which is a satire against the Soviet Union of its time.

I remember Peter Hain was once asked, what are the glories of Western Civilization? Hain of course, an ex-South African liberal Leftist who was head of the anti-apartheid movement when he came to this country, said that there are no triumphs to Western civilization. He said that there's nothing to be proud of at all. All we've created is Hitler and Stalin. Don't forget he's on the Center-Left. So to include Stalin is in a way a *mélange* "own goal" in relation to what could be perceived to be his own side.

The fact that Bond and Sartre—and Hain, who's a much lesser intellect than either of those—compute the same failure is due to the fact that they irreducibly deny the biological basis to civilization.

Race is culture and culture is race, essentially, put very tendentiously and very crudely and far too crudely than many intellectuals would like, or feel comfortable with. But there is a degree to which everything that exists has to come out of something which existed before it. It has to have a primal root. It has to have a foundation. It has to be "racinated," to use Simone Weil's term. It has to come from some egg, or some implantation of self, which gives birth to it.

This is one of the reasons for the pessimism of some of our speakers earlier today, because they don't see any European high culture being created at the present time. And although there's an enormous mélange and superfluity of culture being created at the present time, particularly by the state-subsidized and semi-capitalist arts.

One also has to say, where is the greatness of a universal cultural Western exhibitionism being created today? Because if you look around you don't see it. What you do see is deconstruction on the opera stage. Whereby you will have *Cosi Fan*

Tutte, and you'll have a urinal in the middle of the stage. A urinal, into which men empty their bladders.

Now why is that on the stage? It's because the people who have put that piece of work on are rebelling against the nature of the piece. They're at war with the text. This is what they would tell you. They're attacking the text, even as they're putting it on. It's a sort of masochism in a way, because it means even if they're going forwards they're pummeling themselves in the face, rhetorically, and watching it in a mirror. And they've got a film camera like that one over there, filming them pummeling themselves in the mirror.

Because what they're frightened of is too much authentication. What they're frightened of is too much cultural affirmation. Because if things are culturally affirmed in a prior or an identitarian sort of a way they're conceived to be "too white," or "too European," or too "*ur-*," or "too fascistic," or "too dangerously tribal."

And that's the reason these things are done. Everything is done for a reason. This society, in all of its very complex processes and cultural formations, exists for interconnected sets of reasons. Nothing is purely accidental or contingent. Things may come together by virtue of accident and things feeding off each other in a way that one thing will spawn a concept related to itself. But things are rooted in structures of being and belonging which have either been torn up and thrown to the side, or actually subsist and come out of something that's related prior to their existence.

Why did a Left-wing playwright like Berkoff rewrite *Agamemnon* in the 1960s and 1970s, which is a play by Aeschylus from ancient Greece? Why did Bond rewrite *King Lear*? They did this because they wanted to take some of the primal energy that exists in these amazing cultural forms and use it for their own purposes. They also wanted to have versions of their own of Aeschylus and Shakespeare that they could put on without any filter and without the older texts, which could be perceived as reactionary or unprogressive, or created before the era of progress, created in both cases before the liberal Enlightenment of 200 years ago or more. They wanted a situation where you could refer to a text which is of this present hour and of its present prejudices.

Now Aeschylus's *Agamemnon* is the beginning of a series of tragedies called the *Oresteia* and survives from a Greek competition. Everything in Greece was competitive. Sport was competitive, but art was competitive. When people wrote a tragedy, it would compete with other tragedies, and there would be a vote. And Sophocles and Euripides and Aeschylus, who were the three tragedians that come down to us, won quite a lot of those votes.

This play is about revenge, and it's about the primal, and it's about sources of identity. It's about the aftermath of the Trojan Wars, when Agamemnon comes back from Troy, which they have successfully destroyed after a long siege. He brings with him Cassandra, who may or may not be with child by him. She is the daughter of Priam, the king of Troy, whom he seduced and has kept as a concubine or mistress. He comes back to Argos, the city-state from which he left prior to the Trojan adventure, with the desire to flaunt the fact that Troy has been destroyed, but maybe not to the degree that his wife who's plotting his murder, Clytemnestra, wishes.

Clytemnestra is one of the greatest characters created in Western art. She is the prototype for Lady Macbeth; she is the prototype for all of the powerful women in Western drama, Western cinema, and Western art, who in a sense often adopted a quasi-male role. This is hinted at very much in the early part of the play where she's described as a "man-minded woman," a woman with the mind of a man, a woman who's a woman on the outside and a man on the inside.

She has taken a lover while Agamemnon has been away—because he's taken a few, close to Troy's walls—and the lover is Aegisthus. And Aegisthus is a man who has a bias and a prejudice against the house of Atreus, which is Agamemnon's particular house. And this is because of an act of cannibalism which occurred earlier in the history and trajectory of the house of Atreus, whereby Thyestes served up the sons and daughters of Atreus for his own consumption. And it's because of this blood on the hands and blood in the mouth, and because of this autophagy, this cannibalism which has occurred, that *a curse,* a curse has been placed upon this house by Atreus, and every so often this curse has to ventilate itself.

One of the ways in which the curse ventilated itself is Agamemnon putting to death Iphigenia, one of his daughters he had with Clytemnestra. He did this because the Greek fleet, by myth, was stalled at Aulis and couldn't reach the coast where Troy was. Therefore a sacrifice had to be given the gods. And he was told that he had to sacrifice one of his daughters, Iphigenia, in order to do so. Clytemnestra has never forgiven him for this, and is waiting to revenge herself when he returns to Argos.

When he returns to Argos, she makes him walk upon the purple, or upon the red, in certain of the theatrical versions of this play. It's illicit for a Greek to ape the gods, because the gods are jealous of undue greatness in a human being, which is called hubris, false pride, the pride that portends before a fall. Clytemnestra wants Agamemnon to walk upon the purple, partly because it would justify her later murderous rages and actions against him.

Agamemnon holds out against this, but in the end he walks upon the purple. It's a great moment, when there's a series of doors at the back of the stage, and Agamemnon walks upon the purple as Clytemnestra is at the front of the stage with the chorus, until he finally goes into the palace from which he will not emerge, other than as a corpse.

Whether she murders him in the stagecraft with an axe or a sword, is to me textually unclear: there's evidence for both. Aegisthus gives her a sword, but she also slaughters in the way that you slaughter an animal for sacrifice in accordance with Greek traditions, and this is with an axe. Many of the classical paintings of this play from the 19th century, particularly in English and British art, show Clytemnestra with an axe, either leaning on the axe, or holding the axe over a net. The net is there because these are the curtains, the netting that she actually traps Agamemnon in, prior to giving the blows that kill him in the bath. This is a scenario which has been worked out by Aegisthus, but Aegisthus is regarded as a weakling, because he gets Clytemnestra to do the murder.

One of the greatest scenes in Western drama is when the chorus of Argive elders are talking to the herald, and later then talk to Cassandra as the murder takes place. There's a great cry and a shout, a sort of "Aaahhh!" from offstage. And the chorus hears it and wonders what it is, and they're terrified—the chorus are old men from the city of Argos. And they wonder whether Cassandra's warnings about the possibility of Agamemnon's death are true.

Now Cassandra is in Agamemnon's car, in his chariot, as he pulls up. And she has been afflicted by Apollo with the gift of second sight, so she can see the future. But because she spurned his advances, as a god he has cursed her with the fact that people will only recognize that she has second sight after the event. So she becomes a prophet of illicit loss, if you like. She can only ask the question that others will not accept until they have the evidence before them. So she appears to be a false prophet until she's proved to be right. In other words, her capacity for prophecy never has any positive outcome or goal at the time that she gives it. She's always going to be frustrated in that regard. And the interesting thing is, is that the chorus of Argive elders is partly won over to her complaints, but also rejects her. And this is why in the journalistic tradition that surrounds us today with multiple media platforms, people who warn against a coming danger are often referred to as Cassandras, for adopting the role of Cassandra.

Suddenly, of course, she turns and goes back into the palace, knowing that she will be added to the death total with Agamemnon, because she is killed as his lover with Agamemnon by Clytemnestra at Aegisthus' behalf.

Then this great moment occurs, which is a moment of catharsis in Aristotle's terms. Aristotle believed that the point of tragedy was to put on the stage the negative, or more ferocious, or more diabolical side of man, the non-dualist side of man, in order to overcome it.

Because life is born in pain, dies in pain, and consists of quite a lot of pain during the intermediary stages between birth and death. And in order to overcome and face that, particularly in a stoical way, you needed to take up these negative emotions into yourself and have them purged, have them sublimated, to use a modern word. And the way that you purge them is by watching tragedy.

This is why people have always liked to be entertained by watching unpleasant things. It's a characteristic of our species. And all genres like horror, and all the rest of it, rely upon the fact that people like to see conflict. They like to see contumaciousness; they like to see that which in other circumstances could be perceived as threatening.

And this is what occurs when the doors are flung open at the back of the stage, and Clytemnestra is there with the axe or the sword, and the bath is next to her, and the folds of the net are surrounding and tipping over the outside of the bath, and at the bottom of the bath are the remains of Agamemnon and Cassandra, and they're wheeled, probably by servants or by members of the auxiliary parts of the theatrical troupe, or there's a device that brings them forward to the front of the stage. It's done in a dramatic way. It's often done in silence.

Greek theater, of course, is of such a moment that we don't, even today, completely understand how they did it. There was a lot of dance involved in Greek theater. There was a lot of threnody of the body. The actors were non-personified because they all wore masks. Contrary to the cult of the personality and the actor which we have today, they believed in the depersonalization of the actor, because often different actors would play different parts in the same play, because they would be masked. Nearly all the female parts were played by men, so Clytemnestra would be played by a man, which is a tradition which extends to Elizabethan theater.

Hence the old idea that you should never put your daughter on the stage, because only women of a certain sort were put on the stage until relatively late. Because when the Puritans banned our theatre, when English revolutionaries under Cromwell prevented theatre—yet allowed opera—throughout the period of the interregnum, one of the reasons that they did it was to prevent the prospect of indecency—of pornography, if you like—which always comes, not in a literal pornographic way as would subsist today, but through watching scenes of violence, through watching scenes of transgression, through watching scenes of horror. And also watching scenes which are simulacra.

In all faiths, in Orthodox Judaism, in certain forms of pretty restricted Islam, and in what is called fundamental Christianity, there is the view that because God has created the world as it is, art is a blasphemous simulacrum in relation to this. Most of the people who follow these faiths have no desire to impose upon the arts at all, particularly. But this idea that God made the world, and therefore it is a blasphemy to add to that making, and that all art, even great art—particularly great art—takes away from the unmediated religious experience. Which is why many of the Puritans, like William Prynne and others, oppose the Elizabethan theater, and the Elizabethan stage.

And I want to couple Aeschylus' *Agamemnon* and Shakespeare's *King Lear* together, because the English people achieved an extraordinary thing during the Elizabethan and Jacobean stagecraft. They basically created something which is amongst the elite art that has ever been created on this planet. This small island and the nationality within it, England, produced material at that time which is comparable to the Greeks, and is acknowledged by the whole world to be comparable to the Greeks.

Shakespeare is the greatest of those that were produced at that time, but there were many others, such as Marlowe and Ben Jonson, and Middleton and Rowley, and all of the others: Kyd, and John Webster, the divine John Webster, who could only write tragedy, who would only write dark, treacly pieces—like *The Duchess of Malfi, The White Devil*—could only write tragedy. The highest form, the most cathartic form, the most ennobling form. A form which isn't written today.

Today we have soap operas. Today we have that which is on the tube of the nighttime, the television of the nighttime. It appears that the tragic urge is missing from Western life, and from world civilization. And there is a quite neat fit with that, because the liberal era can only take tragedy if it's restorationalist. There's an enormous archival tradition at the moment, whereby many of the great plays of the past are put on endlessly, in state houses, financed by public money.

One of the more "amusing" features is what's called racially blind casting. You can now have plays like *Julius Caesar,* for example, where a half of the cast is black. And yet there's not a single black character in *Julius Caesar.* This is done so that the audience is desensitized to the fact that that is truly the case. But also it's done because there are an enormous number of talented performers who, if you only did restorationalist pieces, could not perform. Indeed, there's a lot of ideology that plays around the re-presentation of these classic pieces, because nothing is neutral, and everything has to be presented in a particular way.

Othello is a key example. At the beginning of the 20th century, *Othello* would always be played by a white actor blacked-up. In the middle of the 20th century, certain classically trained black actors, particularly from America, were found to play the part. But at the end of the 20th century, and into the 21st century, Othello is played—on the whole, in very progressive theatre companies at any rate—by a white actor who is not blacked-up. Because the play is regarded as a racist play. It's regarded as irredeemably racialist. And therefore to draw attention to this fact, Othello is played white. If people ask why this should be done, it's said, "It's giving a white actor an opportunity that he otherwise wouldn't enjoy."

But there's a degree to which it's being done to draw attention to the fact that this play can't be rewritten in a "Newspeak"-like way, even though certain people would like Shakespeare's plays to be rewritten. *The Merchant of Venice* has been often subjected to the idea that it should be rewritten. Professor David Cesarani at the University of Southampton, has said on many occasions that *The Merchant of Venice* should be textually rewritten, because as a play in its present form it's emblematic of what in *Nineteen Eighty-Four* is called "Crimethink." The whole play could be reduced to the liberal buzz phrase, to the politically-correct buzz phrase, to the Newspeak buzz phrase, if you align it with the language of *Nineteen Eighty-Four*'s "Newspeak," as Crimethink.

I remember he was once asked, on *The Moral Maze*, on Radio Four, "So you're a better writer than Shakespeare?" And he said, "No, not necessarily." Not necessarily. He said, "But we are living in a different era now, and we have different sensibilities. And people's ["people's," don't forget] sensibilities have to be respected and cannot be trampled upon." So it's quite clear that it's only the canonical status of some of these texts, such as Aeschylus, such as Shakespeare, that prevents them from being "messed about with" in terms of the text. But this is only in relation to the body of the text.

The stagecraft, of course, can be transmuted in all sorts of ways. You have Shakespeare set in concentration camps, or in brothels, or in Chinese restaurants, or against banks of tires which have been pleasingly painted red in order to make a particular point. Or in sets—which are slightly traditional in a strange sort of way—sets without any stagecraft or any props at all. Or you have a revivalist current like the Globe, in London, which reacts against the post-modern jiggery-pokery with Shakespeare and other classical texts, and wants to do them in a totally Elizabethan form. And that can be permitted in a strange sort of way, particularly if it becomes part of an enabling, tourist-based experience.

So it's noticeable that all of the classic texts before 1900 have been left, and have not been interfered with except in the way in which they're presented to an audience, as part of the modality of Western civilization. But the texts that exist now, are so politically correct, and so ingrained as such, that no plays that consist of some of the classical verities that I've discussed could be put on now. If somebody wrote *Lear* now, it would not be permitted. The attitude towards illegitimacy is questionable; Lear's patriarchy is questionable in relation to the two to three daughters; the remarks of Kent in relation to Oswald are questionable, particularly psychosexually; the violence would have to be looked at: the blinding scene, when Cornwall blinds Gloucester.

Gloucester is the lower noble underneath Lear who suffers in the subtext of the play. There's two plays, basically, and there's two narratives. And they go along with one another.

Lear suffers spiritually and mentally, whereas Gloucester suffers physically, because he's on the lower level. In order to be redeemed, he actually has to suffer the indignity of having his eyes put out by Cornwall.

Of course, Shakespeare's plays are always morally balanced and seek an Elizabethan equipoise. That's why when Cornwall puts his boot upon Gloucester's eyes, and says, "Out, vile jelly! Where is thy luster now?" when the blinding scene occurs, a servant raises his hand and a dagger against Cornwall in that particular moment. And he does so because Cornwall has rejected the divine pact.

Basically, nobles should not treat an old man, who is a prisoner and who was a guest, in that way. Therefore he's rescinded upon part of a contract which is itself hierarchical and divinely inspired. This means the servant is freed, and can rebel against Cornwall's cruelty in that moment, and in turn mortally wounds Cornwall, although he's finished off himself.

"Ill-timed comes this hurt!" says Cornwall, as he's dragged offstage by his scheming and malevolent wife, who's partly put him up to the blinding of Gloucester anyway. So, even that element of cruelty occurs within a scenario which has a moral framework embedded around it.

This is something which could be said to be missing from Steven Berkoff's version of *Agamemnon*, or Bond's version of *King Lear*, because in Bond's play there's an enormous amount of violence as there is in contemporary cultural material. There's an enormous amount of abattoirial excess, what some call the proletarianization of culture, where everything is reduced to its lowest common denominator.

You see this in horror as a genre. A hundred years ago, horror was Bram Stoker and Wilkie Collins and this sort of thing. Now horror is Stephen King. And beneath Stephen King. And beneath, beneath Stephen King. And beneath, beneath, beneath Stephen King. And so on; you get the message. So there's a degree to which a coarsening and an absence of refinement and a sort of abattoirial statement, whereby the thing is given you neat, is what goes on today and which is on in every multiplex.

Has anyone come across those *Saw* films? *Saw* 1, and *Saw* 2, and *Saw* 3, and there must be a fourth one, so there's *Saw* 4, and this sort of thing, which is sort of sadistic and abbatoirial, although in a sense no one is being harmed, because you're only dealing with puppets.

There's an artistic theory that deals with that area, called the theatre of cruelty, by a surrealist in France in the middle of the 20th century called Antonin Artaud. And there's a degree to which this material is as cruel as Greek tragedy, is a cruel as Elizabethan tragedy, but there's no moral or evidential purpose for it to be so. There's no philosophical reason why it should be so, therefore the thing exists in and of itself.

If you want that degree of abattoirial horror you could go down to your local butcher's, go around the back, and plunge your hands into the offal, and into the meat, and move them around, and bring them up, and have a sort of threnody in that sort of a way. But that's because culturally the thing wouldn't extend beyond that gesture. And that's what's going along with a lot of these pieces, because if you are to make the brutality of life as it's transfigured in tragic art meaningful, you have to transcend those sorts of actions. Or you have to have a vocabulary to transcend them.

But the doctrine of transcendence is a religious doctrine, essentially. Or is a psycho-social, psycho-emotional, and linguistic pattern which portends to religious belief whether one has any religious belief or not. It means that one believes there are things above the things that face you, and there are things above that, and there are things above those things. Or at least there's the possibility that such might be the case.

So you're looking upwards, rather than looking downwards. This is why people go to tragedy and feel exhilarated afterwards, rather than feeling depressed, or out of sorts, or mildly mentally deranged by the depiction of cruelty. It's because it occurs within the context of a spiritual revelation which is transcendent. But the whole purpose of this sort of culture which we live in today, as Evola and other thinkers have put it, is not to have transcendence at all. It's to keep man at a certain level. Ultimately, a level of consumption. The expulsion of energy, the repletion of energy, the consumption of goods, the depletion of the consumption of those goods, the need to consume even more of such goods.

If you keep people at a certain level—and the irony is that this is occurring within a maximally capitalist society, dominated by ideas from the soft Marxian Left. This is one of the great dichotomies that we live in, that we live in a Left-wing market, that we live in a libertarian, Left-leaning, capitalist society. The idea of a capitalist Left, or a Left-leaning market, would have struck most thinkers as totally absurd at the beginning of the 20th century, because the market and all forms of Leftism were supposed to be adversarial. Now we live in a fit, whereby the ideas that the products affirm have been taken from a wide range of the Left's trajectory, whereas the Left itself feels itself to be defeated.

Thirty years ago to have a meeting like this there would have been a riot outside. The Left would not have allowed a meeting of this sort to go ahead unchallenged. But they don't do that now, because they haven't got the personnel to do it now. Not particularly. And the reason for that is their ideas have seemed to have come down, and have been smashed to pieces by history. And they're in a form of oblivion now, partly because the Marxist dystopias that were Soviet-occupied societies in Eastern Europe, real and existing socialism, real and existing cultural Marxism, were such monumental failures for the people who lived under them that they've been sloughed off completely.

And yet, many of the ideas—not the *practice* of lived experience by people who lived under those structures, but many of the *ideas*—have percolated around and never left the West anyway. And you have this strange triumphalist mixture of the massive ingrained market mechanism, which is sucking in money, and goods, and people from all over the world. Because the flip side to capital movements is migration. If people wonder why London is the way it is now, it's because when man can touch a screen in the City of London with his thumb and send hundreds of millions of pounds or dollars or euros or yen, or any other currency, across the world; but money and mankind, money and labor, capital and labor, will move in some sort of distended collaboration which each other. And the reason that all sorts of people want to get into the West in order to work at a median level is the flip side of the ability of enormous masses of interest-bearing money to move around the world at the flick of a switch, or the impress of a thumb upon a computer screen in the City of London or any of its regional counterparts.

So the idea of a Marxian capitalist society or a Left capitalist society which once would have been absurd, and is now dismissed as absurd by most progressive thinkers who think they've lost out continuously to what they call "the Right." Because they believe that the capitalist market is conducive to the Right, and has corralled the society over at the Right end of the spectrum.

Of course, there's a redoubt, there's a range of opinion that exists beyond the alleged Thatcherite and Reaganite Right, which is *nec plus ultra*, which one can never go near, which is a hidden *terra incognita*, which is an area of terror and psychic blasphemy. But apart from that, they believe that the Right has inherited the Earth, when in actual fact much of what this society once stood for has been eradicated to the point of inexistence by the forces that have conquered since 1945 and thereafter.

Can great art be produced in a society such as this one? It's very debatable, given the enormous pressures of conformism and censorship. Political correctness is a form of censorship. Routledge is a well-known Center-Left nonfiction publisher. Routledge now insists, subeditorially, on gender-neutral pronouns. This means everyone has to write "he/she," all of the time. And it's increasingly difficult, if you're going to going to produce anything with any degree of stylistic beauty or felicity at all, to write "he/she/it" all the time, when you mean one thing as against another.

Similarly, politically correct ideology means that a tragical truthfulness to life, which often has a religious dimension to it. Or if it doesn't have a religious dimension to it, it has a higher, profound, philosophical dimension to it. Political correctness, which is based upon the idea that everyone is equal, and everyone is equal in love, doesn't subsist. You click your fingers, and you notice in a moment it isn't true. It isn't true of any form of human life; it isn't true of any form of human interrelationship; it's not true of one relationship between a man and a woman. Therefore, if you are trying to put everything within a paradigm of such radical, enforced linguistic egalitarianism, you will fail instantly, but you will also fail to create great art because it can't be done in such a restricted, in such a stifling context.

It's also difficult to rebel against it. In the past, the playwrights of the 1960s and thereafter used to rebel against the Royal Chamberlain and his censorship of the British theater. They used to rebel against targeted restrictions whereby they couldn't blaspheme against the Christian religion. No one bothers to blaspheme against the Christian religion anymore, because it's perceived to have collapsed, except for some very small groups. And also the enormous amount of blasphemy against the Christian religion which occurred in the '60s, '70s, and '80s, largely wiped the slate clean in relation to the amount of blasphemy that could be encouraged and was felt to be required, because that was another tradition, that was another curtain that had to be ripped down.

The notion of deconstruction is to reduce things to a basis whereby which they're no longer oppressive. It's to deny the rhetoric of oppression within a form. But the problem with that is you end up with nothing. And you end up with a culture that can't affirm itself. And when a culture can't affirm itself—artistically, linguistically, and in other ways—it ceases to have any relevance, and it ceases to have any bite, and it ceases to have any sense of reality.

I remember going to see *Lear—King Lear*, not Bond's travesty—at the Bristol Old Vic, in the West Country when I was about 18 years of age. You have to have a certain element of physical effort to sit through these pieces, because they last between three and three-and-half hours. You have to pace yourself during the performance. There's a sort of *Marathon Man* element to these plays, because they do take quite a bit of resolve to sit through, although there's an intermission after the end of the third act, and prior to the two acts that remain.

The physicality of theater and the physicality of these performances is also important. This is again an irony, because we live in a society of great physicality, and the totalitarian rendition of sport. But at the same time, these types of art are very fleshy, and very physical, and very demanding to perform. Even their travesties like Berkoff's *Agamemnon*, involves an enormous amount of physical acting and mime. And that can actually have a great power, and the audience can have a sense of release through the physical dramaturgy of those who are onstage and depicting these actions in these particular ways.

One of the things that most strikes me now, is the inability to connect to the classical tradition as perceived in great works. There's a cutoff point around 1900 through 1950, when the entire *modus operandi* of Western societies began to change, and began to invert. And we have a culture of inversion, basically. A culture of what was once great, can't be denied its greatness, but is put in a historical niche. It's the historicizing of previous cultural forms, which are not perceived to have any relevance today except when viewed historically. This is what the restorationist culture is all about.

If you noticed, the state subsidization of the arts began in the 1950s. In the past, the Church used to subsidize art, and the aristocracy used to subsidize art, and then the higher bourgeois used to subsidize art. In the socialist and Stalinistic systems, of course, the state agglomerated all art to itself, and put forward any substitute that was thought to be necessary. In Western societies which exist now, you have public provision for the arts, whereby small elite bourgeois audiences pay money to go and see things which are heavily state subsidized, and which are restorational. Now you have the idea of private-public partnerships in relation to the arts, whereby private money comes in because the state can no longer afford to subsidize these things.

It's not that nothing new is being written. But nothing new that's loyal to the creed of political correctness could be performed in a way which is relevant to the classical tradition. So you have a situation where great works may be being written today, but they can't really be put on, because they would be too offensive and too difficult in all sorts of ways.

What is Western civilization? Western civilization is a particular civilization which is reared in Europe—North, East, South, and West—which is expressed through elites, and through individual moments of genius, particularized in particular lives, but that can only be so because of the mass of people that these individuals are drawn from.

Why are people proud that Shakespeare is an Englishman? They're proud that he's an Englishman whether they've opened any of his plays whatsoever at school when they were forced to do them, because he's felt to embody a national consciousness, and he's felt to speak for many who didn't speak, and who couldn't speak. And a people are proud that they have somebody like him in their national trajectory, whether they're interested in his work or not.

Self-pride is very emblematic of an ethnic sense of purpose and also a *joie de vivre* in relation to this life. If you strip that out and take it away from people, they lose something, they lose spirit. They become morbid and depressed. Everyone needs great cultural icons, whether they're interested in them or not. They are part of the fabric that gives an individual life some sort of meaning.

Increasingly, many individuals in this society do not have an overall or an individual meaning. That's why they live moment-to-moment and day-to-day in relation to contingency and consumption. The point of great civilization as expressed in great art, is to raise people out of that particular trough and get them—if only momentarily—looking upwards, looking upwards towards the sky. Looking upwards towards higher forms. Looking upwards towards the prospect of archetypal forms. Looking upwards towards the religions of the past, the present, and the future. Looking upwards towards God or the gods, or the *idea* that they might be there, or the idea that it might be necessary that they're there, even if you don't think that they are. That's the point of great civilization. That's the point of great work. That's the point of great art.

Most of it only exists in the past, now. Or exists as a circular moment in time, whereby these great works are reinterpreted in the present.

But nothing is forever, and I'm quite certain that great works are being written now, are being performed now in the minds of certain individuals, are being conceptualized now, but they don't have an outlet at this time. The point of groups like the New Right on the Continent, here, and in North America—particularly in California, on the far side of the United States—is to create the mental space whereby greatness can come back into culture, to create the mental space for higher works of civilization again.

It's not necessarily to provide those works. That's not its purpose. Its purpose is to provide the space that exists for them. Because if a people cannot affirm itself through great works, it begins to die, whether or not people have any interest in those great works themselves.

Thank you very much!

Counter-Currents/*North American New Right*
June 11, 2012

THE LAST INTERVIEW*

Greg Johnson: Welcome to Counter-Currents Radio. I'm your host Greg Johnson. With us today is Jonathan Bowden. First of all, I need to ask you is it "Bo-den" or "Bow-den"?

Jonathan Bowden: Depends where you are in England basically, if you are in the North of England you say "Bo-den," but if you are from the South of England, and I'm from the South of England, you say "Bow-den."

GJ: Bowden, all right Jonathan Bowden. I know Jonathan Bowden as a writer, as a painter, as an orator, but I don't know much about his past, and so the first thing I'd like to do is find out where you're from, what kind of educational background you have, what kind of family you have, and so forth.

JB: Yes, I was born in Kent in southeast England in 1962, and we moved about a bit, moved to Sussex for a while. But I grew up in Oxfordshire and Berkshire, which are counties in Southern England to the west of London. I went to a Catholic grammar school which was a private school in British terms and went to Cambridge later on, although I regard myself as essentially self-educated in the sense that it never stops.

GJ: Right, what did you take your degree in?

JB: English and History.

GJ: So what did you focus on in your studies of English and History?

JB: English was very much some of the early modernist

---

* Transcript by S. F. and V. S. of an interview recorded in San Francisco on February 26, 2012.

writers such as Wyndham Lewis and some of the late Victorian ideologues and pedagogues like Thomas Carlyle. This is my own schooling of the course, if you like, my own use of the thing for my own purposes. And in history, the English Civil War.

GJ: Tell me, are you influenced by writers like Carlyle and William Morris, certain critics of industrial civilization in the 19th century?

JB: Yes, although part of me perversely likes industrialization in an Ayn Rand sort of a way. I'm critical of the ugliness and debauched modernity that it's led to, a sort of barren and desiccated quality. But on the other hand there's a part of me that admires thrusting modernism, and its energy and achievement, and I'm torn between the utilitarian, sort of dourness that a lot of modernity has become, and the freshness and energy that transpired at its beginning, so I tend to take in a Nietzschean way from different concepts like romanticism and modernism, things which I like. I tend to view things positively rather than negatively. I tend to be dialectical, so there are parts of modernism which I choose to admire and revere, and there's parts that have led on to things which I dislike or despise. So my view doesn't tend to be either/or. It tends to be synthetic in a sense, or syncretic, whereby I take up all sorts of tendencies and use them in a firmament of becoming. That's my own notion anyway.

GJ: I share that same kind of ambivalence. I'm very much attracted to modernism in its more heroic and idealistic manifestations, but there is also a kind of leveling utilitarian modernity that's blighted cities and societies.

JB: Yes, cube-like blocks of endless sugar cubes of concrete festooning cities across the globe.

GJ: Which modern architects do you like, or modern city planners?

JB: After the spirit of Ayn Rand and *The Fountainhead*, in a way I like Mies van der Rohe. I like elements of Le Corbusier, but one thing that's always mistaken with him and with the concept of brutalism in particular, is that the concrete has to be finished, it has to be painted. In England there's been an enormous cult of brutalist concrete architecture lasting from the late '60s until the early '80s; throughout the '70s anyway—and the whole point of that unfinished concrete structure and superstructure was that it should be painted; it should be light; it should be ethereal; it should dance in the sun. There's not much sun in England of course. That's one of the problems. But they just left it in an unpainted and dour state, and it's sort of NCP car park architecture.

GJ: Do you like Frank Lloyd Wright?

JB: Yes, very much so. In particular the private houses that he developed for millionaire clients. But there's two types of modernism, as Bill Hopkins the art critic said to me a long time ago: the modernism for the rich and modernism for the masses, who tend to be poor or poorer. The modernism for the masses tends to be rat-runs and tunnels and sorts of architectonics which are similar to J. G. Ballard's novel *High Rise* where you cram human beings into these enormous blocks in the air and allow them to fester and engage in tumult with each other. And there's the modernism of the rich, where everything works, and it's light and spacious and ethereal, and these blocks which were put up in the 1920s and 1930s in areas like Kensington and Chelsea in West London still work, and are still perfect today.

GJ: One thing that struck me about *From Bauhaus to Our House* . . .

JB: Oh, Tom Wolfe . . .

GJ: Yes. One thing that struck me about Tom Wolfe's *From Bauhaus to Our House* is that he begins by talking about how the rich in the past were really absolute dictators of taste and that if they wanted a mansion, they would get it in whatever chateau style that they demanded. And then with the beginning of modernism, suddenly architects were dictating to the wealthy the kind of buildings that they would live in, the kind of buildings that they would house their factories and offices in. And it struck me that what was going on there was a certain loss of self-confidence among the bourgeoisie that provided an entree for modernism to come in. Does that make sense to you?

JB: Yes, I think very much so. Also it's the concept of the *auteur* in film applied in a different way. It's the romantic ideal of the individual genius artist imposing upon clients, particularly rich clients who are paying for the deed in the first instance. It's always been a fantasy of the 19th and 20th centuries, if nor before, and you had a lot of these modernists who dictated what the new taste was to people who had no idea and were quite scandalized by it but didn't wish to appear as reactionary or as unknowing or as unsophisticated. So they partly privatized their own taste to these artists, who moved in and dictated to them what it should be.

GJ: It seems that an analogous thing happened with modernist painting. Most people when they look at modern art think in the privacy of their own soul, "I don't really like this; I don't find this beautiful," and in the past I think people would have openly stated that they didn't find this beautiful, but there is a sense of a lack of self-confidence in traditions of judgment about what's beautiful, and therefore people became in some ways intimidated into accepting it.

One person that I think is very interesting is Gertrude Stein. There was a big exhibit in San Francisco last year on the Gertrude Stein art collection and the collection of her family. They were great patrons of Matisse and Picasso and other modernist artists. I wandered through this exhibition, and it just struck me that these people were highly susceptible to modern art because of a certain insecurity about their own status and identity, and I thought that that might be a factor in the rise of modern art. Do you think that that makes sense?

JB: Yes, it's partly an outsider's vision. It's partly a psychopathological vision which is re-routed and made to suit insiders. It's also the fact that it's one of the first aesthetics since high Christian art where ugliness is part of the picture. In Christian art of course the ugliness is demonic, and it's the depictions of the Devil and his realm and is the depiction of the hellish in a Hieronymus Bosch sort of way, or in a way of Brueghel or Grünewald.

But in modernist art of course, ugliness is integrated into it because modernist art is dialectical, so it deals with what is traditionally regarded as beautiful and what is traditionally regarded as ugly and plays games between the two of them.

Modernist art is also concerned with concepts like fury and power. Power instead of beauty, or power as beauty, and these aesthetics are not popular. They are elitist aesthetics, but they are elitist aesthetics of the modern world rather than the early-modern, the medieval, the feudal, or the ancient.

And yet they have always existed in art. The depictions of the Gorgon's head in ancient Greek sculpture is the realization of ugliness, the demonic, and the ferocious as a new type of transgressive beauty.

GJ: You are a painter, and a lot of your paintings, all of them really, are modernist. I like some of them quite a lot. I actually bought several of them from you. Yet I am not necessarily a big fan of modern art. I do like Italian Futurism quite a lot; I like its dynamism. I go and look at Picasso though, and I just think, the man doesn't draw very well, he has a penchant for ugliness. So I am a bit of a naïve person when it comes to appreciating modern art. Can you give me a sense of your views of modernism in painting? Who do you think is great, who do you think is bad? What are the standards by which you judge these people?

JB: One of the problems of course is that there are no standards, apart from inbuilt critical reflexivity over time whereby a mass of critics—a critical mass—build up to deify some work and demean others. What's fashionable, what is perceived to be good, what people will spend money on, what has become retrospectively critically acclaimed. These are the taxonomies of the modern. But there's no intrinsic valuation as to what is good or bad in art after about 1860. You can make judgments, however, and my judgment is whether the work makes you feel alive when you look at it or more deadened when you look at it.

I don't care for Picasso particularly, although he has some fine pictures in his overall *oeuvre,* and he's a man of multiple styles rather than one style that's worked out in different areas.

My point about modernism is there are certain works and certain artists who are quite literally extraordinary, and their paintings have never been painted before, and their images have never been seen in the human mind before. It's the belief that things can be made over again. Not in perfection but in ecstatic imperfection.

Take Francis Bacon, for example. Bacon's work is ugly and repellent to many people, and yet the fury and the energy, particularly in the early canvases, is such that some of those images have never been seen before, and they're images which sum up quite a bit of the 20th century in quite an unsentimental way as well. And I regard that as the extraordinary achievement of a type of painting which may well have come to an end.

A couple of hundred years from now, modernism may be looked back on as a *cul-de-sac* actually, that doesn't relate to previous forms of art and doesn't move forward towards anything new. If you look at painting today, the conspicuous thing is its absence. Modern art in the student context is all film and video and installations, which actually relates to more traditional narrative and replicatory and representational forms of art.

Art's about dreaming while you are awake, and quite a lot of modern art, quite a lot of surrealist art for example is nothing more than the reification of dreams.

GJ: Who in your opinion are the greatest modernist painters? Who are the ones who make you feel more alive when you look at their paintings?

JB: In British terms people like Piper and Vaughan and Bacon and Sutherland and Wyndham Lewis and Roberts, but they're just in the British context. In the global context, I reckon Dalí is probably the greatest modern artist of the 20th century.

GJ: I'm a great fan of his work too. There was an exhibit I saw a couple of years ago in Atlanta of his work, spanning his whole artistic career, but they had a lot of the very large canvases from his later years, and they were extremely religious and extremely nationalistic, and it hit me why Dalí became a declassed and unfashionable on the Left because of the Spanish Civil War and the side he took in that.

Who are some of the other painters who you think are really exceptional before the 20th century?

JB: Before the 20th century I think who influenced me are the most imaginative painters. People like Blake, people like Fuseli, people like John Martin, people like Bosch, Grünewald, and Brueghel. People like medieval manuscript illuminators and this sort of thing who are anonymous as far as we are concerned because their names don't come down to us but who can alternate between the angelic and the demonic in marvelous and meaningful ways.

If you take Rembrandt, for example, many of the paintings are indescribably beautiful in their way, and yet the emotional impact for me would be a work like *The Ox Carcass* which would be dismissed as ugly or inhuman or transgressive, in relation to many prior codifications of what people go to art for.

I go to art for a more delineated and expectant form of life. I go to art to see energy and to see energy realized in form. But my tastes tend to be a bit strong really, and I tend to like work which is rather visceral and over the top and imaginative and surreal. But let's put it this way, Botticelli is probably a greater artist than Bosch, artist *qua* artist, and yet Bosch is the most extraordinary artist in the Western tradition, emotionally speaking from my own point of view.

GJ: Would you say that you are more drawn to the sublime in art rather than to the beautiful?

JB: Yes, the sublime and the demonic.

GJ: You are also a writer of fiction and of essays. How would you categorize your fiction for people out there who haven't read it yet and might be curious about it?

JB: They are sort of Gothic fictions really. They are intellectual horror novels and stories. Although I don't care that much for horror as a genre, but I do like the burlesque extremism of it and of the better element of the Gothic tradition. I don't like the way modern horror has developed in the Stephen King sort of way, but I do like intellectual horror that goes back through Lovecraft to Poe and involves people like Ambrose Bierce and people like Algernon Blackwood in the English tradition. I also like the creepy ghost story tradition in English letters which is still not exhausted and you could do quite a bit with.

But I'm interested in the concretization of dreams and the use of narratives that embody fantasy. I think that the point of fiction writers today is to put the reality into life because people are living such fictional lives. I agree with J. G. Ballard that people live through television screens and through video and through the internet to such a degree that it's fantasy piled upon fantasy, and yet the way out of that dilemma is to put some realism back into the fantasy, and that may involve even greater forms of surreality and surrealness.

GJ: You've mentioned Ballard a couple of times, what do you like about his work, and who are some of the other contemporary fiction writers whom you follow?

JB: I've always admired Ballard. He was one of the first adult writers that as an adolescent I came across and who spoke to me directly. It's because he believes that the ferocity of the imagination is the most important artistic attribute, and he's not interested in psychologically realistic and representational work. If you take an earlier work like *The Drowned World*, it's incredibly lush and self-sustaining. It's baroque and overdone in all sorts of ways. It's a rococo and baroque performance, and I do like that "painting in words" element which is very current in his fiction.

As for other people, I like William Golding. I like Anthony Burgess. It's always difficult with people whose reputations are not completely formed by critical opinion because they are too close to the present day. But in American letters, I quite like Truman Capote, even though there are things about him that alienate me, but I quite like his work. I also like the poet Robinson Jeffers, the Californian neo-pagan extremist who corresponded with D. H. Lawrence and is, rhetorically anyway, the most extreme pagan poet in the English language during the last century.

GJ: Do you have any fondness for the writings of Flannery O'Connor?

JB: Yes, very much so. As a Catholic in the Deep South of the United States of America, looking at these crazed, Billy-Bob Protestants, I like all that sort of thing because she's drawn to extreme you see. She's drawn to outsiders. As a Catholic in an ultra-Protestant environment, she feels a bit of an outsider really, and yet she's fascinated by these people who wrestle with snakes in church and fire guns into the roof of the church and can be swayed by these evangelical passions of maudlin excess and emotional debauchery.

GJ: [Laughs] Let me just gather my thoughts here! I had all kinds of images rushing through my mind when you were saying that! Flannery O'Connor has a wonderful essay called "Some Aspects of the Grotesque in Southern Fiction," where she quotes Thomas Mann saying that the grotesque is the ultimate anti-bourgeois style. By that she takes him to mean that the grotesque is what resists the whole modern narrative of moral progress and also technological and scientific progress. The progressive mind believes that we are going to create a world where everybody's healthy with gleaming teeth, their minds are healthy, and evil is progressively mitigated. And so she cleaves to the grotesque because she wants to disrupt the kind of modern optimism and instead give you a sense that there's another order of the world that resists that kind of ironing out and straightening up.

JB: Well, there's bound to be a Protestant element in a Catholic who's so transfigured by Protestant culture, so she's bound to be a bit of a Jansenist and a bit of a pessimist. A sort of emotive pessimist; and yes, the grotesque is within the romantic sensibility and the early modern sensibility a way of projecting anti-bourgeois sentiment and morally licentious extremism in prose, on film, and in pictorial art.

Yes, I suppose I am a bit of an anti-bourgeois artist in a way. I'm not conservative when it comes to aesthetic matters but then I regard myself as a revolutionary conservative in any respect.

GJ: Another contemporary person who's aesthetic is I think very Flannery O'Connoresque, and for the same metaphysical reasons and with the same kind of political agenda that's anti-progressive, is the filmmaker David Lynch. What do you think of Lynch?

JB: Yes, I like Lynch. The cultivation of the supernumerary beheading is part and parcel of his attitude towards life. I think that the intrusion of the surreal and the overheated into otherwise normative narratives is what makes them startling, what makes them forbidding. They're dreams, although dreams are often not that interesting in a strange sort of way. What's interesting is lucid dreaming, dreaming while you are awake and sentient.

J. G. Ballard has a doctrine called The Death of Affect, and he has another doctrine called The Normalization of the Psychopathic, and both are evident in Lynch's cinema and similar types of grotesque, post-modernist art in certain respects. The Death of Affect is the fact that we are surrounded by such an overkill of media that it's only by retreating into the private fantasies of the living mind that we can find an individual way out though all of these other myths that people would have us live within. And the psychopathological urge is the fact that people are bored. There's a comedian in Britain who has a slogan for the mass of the population which is "Live, Work, Consume, Die. You are bored, this is the antidote." And a lot of art in contemporary circumstances is an attempt to get people to live more realistic fictions.

GJ: So let's talk about film. Who are you favorite filmmakers? And what do you think of the aesthetic nature and the aesthetic potential of film.

JB: Film's aesthetic potential is limitless. I've made a few films of my own. I've made one film called *Venus Flytrap,* which is about a mad scientist who wants to take over the world with plants that feed on human flesh. It's a sort of Roger Cormanesque B-movie but with Nietzschean and Odinic themes and shot in a sort of post-modern way. I made another film about Punch and Judy called *Grand Guignol*. Punch and Judy has always obsessed me because it's part of the British folk tradition. But it's also so unbelievably violent and demotic and anti-bourgeois in its unconstrained glee, sadism, pitilessness, and love of the burlesque.

Filmmakers who influenced me: I like Syberberg's work a great deal. I like Tarkovsy's work a great deal. I like Powell's work a great deal. It would be Michael Powell rather than David Lean for me in terms of British cinema, just to look narrowly at one's own national tradition. I like a lot of *film noir*. I like Fritz Lang, particularly the films he made before he left Germany which are quite truly extraordinary. I like the early Soviet cinema as well.

I like Riefenstahl's films, even though she's a sort of, almost a delinquent romantic in a way. The romanticism is so obsessional and so *ur*-conscious and so yearning, it's almost amusing in a way. I know that sounds a bit blasphemous in relation to a film like *Triumph of the Will*. But there is a sort of undercurrent of yearning expectancy that is explosively anti-bourgeois in its fullness and extent, and although I've got a certain sympathy for the bourgeoisie as a class, and I'm not anti-bourgeois politically, culturally and aesthetically, I'm always drawn to the extreme and to that which is partly outside the circle of what is accepted. But I wouldn't consider my own tastes to be countercultural in a Leftist sense. I consider them to be counter-current in terms of what might be said to exist in the mainstream, that ought to be mainstream and is the most interesting part of the mainstream.

GJ: Let's talk about opera. One of my favorite Riefenstahl films is *Tiefland*, which is actually a film based on a romantic opera. Do you like opera and, if so, what sort of opera? What composers, and what do you think is aesthetically powerful about opera? Why does it work?

JB: It works because it is so unconstrained, and there is no constraint placed upon the remit of its emotional extremism and lustful range. In terms of contemporary opera I like Harrison Birtwistle quite a lot. He wrote an opera called *Punch and Judy* which is very violent and episodic and picaresque. Wagner I suppose above all, and in the 20th century, people like Berg. I like *Wozzeck* and *Lulu*, again for their extremity and their coming to terms with the nature of man in a way which is stylistically accomplished but very near the edge of what can be expressed.

GJ: Yet for all of your interest in modernism and art and painting and sculpture and architecture, you are also something of a traditionalist and a conservative. You are one of the leading people in the New Right scene in Great Britain. How do your reconcile these things? Most people would think that that is simply contradictory and makes no sense.

JB: Yes, it's an odd one. I think that the only way that things can be reconciled is to say that I am an elitist and an inegalitarian, and the moral Left in art, if there is such a thing, tends to egalitarianism and equality in its judgments. So if I favor the modern world or parts of the modern world, I want the modern world to be as unequal as possible and elitist in spirit, and therefore what appears superficially to maybe be Left-wing, from a very sort of staid and conservative perspective, is nothing of the kind.

It's a sort of very radical revolutionary Right wing, in that all forms lead onto other forms which are above them, and the degree to which you can never quite take out the prospect of something which is above something else, because there will always be at least the prospect of something above you, and above that which you might seek to achieve, so I see a commitment to certain aesthetics as non-transgressive in the usual way. I don't see an easy parallel between a commitment to the radical revolutionary Left in art and a commitment to the modern and the new in art. Anyway, moderns only stand on the shoulders of giants that existed before them that enable them to cut loose and do their mad capers so everything builds on something that existed before you and without the concrete that is underneath your feet you're lost and aimless and atomized.

GJ: So, you think that modernism is traditional in the sense that it is an outgrowth of a past tradition rather than being something that is revolutionary, Leftist in a revolutionary sense, and you think that modernism is not Leftist because it is not egalitarian, meaning that it is not easy for the masses to appreciate. If that is the case, what do you think would be the most consistent artistic style if you were a revolutionary egalitarian Leftist?

JB: MTV [laughs].

GJ: Okay, that makes a lot of sense. It is very peculiar how a lot of people who profess radical egalitarian ideas cleave to radically inegalitarian forms of art, and maybe it's a bit of repressed elitism, sublimated elitism on their part. It was quite extraordinary how the high tradition of Western classical music and opera for instance, was kept alive in communist countries. You'd think that that would be the first thing to go, and it would all be replaced with MTV or pop music. Yet they were very anti-Beatles in the USSR and very pro-Tchaikovsky. They weren't pro-modernist, but they were pro-high art.

JB: Yes. They had the view that the people, the masses could be raised to a higher cultural level and the masses might be capable of being raised to a higher cultural level. I don't give up on that possibility, although you'd need to control the mass media and certain parts of the internet in order to do that. But it would be an indoctrination. High art is not for the masses and is not for the majority of people, and it can't be and it is only an ideological statement to say that it ought to be. You could impress these things upon people, you could raise people's cultural level, you could educate them better, but a lot of that is tokenistic.

In the end, the cultural industry, as Adorno once described it—which we have all around us, and which follows us from cradle to grave and is available 24 hours a day, seven days a week, 360-odd days a year—this sort of cultural industry is what the masses partly want. It's not just imposed upon them, it's their level which is being appealed down to, and they're being brought up to meet it with the cash nexus as the commercialization of the thing which propels it along. But the idea that the masses are degraded by this material is only partly true. It's a degradation that they wish to enter in to with fecund glee and foreknowledge, and so I'm very much a conceptual elitist of rather a stark sort.

GJ: I very much like a lot of socialist realist art. I like a lot of socialist realist painting. I like a number of the composers who composed in the USSR, and in some ways I think that Stalin had fairly good taste in art. I think that Shostakovich was heading in the wrong direction before Stalin scared him into writing his greatest symphony, which is the Fifth Symphony.

JB: But they're all about Stalin those works, aren't they?

GJ: Yes. Do you think that there's value in socialist, specifically Soviet art?

JB: Yes, unfortunately in a way, because it doesn't always fit my thesis in other respects. But you can be steeped in the classical and you can be steeped in the modern. The problem with viewing everything undialectically is to think that you have to make a choice. You have to go with that which is perceived to be classical or that which is perceived as modern. There's no art that's more hated than neo-classicism amongst the present parvenus of the modern, and yet in actual fact, Breker and Kolbe are not outside the remit of the modern at all, even in their use of planes and their use of the dynamic tension in the body. You seek or relay correlatives with elements in modern art but that's not really the important point. The important point is that you can do excellent work in all sorts of areas. It's the energy that you bring to things and the degree to which you can impress a vision of life and death upon the spirit of the material before you.

The eugenic element in Soviet art is probably what makes it interesting because they were attempting to raise mass taste. Which means that you have to go down to meet mass taste in order to be capable of raising it up. Where they made a mistake, in my view, is preventing people from individual self-expression and contributing to art in a modern way by the sort of ludicrous specificity whereby the regime imposes the aesthetic tastes on the entire intellectual *avant-garde*. That never works. As soon as the Soviet Union collapsed, they all reverted to doing what they wished to do anyway.

So my view is that you take the best work from all sorts of areas and you corral it together because work's never acceptable and never respectable all the way around. Aesthetically, if you could depoliticize it, Nazi sculpture for example, is—post Rodin—extraordinarily close to what mass sensibility and the concept of the beautiful is, and yet there's nothing more shocking, nothing more appalling to the contemporary liberal mind than that sort of work.

GJ: I don't know of any great Soviet painters or sculptors, but I do know of a number of great Soviet composers. I think that Shostakovich was a great composer. I think that Prokofiev did some great work in the USSR. I like a lot of Khachaturian's compositions. What do you think of them as composers, and why do you think that there was greater music composed in the USSR than there was say, visual art or sculpture or architecture?

JB: Because you could express yourself in a way which the regime couldn't tease into censorship because music works on another level. It was harder to censor as long as you didn't make ultra-modernist quotations and as long as you didn't veer into what they regarded as sheer formalism, you could get away with quite a lot of an emotional range. So Shostakovich could do anthems to the Soviet police, and yet they could be fine works. Those are just titles, portmanteau titles that could be taken off the work retrospectively and largely, in terms of Shostakovich's Western reputation, have been.

I think that the reason that Soviet music reached such heights is partly the restrictions that were placed upon it. So although I don't really agree with putting restrictions on artists, if you want great work, you often have to put certain restrictions on. It's like the Hollywood code for films, because they enforced bourgeois standards of taste and decency, and because they enforced a degree of compulsive sexlessness, they made filmmakers extraordinarily imaginative in their recrudescence of the erotic. When you allow people to be very blatant, and to be very crude, which is partly what has happened, you lower the tone and you lower the standards all the way round.

GJ: Isn't classicism in the broadest sense simply the creation of those kinds of constrictions and rules that allow the imagination to express itself by giving it a channel through which it has to focus itself. It actually can stimulate creativity rather than constrict it.

JB: Yes, although sometimes classicism can sort of devour itself, like the Promethean eagle devouring the vitals. There is a degree to which at times classicism can become tired, and it needs to be renewed. The modern movement was an attempt to renew, it's the cleaning of the blades prior to the cultivation of new work.

GJ: Who are your favorite poets?

JB: I like T. S. Eliot, although emotionally I don't warm to him. I like D. H. Lawrence, although he's probably a greater prose writer than he is a poet. I do rather adore Robinson Jeffers, although he's an acquired taste, I admit that. I like Emily Dickinson actually, in various ways. She amuses me, although there is a sort of innocent-minded nature worship and pantheism to her work which isn't necessarily that interesting. What is interesting is the Calvinist spirit of death-consciousness that lurks at the heart of tiny little poetic haikus about bees and birds and what she's seen going on in the garden of her reclusive life. Who else? I like . . .

GJ: Do you like Blake as a poet as well as a painter?

JB: I prefer him as a painter, really. Blake is probably England's greatest artist actually. In terms of sheer imaginative power. And he created his own religion; he created his own world. Blake's art is very close to madness in the sense that it's the desire for solipsism in the creation of a totally alternative space within which art can be itself. I think that you've got to be a little less pure than that, otherwise you are shading over into insanity. But art and insanity are very close, and the entire modern movement is partly based, *sub specie aeternitatis,* on the art of the insane.

GJ: You are an author as well as a reader of comics and graphic novels.

JB: Yes, when I was a child and an adolescent. Yes.

GJ: That's a quintessentially popular art form. It's directed primarily to children and young adults, and yet you think that it has a great deal of aesthetic potential. Can you talk a little bit about your sense of that?

JB: Yes, it's an interesting one because that's very much an art for and of the masses. And although I am an elitist, there are moments when you wish to communicate with the majority of people. I suppose the thing that attracted me to them when I was very young was the heroic. The heroic is denied in our culture in all sorts of ways and has been disprivileged. Those forces that animated the great epics and Homer have been forced down to the level of comic books literally. Because the heroic is not seen as a necessary or requisite part of a high culture.

When you have liberal values supervising the novel and the elite play and the elite film, the heroic will go down into the lowest forms of mass culture. And yet really what are comics? They're films on paper, and in certain cultures, like Japan and so on, they're considered to be genuine art forms of quite a high sort. That isn't true in the West, but because they are representational and yet very imaginative. You can communicate with a large number of people instantaneously, and you can also be stereotypical in relation to the heroic which is more difficult with more complicated forms.

There is also a degree to which the art can be actually quite abstract, because it's draughtsmanship *par excellence,* and it's only lines on paper. And if you look at the imaginative input into what is purely a commercial area, there's this odd trade-off between the aesthetic quality and the risible quality in terms of psychological realism and sociological appropriateness.

But that's not what these things are about. They are also a pure form of escape and a pure form of sub-literary escapism, and I quite like art as a sort of escapism, because we're all born, we're all going to die, and there needs to be something to fill the gap in between.

GJ: The graphic novel has emerged as a more artistically serious form of comic book, and for a long time I have to admit that I was somewhat dismissive of this. First of all, people were touting Spiegelman's *Maus*, and I thought that this was very tendentious anti-cat propaganda. How is this an improvement on the comic book, and how is this serious as art?

Then I started discovering that movies that I thought were really rather good, like *A History of Violence*, were based on graphic novels, and so I started looking into them. I really am very impressed specifically with the graphic novel *Watchmen*, which I think is as a novel really on the level of some 19th-century romantic novels of the highest order. What do you think of the graphic novel, and what do you think its future is, its potential is?

JB: Well, its potential . . . because they really are films on paper. There's no denying that they are what it says on the tin. Therefore, the commercial pressures aside, their artistic future is limitless, because it's as limitless as the capacity to create stories and to visualise them. So, all that will hold them back is the absence of seriousness with which they are viewed by the general, more literate culture. It's probably true that mass culture is more visual than elite culture. Because elite culture tends to be more conceptual and tends to be bound by words.

Now, in these types of graphic novels you have sequential art with a storyboard that is a film on paper and so you do have the ability to create films very cheaply. In some ways, it's a marvellous medium because it approximates to Wagner's total art form, because with the exception of music you've got almost everything combined.

There's always something slightly ridiculous about comics, even the highfalutin ones that we're discussing at the moment, but that's part of their charm. They do have a charm. They do have a kitsch, which is part of their romantic allure. Because the first literature that most children fall in love with actually, long before they come to books, they look at this sort of material. Even if they quickly outgrow it.

GJ: Who do you think are the best graphic novelists and what are the best graphic novels?

JB: There's a Batman called *Arkham Asylum* which is by Dave McKean—visually anyway—and which is quite extraordinary. That was done before computers became fashionable. To paint on a computer screen and to print it out is how that sort of art form is now done, but McKean did individual paintings. Each of those panels is an individual painting situated within a larger conspectus.

I suppose Alan Moore. I don't care for Alan Moore's sort of politics particularly, insofar as it's subliminally present in his work, but he would have to be considered as a major talent in the area that he's chosen to concentrate in.

Again, you tend to scan this sort of material. You don't so much read it as you scan it. It's very much like watching film. You absorb it. It's like the windscreen wipers in a car—flick, flick—and then you go to the next page, and you absorb it almost osmotically. You float in this material and then put it down.

In this sense it's probably more powerful than visual art, although visual art can reach parts of the mind that nothing else can, because it's not bounded by narrative, and yet if you bound images by narrative, you have the possibility of reaching very large numbers of people. It's surprising in some ways that graphic novels haven't even been even more successful than they could be, but that's probably because television is in the way and the DVD is in the way. If those forms were less pronounced, probably they'd have an even greater articulacy than they do at the present time.

GJ: You said that the graphic novel is like the Wagnerian total work of art except that it lacks music, which brings to mind the movies that have been made from graphic novels, which of course include music. One of my theses is that the movie really is the thing that most closely approximates Wagner's idea of the complete work of art, because with Wagner you still had the staging necessities of the theatre that sort of constrict your points of view, whereas film doesn't have those constrictions, and therefore it's more versatile, yet it can incorporate all the other art forms like the complete work of art was supposed to do. Do you think that's a sensible thesis?

JB: Very much so. Yes. Film is the ultimate art form of the 20th century and contains all the other arts within itself. That's why it was important to try and make films. Film is the most frustrating thing to do, however. Because it involves radical collaboration with other people and with other egos, and it's costly, and it's extraordinarily time-consuming to do properly. It involves great technical skill and ingenuity.

However, digital film-making has democratized the film industry even though in the end these films are just cut up and put on YouTube or its equivalent. But you can now make films for very little money. The films that I've made cost £800 pounds each, which is totally ridiculous in relation to what film technology once cost in the past.

But, yes, I've always wanted to make films actually because films are the total way in which you can live a dream which can impact upon other people and also can be seen in a relatively short and sequential period of time. It takes maybe 8, 10, 16, 24 hours to read a book sequentially over a period. An image can be accessed in seconds, that's true. But a film you can put life, death and everything else into a spectacle that lasts for one hour. There is probably nothing like it.

GJ: Let's switch our topics to some philosophical issues. You seem to be quite conversant with a wide range of ideas, especially ideas on the Right. But there's a great deal of intellectual diversity and deep philosophical divisions amongst various Rightists. For instance, I know people who are Guénonian Traditionalists, and I know people who are Darwinists, and they have very different accounts of the evolution or devolution of man, for instance. Where do you stand on issues like that? Are you a Traditionalist? Are you a Darwinist? Are you a materialist? Are you a dualist? What philosophical outlook do you think is most adequate?

JB: I'd probably be described by a critic looking on from the outside as a Nietzschean, and as a Right-wing Nietzschean, in love with paradox, possibly for its own sake. I'm not technically a Traditionalist in the purest sense, because I don't necessarily believe that there's one tradition that one can get back to. The problem with all forms of Perennialism is that there's no agreement on what one should get back to in relation to a prospective Golden Age.

But the real division for me is between those that are metaphysically objectivist and those that are metaphysically subjectivist. All liberal Left-wing thought is metaphysically subjectivist, which means, put very simply, that you make it up as you go along or that life is endlessly socialized in its impact and import.

Metaphysical objectivism is the idea that there are standards outside life and there are concepts which pre-exist man and his consciousness of himself and that are absolute and that lack variation and can always be subscribed to by looking back at them, whereas Nietzsche had the view that, in a sense, such objectivist standards do exist, but we don't entirely know what they are, because we're not divine, and we cannot perceive the world from its outside by virtue of the fact that we're meshed in it and its fleshy and contingent circumstances.

So, what you have to do, is you have to become actualized in the space that you're in, and, by subjectively understanding the possibility of the objective that remains behind you, you achieve maximum insight through a morality of strenuousness. So, that's what I would tend to believe.

In relation to things like Darwinism or regression of man theories *à la* Evola, I would take the view that perspectivally both can be right. We've evolved from lower forms, but you can also see the apes as falling away from one of our particular trajectories in relation to ascent. But it doesn't bother me. The animalism of man doesn't bother me as a concept. You only have to look around you in your local Wal-Mart.

GJ: I think that one way to somewhat reduce the tension between the Darwinists and the Traditionalists is simply to recognize that Traditionalism is not necessarily an account of how things actually happened. It's first and foremost a collocation and synthesis of mythology, and mythology doesn't necessarily have to be literally true in order to be extremely useful, and I don't care how silly the idea of man's devolution from higher beings is from a biological or evolutionary standpoint. When I go to Wal-Mart it makes a lot of sense, and so it's got its own power and its own truth, and it doesn't necessarily have to have the kind of truth that competes with scientific truth.

JB: Yes, that's right. There are different forms of truth, and it's a Gradgrind human mind that can't see that. But that's inevitable. Politics is a rather dry area, and people who are very politically-minded, on the whole, want rather tough, affirmative single-track causations, don't wish to mix things together, and don't want to be too philosophically complicated. After all, in the end, politics is about influencing the mass of people, and these issues are of no importance at all to the mass of people, who wish to see their areas less crime-ridden or wish to see their cities with less immigrants in them or more immigrants in them, depending on their point of view.

But these philosophical niceties are actually very important. Religions are enormous psychic novels, and the myths that sustain them are the poetic tropes that give reality and variety to their endless and teeming dreaming.

GJ: Let's talk about religion. Where do you stand on religious issues? Did you receive any kind of religious training as a young man, and did it stick? How has your religious thinking evolved over time?

JB: Yes, that's interesting. Emotionally, I'm drawn to religiosity. Although, I suppose if you wish to be very tough-minded and literal about things then I'm an atheist. But I don't care for atheism as a position emotionally and psychologically because it's such a desiccated and empty and banal position. All the musical traditions of any import are on the other side. So, I'm very much close to the Existentialists of the 1950s, who, although they framed all their religious concerns within what might be perceived as a rationalist purview, were obsessively religious in their attitude towards life and yet didn't have a coherent religious system, Christian or otherwise. I'm a bit like that really.

I went to a Catholic school where, contrary to the idea it was sort of a torture chamber with a bit of added excess and brothers dressed in dresses flogging boys whilst you conjugated Latin verbs, it was actually a very good education and set oneself up for adult life in a very adequate way. But religiously, though I admire the myths, I've never really been that much of a Christian, although I can be moved by a film like Mel Gibson's *The Passion of the Christ*, which struck me as a genuinely religious film and an extraordinarily accomplished artistic film as well; the two combined.

So, I'm emotionally drawn to religion, but I would not in a hard, factual sense be described as a religious person.

GJ: Are you more drawn to Christian or pagan mythology?

JB: No, I've been much more drawn to pagan mythology, although there's a lot of Christian artistic inheritance that would influence me a great deal. But no, I'm emotionally and belletristically and aesthetically and psychosexually, I'm a pagan.

GJ: We were having a conversation a few days ago about astrology, and you said that you had the astrological profile of a fascist dictator, and that brings me to the next question which is: What do you think the ideal political system is?

JB: That's very difficult at this moment in time to answer. I think the best political system is the most conservative system imaginable combined with the most revolutionary system imaginable. So, it's something which is classical and flexible. It will be the equivalent of a classical modernism, really, in terms of its stylistic aesthetics, but beyond just style and/or aesthetics, its meaning and its sense of itself. It has probably never existed. It's the lifestyle of Ernst Jünger conceived as the management of a state.

GJ: Are there historical regimes that you think most closely approximate that?

JB: No, not really. It's why I'm not in love with any particular dictatorship or any particular form of democratic organization. All of them have positive features. All of them have negative features. I perceive of life as essentially dynamic, and therefore there's never been a static society which was perfect. But humans aren't perfect. And there's no such thing as human perfectibility.

My interest in the grotesque is because man is so lopsided and so deliriously imperfect that the idea of utopia is itself slightly risible and will lead to dystopia anyway. But one should attempt to achieve one's own utopias as long as one realizes that there always imperfect and approximate. Just as human life begins with childhood and ends with the idiocy of pre-senility, societies need to endlessly renew themselves.

My vision of not a just society but a society that's come to terms with the nature of its own injustice is a quivering sword in a fencer's hand—morality and social climbing perceived as a form of mountaineering. It's a society that's more dangerous than the present one, even though the present one has all sorts of dangers, and is more alive and is more percussively inegalitarian and elitist.

I suppose the open-minded rule of a traditional aristocracy that partly believed that the patronage of the arts was one of the most important things that it could do as well as officiating at religious ceremonies would be the sort of sensibility that I favor.

GJ: What thinkers or writers have influenced your views of politics most?

JB: The most is probably Carlyle and Wyndham Lewis and Machiavelli and, although he's not really political in a narrow sense, Friedrich Nietzsche, and Georges Sorel as well, and Curzio Malaparte and D'Annunzio and D. H. Lawrence. But again, the people who've influenced me tend to splurge over into the artistic area and are not narrowly political. I suppose Plato, in a way: both to approximate to, to ascribe to and to reject simultaneously.

Amongst contemporary theorists, amongst contemporary politicians, Enoch Powell was an interesting classicist who wrote poetry, and there's an existential subtext to some of his articulations. We're talking in a British context here. Who else? I'm certainly not influenced by Michael Oakeshott and sort of milksop conservatives of that sort. But then again, I've always been too revolutionary to be a complete conservative and too conservative to be a complete revolutionary.

I believe in a mixture of the past and the present. I'm an optimistic person, actually. I believe very much in the future. I don't share the pessimism that most Right-wing people do. Most Right-wingers are pessimistic people and have a strong streak of puritanism in their personalities. Although there are puritanical sides to me, they tend to be part of a starkness and part of an aesthetic that is thrown beyond itself.

To me, artistic things are so much more important than anything else, and politics is a way to achieve certain artistic goals that otherwise would fall fallow.

GJ: Ayn Rand had an essay called "Bootleg Romanticism" where she talked about certain forms of popular literature in the 20th century that she thought were a refuge where 19th-century romanticism had fled because it had been purged by naturalism and modernism and the sort of higher letters. She talks about things like spy shows. She talks about *The Man from U.N.C.L.E.*, although she dropped that from the published version of that essay when she put it in her book *The Romantic Manifesto*. She talks about the Bond films. She talks about pulp adventure novels and things like that.

You have a great interest in pulp novels . . .

JB: . . . Raymond Chandler . . .

GJ: You have an interest in pulp and popular fiction. Is that true?

JB: Yes, partly because its crudity is endlessly amusing and also its love of the extreme and its love of the radical situation is compelling.

I'm drawn to extremism. I've always been an extremist. But I'm not drawn to the usual forms of counter-bourgeois extremism that exist on the Left. So, with me, the elitist spine that has to subsist in everything prevents me from going in a Leftwards direction because egalitarianism is a bore. There's nothing more boring than egalitarianism. There's nothing more aesthetically sterile. And that's why the truth is on the Right side of the equation.

As for popular forms: popular forms can be very mass-oriented and degraded, but they can also be endlessly charming and full of life and brio and energy, and in their very crudity they can escape some of the halting steps that the naturalist aesthetic might place upon things. It's the very abnaturalism and non-naturalism of elements of the popular imagination, as perceived artistically in mass culture, that can render the grotesque even more baleful, even more illuminating, even more distressingly actual.

GJ: You like Robert E. Howard. You've done a lot of writing about his *Conan* works and other writings. Again, this is a fellow who created a lot of popular literature, yet you are drawn to it even as an anti-egalitarian elitist.

JB: Yes, that's right. Partly just because of the heroic metaphysic which is itself a form of elitism, as Rand rightly pointed out. Things are never destroyed in culture. They're just displaced, and therefore they find new levels for themselves through which they can articulate what they are or might be. So, naturalistic fiction displaced fantasy fiction, which went down into genres like fantasy and science fiction and the rest of it, and those come up again and become more literary in the hands of somebody like Ballard.

Whereas popular work and elitist work fertilize each other and interrelate. With me things are never either/or but yes/and, and there's a degree to which you can see ramifications of the elite in the popular, and you can see dithyrambic populism in elitism. It's more the treatment and the self-overbecoming which is involved in any creative moment. It's less whether there's something that's popular or whether something is populist or whether something is elitist. Life and history will determine that.

Howard is now regarded in part as a sort of, not as an elite writer, but as a qualified elite writer—certainly as a literary writer, which as pulpster he

was never considered to be. Indeed, the triumvirate of the *Weird Tales* three—Lovecraft and Clark Ashton Smith and Robert E. Howard—are now considered to be essentially elitist writers who went slumming.

GJ: When I read Rand's essay it occurred to me that you could run a similar argument regarding music in this sense that in the late 19th-, early 20th-century romanticism was dominant in music and then modernism came in, and the romantic sensibility was driven off the concert stages, and it showed up in Hollywood, and so you had a lot of film composers who were carrying on the romantic tradition in ways that more "serious" academic composers were not. What do you think of film music?

JB: I like film music. Partly because it's an extension of film as the total artwork. It'd be interesting to have film music with a totally blank screen, wouldn't it? Whereby you actually had a film that was rendered musicological, and then you voided the screen, and just played the music so you had a concert response to what might be programmatic or filmic music.

Yes, I like film music, although its composers are not individually that important, because you can't abstract it from the film which their product is a part of. But no, a film without music is a deader film. If you ever sit through films which have very little music, you've lost a part of the overall experience.

One of the things that interests me a great deal is that ultra-modern music and horror films go very much together. Partly because the Hammer films in Britain could get modernist composers very cheaply, like Elisabeth Lutyens and this sort of thing, to do these amazing scores which are completely over the top and, from a naturalistic point of view, utterly ridiculous and yet suit that sort of hedonistic and abstracted material even at its most popular and deranged.

So, I quite like that sort of combination of sort of Charles Ives *manqué* and Hammer horror.

GJ: Kerry Bolton has done a lot of writing for Counter-Currents since our website got started, and he's published a lot of essays on artists of the Right. We're going to bring out two volumes of these essays now.[1] He's written so much that it has exceeded the length of one volume.

It is really quite remarkable that some of the greatest artists of the 20th century, especially the first half of the 20th century, were political Rightists and sometimes rather radical Rightists. It's interesting to me how Counter-Currents as a metapolitical project embraces the attempt to cultivate artists. One of the things that I would very much like to do is, to the extent that it's possible for a journal to cultivate artists, I would very much like to encourage a new artistic scene on the Right. It would be very nice if some of the great artists in the 21st century turned out to be Rightists as well.

What are your thoughts about how one can cultivate an artistic/political subculture? Do you think that can be cultivated or does that just happen in ways that can never be predicted or controlled?

---

[1] The first volume is Kerry Bolton, *Artists of the Right: Resisting Decadence*, ed. Greg Johnson (San Francisco: Counter-Currents, 2011).

JB: I think it's more likely to happen in the latter way in which you just described it. It's difficult to stimulate such a thing into being, but you can help that which exists. I think that probably works like Bolton's are very important because what they're doing is they're engaging in cultural revisionism. What they're doing is they're bringing back into focus all of the people who existed between about 1900 or 1890 and 1945. The great fall off, of course, is the effect of the Second World War. If you wish to get anywhere in the arts since the Second World War you've had to have liberal opinions because civilized people couldn't have illiberal opinions because they could be perceived as leading in a fascistic direction.

But we're living in a new era now, and we're living in a post-modern or a post-post-modern or a hyper-real era, and I feel it's time to bring back all of these titans from the first part of the 20th century to give people the courage and the energy to say that they believe in new forms of art which are radically unequal and radically inegalitarian in their responses to life.

I feel that the best thing that can be done is to take people up when they appear and to manifest interest in their work and to project them without fear or favor when you're aware of the nature of their existence. I don't think you can synthetically bring into being a Right-wing cultural and artistic movement, but you can pick and choose from a large number of people who will come forward in the next ten years or so, or who have created silently and without being recognized since 1945.

GJ: It strikes me that things that I can do as an editor of a journal are really twofold: Publishing articles like Kerry Bolton's gives people today a whole pantheon of models that they can look to which can be inspiring and the other thing that's possible is to provide critical feedback and exposure to contemporary artists who are working in a sort of Right-wing subculture, and I think that's really the best that I can do. If there's more, I would like to know. If there are people out there who want to contact me, we'll do our best to give you critical feedback and to give your work exposure. And one hopes that there's a genius out there listening; the next Ezra Pound or the next Roy Campbell. And really, that's the best we can do.

JB: Yes, I think that's the best that can be done and what ought to be done and what should be done and what is being done.

GJ: Well, Jonathan, thank you very much. This has been very, very enjoyable, and I hope to talk to you again soon for another Counter-Currents Radio show.

JB: Thanks very much.

Counter-Currents/*North American New Right*
January 25, 2013 & April 29, 2013

INDEX

This index lists all occurrences of proper names plus definitions and discussions of important concepts. Numbers in bold refer to a whole chapter devoted to a particular topic.

ABOUT THE AUTHOR

JONATHAN BOWDEN, April 12, 1962–March 29, 2012, was a British novelist, playwright, essayist, painter, actor, and orator, and a leading thinker and spokesman of the British New Right.

Born in Kent and largely self-educated, Bowden was a popular speaker for a succession of Right-wing groups, including the Monday Club, the Western Goals Institute, the Revolutionary Conservative Caucus, the Freedom Party, the Bloomsbury Forum, the British National Party, and finally the New Right (London), of which he was the Chairman.

His books include *Mad* (1989), *Aryan* (1990), *Sade* (Egotist, 1992), *Brute* (Egotist, 1992), *Skin* (Egotist, 1992), *Axe* (Egotist, n.d.), *Craze* (Egotist, 1993), *Right* (European Books Society, 1993), *Collected Works* (Avant-garde, 1995), *Standardbearers: British Roots of the New Right*, edited with Adrian Davies and Eddy Butler (Beckenham, Kent: The Bloomsbury Forum, 1999), *Apocalypse TV* (London: The Spinning Top Club, 2007), *The Fanatical Pursuit of Purity* (London: The Spinning Top Club, 2008), *Al-Qa'eda MOTH* (London: The Spinning Top Club, 2008), *Kratos* (London: The Spinning Top Club, 2008), *A Ballet of Wasps* (London: The Spinning Top Club, 2008), *Goodbye Homunculus!* (London: The Spinning Top Club, 2009), *Lilith Before Eve* (London: The Spinning Top Club, 2009), *Louisiana Half-Face* (London: The Spinning Top Club, 2010), *Colonel Sodom Goes to Gomorrah* (London: The Spinning Top Club, 2011), *Our Name is Legion* (London: The Spinning Top Club, 2011), *Locusts Devour a Carcass* (London: The Spinning Top Club, 2012), and *Spiders are Not Insects* (London: The Spinning Top Club, 2012), and *Pulp Fascism: Right-Wing Themes in Comics, Graphic Novels, and Popular Literature*, ed. Greg Johnson (San Francisco: Counter-Currents, 2013).

Bowden's art is published in *The Art of Jonathan Bowden (1974–2007)* (London: The Spinning Top Club, 2007), *The Art of Jonathan Bowden, Vol. 2 (1968–1974)* (London: The Spinning Top Club, 2009), and *The Art of Jonathan Bowden, Vol. 3 (1967–1974)* (London: The Spinning Top Club, 2010).

www.ingramcontent.com/pod-product-compliance
Lightning Source LLC
LaVergne TN
LVHW091052080826
845145LV00002B/717

* 9 7 8 1 9 3 5 9 6 5 7 7 0 *